Adobe Animate

2024 Release

Classroom in a Book®
The official training workbook from Adobe

Russell Chun

Adobe Animate Classroom in a Book® 2024 Release

Chapter 10 Asset Credits
Running shoes_62402566 © Robert Babczynski/Shutterstock
Sports runners situated in a shoe box_109846007 © Kitch Bain/Shutterstock
Sport and healthy lifestyle_1117120196 © RomarioIen/Shutterstock

Executive Editor: Laura Norman
Senior Production Editor: Tracey Croom
Adobe Press Associate Editor: Anshul Sharma
Development Editor: Stephen Nathans-Kelly
Project Editor: Maureen Forys,
            Happenstance Type-O-Rama
Copy Editor: Audrey Doyle
Proofreader: James Fraleigh

Technical Reviewer: Joseph Labrecque
Keystroker: Megan Ahearn
Compositor: Cody Gates,
            Happenstance Type-O-Rama
Indexer: Rachel Kuhn
Cover Illustration: Nurul Kusumaningrum,
            behance.net/Nuymotion
Interior Designer: Mimi Heft

ISBN-13: 978-0-13-831771-3
ISBN-10: 0-13-831771-2

1 2023

WHERE ARE THE LESSON FILES?

Purchase of this Classroom in a Book in any format gives you access to the lesson files you'll need to complete the exercises in the book.

1 Go to peachpit.com/AnimateCIB2024.

2 Sign in or create a new account.

3 Click Submit.

⬤ **Note** If you encounter problems registering your product or accessing the lesson files or web edition, go to peachpit.com/support for assistance.

4 Answer the questions as proof of purchase.

5 The lesson files can be accessed through the Registered Products tab on your Account page.

6 Click the Access Bonus Content link below the title of your product to proceed to the download page. Click the lesson file links to download them to your computer.

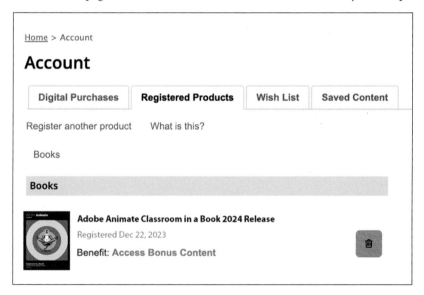

⬤ **Note** If you purchased a digital product directly from peachpit.com, your product will already be registered. Look for the Access Bonus Content link on the Registered Products tab in your account.

CONTENTS AT A GLANCE

CONTENTS

GETTING STARTED

The 2024 release of Adobe Animate provides a comprehensive authoring environment for creating sophisticated animations and interactive, media-rich applications that you can publish to a variety of platforms. Animate is widely used in the creative industry to develop engaging projects that integrate sound, graphics, and animation. You can create original content in Animate or import assets from other Adobe applications such as Photoshop and Illustrator, quickly design animation and multimedia, and use code to integrate sophisticated interactivity.

Use Animate to generate graphics and animation assets, publish broadcast-quality animation, build innovative and immersive websites, create stand-alone desktop applications, and create apps to distribute to mobile devices running on Android or iOS.

With extensive controls for animation, intuitive and flexible drawing tools, and output options for HD video, HTML5, WebGL, SVG, mobile apps, and desktop applications, Adobe Animate is a robust multimedia authoring environment that enables your imagination to become reality.

About Classroom in a Book

Adobe Animate Classroom in a Book 2024 Release is part of the official training series for Adobe graphics and publishing software developed with the support of Adobe product experts. The lessons are designed so that you can learn at your own pace. If you're new to Animate, you'll learn the fundamental concepts and features you'll need to use the program. Classroom in a Book also teaches many advanced features, including tips and techniques for using the latest version of this application.

Although each lesson provides step-by-step instructions for creating a specific project, there's room for exploration and experimentation. You can follow the book from start to finish or do only the lessons that correspond to your interests and needs. Each lesson concludes with review questions to reinforce what you've learned.

What's new

The 2024 release of Adobe Animate provides a sleek new user interface for a consistent experience across Creative Cloud applications, and native Apple Silicon M1 and M2 support for significant performance boosts. Enhancements to animation controls such as resetting warped asset puppet pins and Frame Picker panel updates make creating animations easier and faster.

The lessons in this book provide opportunities to use some of the updated features and improvements in Animate, including the following:

• The sleek new user interface

• The ability to reset puppet pins on a warped asset to their initial state with a single click

In addition, new lesson graphics in the book give readers fresh animation exercises and challenges to learn and master animation techniques.

Prerequisites

Before you begin using *Adobe Animate Classroom in a Book 2024 Release*, make sure your system is set up correctly and that you've installed the required software. You should have a working knowledge of your computer and operating system. You should know how to use the mouse and standard menus and commands and also how to open, save, and close files. If you need to review these techniques, see the printed or online documentation included with your macOS or Microsoft Windows software.

Installing Animate

You must purchase the Adobe Animate application as part of Adobe Creative Cloud. The following specifications are the minimum required system configurations.

macOS

- Multicore Intel processor with 64-bit support ARM-based Apple silicon processor

- macOS version 12 (Monterey), version 13 (Ventura)

- 8 GB of RAM (16 GB recommended)

- 1024x900 display (1280x1024 recommended)

- QuickTime 10.x software recommended

- 6 GB of available hard-disk space for installation; more free space required during installation (cannot install on a volume that uses a case-sensitive file system or on removable flash storage devices)

- OpenGL version 3.3 or higher (Metal Support recommended)

- Broadband internet connection and registration necessary for required software activation, validation of subscriptions, and access to online services

Windows

- Intel Pentium® 4, Intel Centrino®, Intel Xeon®, or Intel Core™ Duo (or compatible) processor (2 GHz or faster processor)

- Windows 10 version v22H2, Windows 11 version v21H2, v22H2

- 8 GB of RAM (16 GB recommended)

- 1024x900 display (1280x1024 recommended)

- 4 GB of available hard-disk space for installation; more free space required during installation (cannot install on removable flash storage devices)

- OpenGL™ version 3.3 or higher (DirectX® 12 with feature level 12_0 recommended)

- Broadband internet connection and registration necessary for required software activation, validation of subscriptions, and access to online services

For updates on system requirements and complete instructions for installing the software, visit helpx.adobe.com/animate/system-requirements.html.

Install Animate from Adobe Creative Cloud at creative.adobe.com and make sure that you have your login and password accessible.

Online content

Your purchase of this Classroom in a Book includes online materials provided by way of your Account page on peachpit.com. These include the following.

Lesson files

To work through the projects in this book, you will need to download the lesson files by following the instructions below.

Web Edition

● **Note** If you
encounter problems
registering your product
or accessing the lesson
files or Web Edition,
go to peachpit.com/
support for assistance.

The Web Edition is an online interactive version of the book providing an enhanced learning experience. Your Web Edition can be accessed from any device with a connection to the internet, and it contains the following:

*   The complete text of the book

*   Hours of instructional video keyed to the text

*   Interactive quizzes

Accessing the lesson files and Web Edition

● **Note** If you
purchased a digital
product directly from
peachpit.com, your
product will already be
registered. Look for the
Access Bonus Content
link on the Registered
Products tab in your
account.

You must register your purchase on peachpit.com in order to access the online content:

1   Go to peachpit.com/AnimateCIB2024.

2   Sign in or create a new account.

3   Click Submit.

4   Answer the question as proof of purchase.

5   The lesson files can be accessed from the Registered Products tab on your Account page. Click the Access Bonus Content link below the title of your product to proceed to the download page. Click the lesson file link(s) to download the files to your computer.

   The Web Edition can be accessed from the Digital Purchases tab on your Account page. Click the Launch link to access the product.

How to use the lessons

Each lesson in this book provides step-by-step instructions for creating one or more specific elements of a real-world project. All the lessons build on one another in terms of concepts and skills, so the best way to learn from this book is to proceed through the lessons in sequential order. In this book, some techniques and processes are explained and described in detail only the first few times you perform them.

You will create and publish a variety of final project files, such as animated GIFs, HTML files, and videos, in the lessons in this book. The files in the End folders (01End, 02End, and so on) within the lesson folders are samples of completed projects for each lesson. Use these files for reference if you want to compare your work in progress with the project files used to generate the sample projects.

The organization of the lessons is also project oriented rather than feature oriented. That means, for example, that you'll work with symbols on real-world design projects over several lessons rather than in just one lesson.

Additional resources

Adobe Animate Classroom in a Book 2024 Release is not meant to replace documentation that comes with the program or to be a comprehensive reference for every feature. Only the commands and options used in the lessons are explained in this book. For comprehensive information about program features and tutorials, refer to the following resources, which you can reach by choosing commands on the Help menu or by clicking links in the Start screen.

Adobe Animate Learn & Support: You'll find and browse Help and Support content at helpx.adobe.com/animate.html. You can also reach that page by choosing Help > Animate Help or by pressing F1. On the Learn & Support page, click User Guide for documentation on individual features, or visit helpx.adobe.com/animate/topics.html.

Animate in-app tutorials: For a range of interactive tutorials on Animate, choose the Learn tab from the Start screen, or choose Help > Hands-on Tutorial. The short tutorials let you follow step-by-step instructions in the app itself so that you can quickly learn how to animate with graphics already provided for you.

Animate web tutorials: Explore the extensive list of video tutorials on the web by choosing the Learn tab from the Start screen. The video tutorials appear below the hands-on in-app tutorials. You can also choose Help > Online Tutorial. You can sort the tutorials by Beginner or Experienced, and sample files are provided for you to practice with.

Adobe Creative Cloud tutorials: For inspiration, key techniques, cross-product workflows, and updates on new features, go to the Creative Cloud tutorials page, helpx.adobe.com/creative-cloud/tutorials.html. Available to all.

Adobe Animate Assets panel: The Assets panel comes loaded with finished animations using a variety of techniques, such as frame-by-frame animation, tweens, and inverse kinematics with the Bone tool.

Simply drag the asset from the Assets panel onto your Stage. Take your time to explore how the animation is put together, customize it, and feel free to use it in your own projects. Studying other artists' work is a great way to learn as well as to get inspired. New assets are always being added, so check the Download Assets icon at the bottom of the panel for updated content.

Adobe forums: Tap into peer-to-peer discussions, questions, and answers on Adobe products at forums.adobe.com. The Adobe Animate forum is accessible by choosing Help > Animate Community Forum.

Adobe *Create*: The online magazine *Create* offers thoughtful articles on design and design issues, a gallery showcasing the work of top-notch designers, tutorials, and more. Check it out at create.adobe.com.

Resources for educators: www.adobe.com/education and edex.adobe.com offer a treasure trove of information for instructors who teach classes on Adobe software. Find solutions for education at all levels, including free curricula that use an integrated approach to teaching Adobe software and can be used to prepare for the Adobe Certified Professional exams.

Also check out these useful sites:

- **Adobe Extensions:** https://exchange.adobe.com/creativecloud.html is a central resource for finding tools, services, extensions, code samples, and more to supplement and extend your Adobe products.

- **Adobe Animate product home page:** www.adobe.com/products/animate.html.

Adobe Authorized Training Centers

Adobe Authorized Training Centers offer instructor-led courses and training on Adobe products. A directory of AATCs is available at https://learning.adobe.com/.

About the Author

Russell Chun is an associate professor at the Lawrence Herbert School of Communication at Hofstra University, where he teaches multimedia storytelling, data journalism, and information design. His research examines effective visual communication and has been published in *Journal of Visual Literacy*, *Proceedings of the New York State Communication Association*, *Visual Studies*, and *Visual Communication Quarterly*, where he serves as an associate editor. He has been writing books on Adobe Animate and its predecessor, Flash, since 2001. He lives in Brooklyn, New York, with his wife and three children.

1 GETTING ACQUAINTED

Lesson overview

In this lesson, you'll learn how to do the following:

- Create a new file in Adobe Animate.
- Understand the different Animate document types.
- Adjust Stage settings and document properties and customize your workspace.
- Open and work with panels.
- Select and use tools in the Tools panel.
- Add layers using the Timeline panel.
- Understand and manage keyframes in the timeline.
- Add filters and color effects to keyframes.
- Work with imported images in the Library panel.
- Move and reposition objects on the Stage.
- Preview and publish your animation.
- Save your file.

 This lesson will take less than 1 hour to complete.

To get the lesson files used in this chapter, download them from the web page for this book at peachpit.com/AnimateCIB2024. For more information, see "Accessing the lesson files and Web Edition" in the Getting Started section at the beginning of this book.

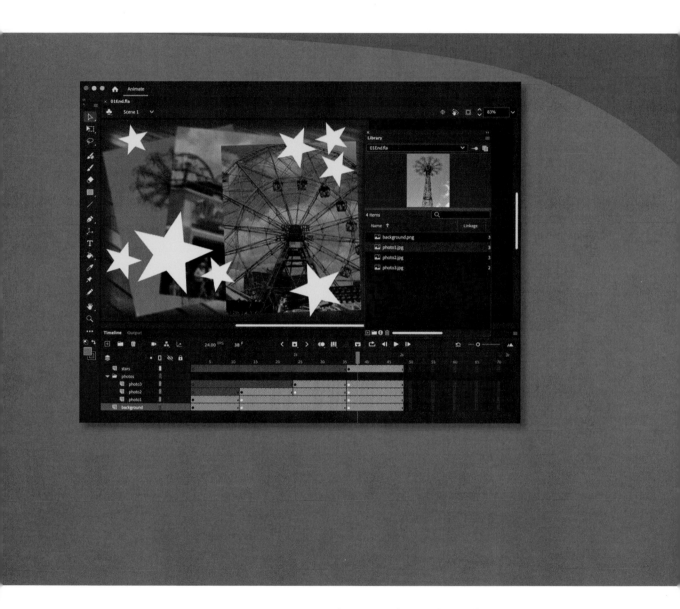

In Animate, the Stage is where you lay out all your visual elements, the Timeline panel is where you organize frames and layers, and other panels let you edit and control your creation.

Starting Adobe Animate and opening a file

The first time you start Adobe Animate you'll see the Home screen, which also serves as a place to create a new document or open a saved document. It displays the kinds of projects you can build along with any recently opened files.

Note If you have not already downloaded the project files for this lesson to your computer from your Account page on peachpit.com, make sure to do so now. See Getting Started at the beginning of the book.

Tip You can also start Animate by double-clicking an Animate file (*.fla or *.xfl), such as the 01End.fla file that is provided to show you the completed project.

In this lesson, you'll create a simple slideshow-type animation to showcase a few vacation snapshots. You'll add a background, photos, and some decorative elements, and in the process you'll learn about positioning elements on the Stage and placing them along the timeline of the animation so that they appear one at a time, in sequence. You'll begin learning how to use the Stage to organize your visual elements spatially and how to use the Timeline panel to organize your elements temporally.

1   Start Animate. In macOS, double-click Adobe Animate 2024 in the Adobe Animate 2024 folder in the Applications folder. In Windows, choose Start > Programs > Adobe Animate.

2   Choose the Open button or choose File > Open (Command+O/Ctrl+O). In the Open dialog box, select the 01End.fla file in the 01/01End folder and click Open to see the final project.

3   Choose the Test Movie button in the upper-right corner of the application interface, or choose Control > Test.

Animate exports the project and opens it in a new window.

An animation plays. During the animation, several overlapping photos appear one by one, with stars appearing at the end. As the new photos appear, the previous photos become blurry, receding into the background.

4   Close the preview window and the FLA file.

Understanding document types and creating a new document

Animate is an animation and multimedia authoring tool that creates media for multiple platforms and playback technologies. Knowing where your final animation will play determines what type of document you'll choose when you create a new file.

Playback environment

The playback, or runtime, environment is the technology that your final published files use to play. Your animation could play in a browser with HTML5 and JavaScript. Perhaps your animation will be exported as a video to be uploaded to YouTube or an animated GIF on social media. Or your project could play as an app on a mobile device or even as a virtual reality immersive experience. You should make that decision first so that you can choose the appropriate document type.

● **Note** Not all features are supported across all document types. For example, HTML5 Canvas documents don't support the 3D Rotation tool or the 3D Translation tool. Tools that are not supported by the current document type are dimmed in the Animate interface.

Document types

There are nine types of documents, but you'll likely work with only the first two or three described below, as they are the most common. The nine documents target different playback environments that determine some of the animation and interactivity features. Your choices for Animate documents are the following:

● **Note** The ActionScript 3.0 document also supports publishing content as a projector for either Windows or macOS. A projector plays as a stand-alone application on the desktop, without needing a browser.

- Choose ActionScript 3.0 to create animation to export to video or to export graphics and animation assets, such as spritesheets or PNG sequences. ActionScript is the native scripting language in Animate and is similar to JavaScript, but choosing an ActionScript 3.0 document doesn't mean you have to include ActionScript code.

- Choose HTML5 Canvas to create projects that play back in a modern browser using HTML5 and JavaScript. You can add interactivity by inserting JavaScript within Animate or adding it to the final published files.

- Choose WebGL glTF Extended or WebGL glTF Standard for interactive animated assets to take advantage of hardware-accelerated support of graphics or for supported 3D graphics.

- Choose AIR for Desktop to create animation that plays as an application on Windows or macOS desktops, without needing a browser. You can add interactivity in an AIR document using ActionScript 3.0.

- Choose AIR for Android or AIR for iOS to publish an app for an Android or Apple mobile device. You can add interactivity to your mobile app using ActionScript 3.0.

▶ **Tip** You can easily switch from one document type to another. For example, you can convert an ActionScript 3.0 document into an HTML5 Canvas document if you have an old Flash banner ad animation that you want to update. Choose File > Convert To > [*new document type*]. Some functionality and features may be lost in the conversion, however. For example, conversion to an HTML5 Canvas document will comment out ActionScript code.

- Choose VR Panorama or VR 360 to publish a virtual reality project for a web browser that lets your audience look in all directions. You can add animation or interactivity to your immersive environments.

Regardless of the playback environment and document type, all documents are saved as FLA or XFL (Animate) files. The difference is that each document type is configured to export different final published files.

Creating a new document

You'll create the simple animation that you previewed earlier by starting a new document.

1 Start at the Home screen in Animate, which is the default workspace when you launch the application. You can also get to the Home screen by pressing the Home button at the top left of the interface.

The Home screen displays preset options for different playback environments and layout sizes.

For example, when you select More Presets and choose the Full HD option under Character Animation, Animate creates a new ActionScript 3.0 document meant to export video at 1920x1080 pixels. The Square option under Ads creates a new HTML Canvas document at 250x250 pixels meant for playback in a browser.

2   Choose More Presets or choose Create New (File > New).

The New Document dialog box appears. The row at the top contains six categories of intended uses; click a category to display the preset size layouts it contains in the center of the dialog box. You can either use the presets as given or fine-tune their settings using the Details section on the right side of the dialog box.

3 Select the Advanced category at the far right.

The center of the dialog box now displays all the available platforms. You can select a document type and type your document's dimensions into the Width and Height boxes.

4 In the Platforms area in the center of the dialog box, select ActionScript 3.0. In the Details area on the right side of the dialog box, choose the dimensions of the Stage by entering new pixel values for the Width and Height. Enter **800** for Width and **600** for Height. Enter 30 for the Frame Rate.

5 Click Create.

Animate creates a new ActionScript 3.0 document with the specified Stage dimensions.

● **Note** If you save your Animate document as an Animate Uncompressed Document (.xfl), your document is saved as a collection of files in folders and not as a single document. This exposes the contents of your document to you and to other developers to swap assets easily. XFL is a more advanced format that you won't be using in this book.

6 Choose File > Save. Name the file **01_workingcopy.fla**, and from the File Format/Save As Type menu, choose Animate Document (*.fla). Although the software application is called Animate, be aware that the file extension is .fla or .xfl, both of which preserve echoes of the name of the ancestor of Animate: Flash. Navigate to the 01Start folder and click Save.

Saving your file right away is a good working habit that ensures your work won't be lost if the application or your computer crashes. You should always save your Animate file with the extension .fla (or .xfl if you save it as an Animate Uncompressed Document) to identify it as the Animate source file.

Getting to know the workspace

The first time you run Animate, you'll be asked what kind of user you are—beginner or expert, for example. Your answer will determine how the interface is configured. Don't worry about your choice, as you can customize your workspace to whatever makes you comfortable. You will also learn to configure the workspace to match how it appears in this book.

The Animate work area includes the command menus at the top of the screen and a variety of tools and panels for editing and adding elements to your movie. You can create all the objects for your animation in Animate, or you can import elements you've created in Adobe Illustrator, Adobe Photoshop, Adobe After Effects, or other compatible applications.

There are many different interface configurations, but in the Essentials workspace, Animate displays the menu bar, Timeline panel, Stage, Tools panel, Properties panel, and Edit bar, along with a few other panels. As you work in Animate, you can open, close, group, ungroup, dock, undock, and move panels around the screen to fit your work style or your screen resolution.

Tools panel

Edit bar

Application bar

Stage

Properties panel

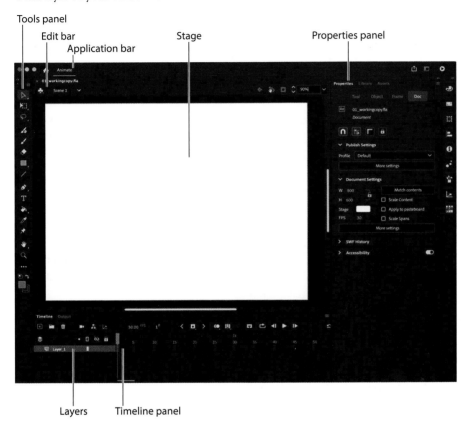

Layers   Timeline panel

Choosing a new workspace

Animate also provides a few preset panel arrangements ("workspaces") that may better suit the needs of particular users. Use the Window > Workspaces submenu or the workspace switcher at the top right of the interface to choose a different work-space or to save a new one.

1   Click the workspace switcher and choose a new workspace.

The various panels are rearranged and resized according to their importance in the chosen workspace. For example, the Animator and Designer workspaces put the Timeline panel at the top of the work area for easy and frequent access.

2 Select the Essentials workspace.

This book shows the step-by-step lessons in the Essentials workspace. It provides a good balance of access to the Stage and the most commonly used panels.

3 If you have moved some of the panels around and want to return to one of the prearranged workspaces, choose Window > Workspaces > Reset [*preset name*] and click Yes in the confirmation dialog box. Or, from the workspace switcher, choose the reset icon to the right of the workspace name.

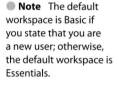
Note The default workspace is Basic if you state that you are a new user; otherwise, the default workspace is Essentials.

Saving your workspace

If you find an arrangement of panels that suits your style of work, you can save it as a custom workspace and return to it at a later date.

1 Open the workspace switcher and enter a name for your new workspace in the field below New Workspace.

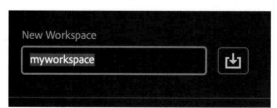

2 Click the Save Workspace icon next to the new name.

Animate saves the current arrangement of panels and adds it to the options in the Workspace menu, which you can access at any time.

▶ **Tip** If you want to save and share your workspace preferences (in addition to other customizations), you can export them into an ANP file. Choose Animate > Settings > Export Preferences to save a file that others can import.

3 By default, the Animate interface is dark gray. However, you can change the interface to a lighter gray if you prefer. Choose Animate > Settings > Edit Preferences (macOS) or Edit > Preferences (Windows), and in the Interface preferences category, choose a different level of gray.

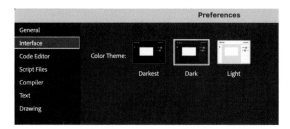

In this book, the screenshots are shown in the Dark mode.

About the Stage

The big white rectangle in the middle of your screen is called the Stage. As with a theater stage, the Stage in Animate is the area that viewers see when a movie is playing. It contains the text, images, and video that appear on the screen. You move elements on and off the Stage to place them in and out of view. You can use the rulers (View > Rulers) or grids (View > Grid > Show Grid) to help you position items on the Stage.

Additional positioning aids include guides (pulled from the top or side rulers; View > Guides) and the Align panel, among others. You'll learn about these tools in later lessons in this book.

By default, you'll see the gray area off the Stage where you can place elements that won't be visible to your audience. The gray area is called the *pasteboard*. To see only the Stage, choose View > Magnification > Clip To Stage to select the option. For now, leave Clip To Stage deselected, allowing the pasteboard to remain in view.

You can also click the Clip Content Outside The Stage button to crop the graphic elements that fall beyond the Stage area so that you can see how your audience will view your final project.

▶ **Tip** You can view
the Stage in full-
screen mode without
the distraction of
the various panels
by choosing View >
Screen Mode >
Full Screen Mode. Press
F4 to toggle the panels,
and press the Esc key
to return to Standard
Screen Mode.

To scale the Stage so that it fits completely in the application window, choose View > Magnification > Fit In Window. You can also choose different magnification view options from the menu just above the Stage.

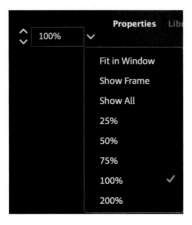

Changing the Stage properties

Now you'll change the color of the Stage. The Stage color, along with document properties such as the Stage dimensions and frame rate, is available in the Properties panel, which is the vertical panel just to the right of the Stage.

1 In the Document Settings section of the Properties panel, note that the dimensions of the current Stage (the Size parameters) are set at 800x600 pixels, which you chose when you created the new document.

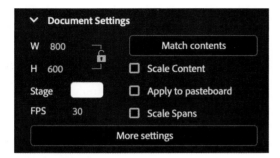

2 Also in the Properties panel, click the Background Color box next to the Stage and choose a new color from the color palette. Choose dark gray (#333333).

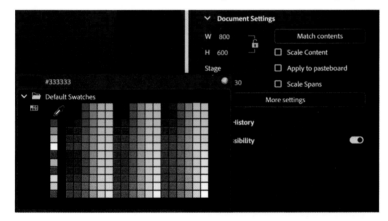

Your Stage is now a different color. You can change the Stage properties at any time.

Working with the Library panel

The Library panel is accessible from a tab just to the right of the Properties panel. The Library panel displays the contents of your document's library, which is where you store and organize symbols created in Animate, as well as warped assets and imported files, including bitmaps, graphics, sound files, and certain video clips. Symbols and warped assets are graphics used for animation.

● **Note** You'll learn much more about symbols in Lesson 2, "Creating Graphics and Text."

About the Library panel

The Library panel lets you organize library items in folders, see how often an item is used in a document, and sort items by type. You can also create folders in your Library panel to help you group items. When you import items into Animate, you

Tip You can also save assets in the Assets panel (Window > Assets), or save them to share across Adobe products by clicking the CC Libraries icon (Window > CC Libraries) and storing them in your Creative Cloud account.

Tip If the Enable menu isn't visible, click the Options button to activate it.

can import them directly onto the Stage or into the library. However, any item you import onto the Stage is also added to the library, as are any symbols you create. You can then easily access the items to add them to the Stage again, edit them, or see their properties.

To display the Library panel, choose Window > Library, or press Command+L/Ctrl+L.

Importing an item to the Library panel

Often, you'll create graphics directly with the drawing tools in Animate and save them as symbols, which are stored in the library. At other times you'll use the Asset Warp tool to create a rig inside imported graphics, which are also stored in the library. You can also import media such as JPEG images or MP3 sound files, and they, too, are stored in the library. In this lesson, you'll import several images into the library to be used in the animation.

1   Choose File > Import > Import To Library. In the Import To Library dialog box, select the background.png file in the 01/01Start folder and click Open. Choose All Files (*.*) from the Enable menu if the image files are dimmed.

Animate imports the selected PNG image and places it in the Library panel.

2   Continue importing photo1.jpg, photo2.jpg, and photo3.jpg from the 01Start folder.

You can also hold down the Shift key to select multiple files and import all the images at once.

The Library panel lists the filenames of all the imported images and provides a thumbnail preview of any selected file. These images are now available to be used in your Animate document.

Adding an item from the Library panel to the Stage

Tip You can also choose File > Import > Import To Stage, or press Command+R/ Ctrl+R, to import an image file to the library and put it on the Stage, all in one step.

To use an imported image, simply drag it from the Library panel onto the Stage.

1 Choose Window > Library to open the Library panel if it isn't already open.

2 Drag the background.png item onto the Stage and place it approximately in the center of the Stage.

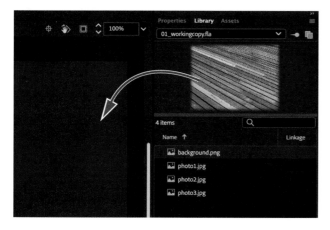

Understanding the Timeline panel

In the Essentials workspace, the Timeline panel is located below the Stage. The Timeline panel contains playback controls for your animation as well as the timeline itself, which displays the sequence of events in the animation from left to right. An Animate movie measures time in frames, just as in a filmstrip. As the movie plays, the playhead, shown as a blue vertical line, advances through the frames shown in the timeline. You can change the content on the Stage for different frames. To display a frame's content on the Stage for any particular time, move the playhead to that frame in the timeline.

At the top of the Timeline panel, Animate indicates the selected frame number and the current frame rate (how many frames play per second).

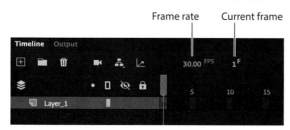

The timeline portion of the Timeline panel also displays layers, which help you organize the artwork in your document. At the moment, your project has only one layer, which is called Layer_1. Think of layers as multiple filmstrips stacked on top of one another. Each layer can contain a different image that appears on the Stage, and you can draw and edit objects on one layer without affecting objects on another layer. The layers are stacked in the order in which they overlap each other so that objects on the bottom layer in the timeline are on the bottom of the stack on the Stage. You can hide, lock, or show the contents of layers as outlines by clicking the dots or the square in the layer under the layer option icons.

If you have multiple layers, you can use the View Only Active Layer option above the timeline to show only the currently selected layer.

Changing the appearance of the timeline

You can adjust the timeline's appearance to accommodate your workflow. When you want to see more layers, choose Short from the Frame View menu in the upper-right corner of the Timeline panel. The Short option decreases the height of the frame cell rows. The Preview and Preview In Context options display thumbnail versions of the contents of your keyframes in the timeline.

Reset Timeline Zoom To The Default Level

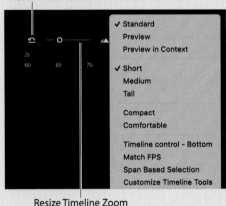

Resize Timeline Zoom

For finer control over the timeline frame sizes, drag the Resize Timeline Zoom slider. The slider adjusts the size of the frames so that you can see more or less of the timeline. Click the Reset Timeline Zoom To The Default Level button to revert the timeline view to its normal size.

To position different animation options on your timeline for quick access, click the options menu at the corner of the timeline and choose Customize Timeline Tools. The Customize Timeline menu appears, which contains all the available tools you can choose to display or to hide. The highlighted icons are those that are, by default, on the top of the timeline.

Click to add or remove a tool. Click the Reset Timeline Controls button to reset the timeline to its original appearance.

Renaming a layer

It's a good idea to separate your content on different layers and name each layer to indicate its contents so that you can easily find the layer you need later.

1　Double-click the name of the existing layer, Layer_1, to rename it, and type **background**.

2　Click outside the name box to apply the new name.

3　Click below the lock icon to lock the layer. Locking a layer prevents you from accidentally moving or making changes to whatever is inside that layer.

A lock icon appears in the layer. The lock icon indicates that you can't make edits to the layer, because it is locked.

Adding a layer

A new Animate document contains only one layer, but you can add as many layers as you need. Objects in the top layers will overlap objects in the bottom layers, unless you change the layer depth with the Layer Depth panel. You'll learn more about this option in Lesson 7, "Animating the Camera."

1 Select the background layer in the timeline.

2 Choose Insert > Timeline > Layer. You can also click the New Layer button above the timeline.

A new layer appears above the background layer.

3 Double-click the new layer to rename it, and type **photo1**. Click outside the name box to apply the new name.

Your timeline now has two layers. The background layer contains the background photo, and the newly created photo1 layer above it is empty.

4 Select the top layer, called photo1.

5 Choose Window > Library to open the Library panel if it isn't already open.

▶ **Tip** As you add more layers and your overlapping graphics become more complicated, click the dot below the eye icon in any layer to hide its contents. Alternatively, hold down the Shift key and click the dot below the eye icon to make the layer partially transparent so that you can see what's below it. Hiding or making a layer transparent affects only how you see your project in Animate—it doesn't affect your final exported project. Double-click the Layer icon to modify the level of transparency in the Layer Properties dialog box.

6 Drag the library item called photo1.jpg from the library onto the Stage.

The photo1 image appears on the Stage and overlaps the background image.

7 Choose Insert > Timeline > Layer, or click the New Layer button above the timeline, to add a third layer.

8 Rename the third layer **photo2**.

Working with layers

If you don't want a layer, you can easily delete it by selecting it and then clicking the Delete button above the timeline.

If you want to rearrange your layers and change how your graphics overlap each other, simply drag any layer up or down to move it to a new position in the layer stack.

Inserting frames

So far, you have a background photo and another overlapping photo on the Stage, but your entire animation exists for only a single frame, which is only a fraction of a second. To create more time on the timeline and make this animation run for a longer duration, you must add additional frames.

1   Select frame 48 in the background layer. Use the Resize Timeline View slider at the upper-right corner of the Timeline panel to expand the timeline frames to make it easier to identify frame 48.

2   Choose Insert > Timeline > Frame (F5). You can also choose Frame from the menu above the timeline (if you have the Frames Group option enabled from Customize Timeline Tools), or you can right-click frame 48 and choose Insert Frame from the context menu that appears.

Animate adds frames in the background layer up to the selected frame, frame 48.

3 Select frame 48 in the photo1 layer.

4 Choose Insert > Timeline > Frame (F5), choose Insert Frame above the timeline, or right-click and choose Insert Frame to add frames in the photo1 layer up to frame 48.

5 Select frame 48 in the photo2 layer and insert frames on this layer.

You now have three layers, all with 48 frames on the timeline. Since the frame rate of your Animate document is 24 frames per second, your current animation lasts 2 seconds.

Selecting multiple frames

Just as you can hold down the Shift key to select multiple files on your desktop, you can hold down Shift to select multiple frames on the Animate timeline. If you have several layers and want to insert frames into all of them, select a frame in the first layer and then Shift-click the same frame in the last layer to select all the frames in the layers in between, or drag to select multiple layers. Then choose Insert > Timeline > Frame.

Creating a keyframe

A keyframe indicates a change in content on the Stage. Keyframes are indicated on the timeline as a circle. An empty circle means there is nothing in that particular layer at that particular time. A filled-in black circle means there is something in that layer at that time. The background layer, for example, contains a filled keyframe (black circle) in the first frame. The photo1 layer also contains a filled keyframe in its first frame. Both layers contain photos. The photo2 layer, however, contains an empty keyframe in the first frame, indicating that it is currently empty.

Empty keyframe   Filled keyframe

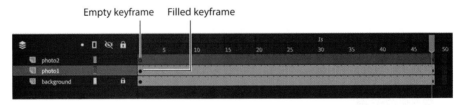

Understanding Auto Keyframe mode

There are two modes for creating keyframes. The Auto Keyframe option above your timeline can be either enabled or disabled.

If it is enabled (if the keyframe icon displays a letter "A"), adding or editing content on the Stage automatically creates a new keyframe at that point in time. If it is disabled, you create keyframes manually, as described in this task. Generally, for the projects in this book, you'll want to keep the Auto Keyframe option disabled. This way, you will learn to create a keyframe only when you specifically want one, and you will avoid accidentally creating keyframes.

In the next task, you'll insert a keyframe in the photo2 layer at the point in time when you want the next photo to appear.

To turn Auto Keyframe on or off, select the Customize Timeline Tools option in the upper-right corner of the timeline (see the sidebar "Changing the appearance of the timeline" earlier in this lesson). Select the Auto Keyframe icon to add it to your Timeline controls and enable it, or deselect the Auto Keyframe icon to remove it from your Timeline controls and disable it.

In this book, the Auto Keyframe option is turned off (unless otherwise specified), and the Frames Group above your timeline is added from the Customize Timeline Tools option in the upper-right corner of your timeline.

1 Make sure the Auto Keyframe option is off. Select frame 24 on the photo2 layer. The frame number of a selected frame is displayed above the left end of the timeline.

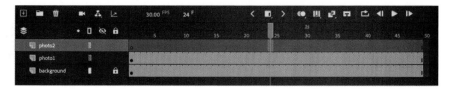

2 Choose Insert Keyframe from the menu above the timeline, or choose Insert > Timeline > Keyframe (F6).

A new keyframe, indicated by an empty circle, appears in the photo2 layer in frame 24.

3 Drag photo2.jpg from your library onto the Stage.

The empty circle at frame 24 becomes filled, indicating that there is now content in the photo2 layer. When your animation plays, your photo appears on the Stage at frame 24. You can drag the blue playhead along the top of the timeline to "scrub," or show what's happening on the Stage, at any point along the timeline. You'll see that the background photo and photo1 remain on the Stage throughout the timeline but that photo2 appears only at frame 24.

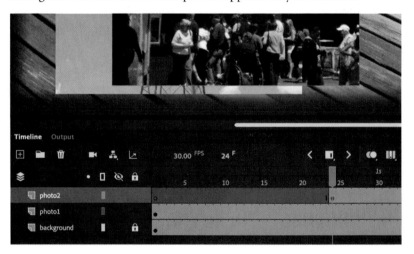

Understanding frames and keyframes is essential for mastering Animate. Be sure you understand how the photo2 layer contains 48 frames with two keyframes—an empty keyframe at frame 1 and a filled keyframe at frame 24.

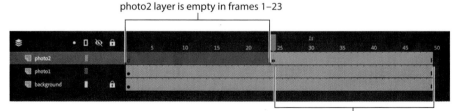

photo2 layer is empty in frames 1–23

photo2 layer contains content in frames 24–48

Moving a keyframe

If you want photo2.jpg to appear later or earlier in time, you need to move the keyframe in which it appears closer to or farther from the right on the timeline. You can easily move any keyframe by simply dragging it to a new position.

1 Select the keyframe in frame 24 on the photo2 layer.

2 Drag the keyframe to frame 12 in the photo2 layer. As you drag, you'll see a box icon appear under your cursor, indicating that you are repositioning the keyframe.

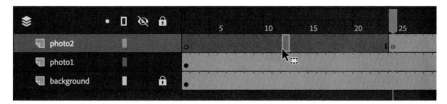

The photo2.jpg file now appears on the Stage much earlier in the animation.

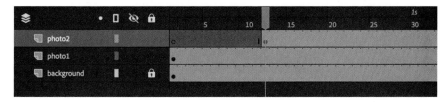

Removing a keyframe

If you want to remove a keyframe, do not press the Delete/Backspace key! Doing so will delete only the contents of that keyframe on the Stage, leaving you with an empty keyframe.

Instead, select the keyframe and choose Modify > Timeline > Clear Keyframe (Shift+F6).

Your keyframe (and its contents) will be removed from the timeline.

Organizing layers in a timeline

At this point, your working Animate file has only three layers: a background layer, a photo1 layer, and a photo2 layer. You'll be adding more layers for this project, and as in most other projects, you'll end up having to manage multiple layers. Layer folders help you group related layers to keep your timeline organized and manageable, just as you make folders for related documents on your desktop. Although it may take some time to create the folders, you'll save time later because you'll know exactly where to look for a specific layer.

Creating layer folders

For this project, you'll continue to add layers for additional photos, and you'll place those layers in a layer folder.

1   Select the photo2 layer and click the New Layer button above the timeline.

2   Name the layer **photo3**.

3   Insert a keyframe at frame 24.

4   Drag photo3.jpg from the library onto the Stage.

You now have four layers. The top three contain photos of scenes from Coney Island that appear at different keyframes.

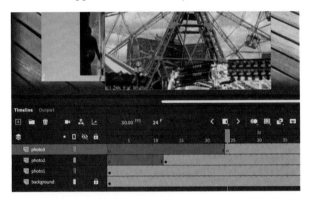

5   Select the photo3 layer and click the New Folder icon at the top of the Timeline panel.

A new layer folder appears above the photo3 layer.

6   Name the folder **photos**.

Adding layers to layer folders

Now you'll add the photo layers to the photos folder. As you arrange layers, remember that Animate displays the content in the layers in the order in which they appear in the timeline, with the top layer's content at the front and the bottom layer's content at the back.

1   Drag the photo1 layer into the photos folder.

Notice how the bold line indicates the destination of your layer. When you place a layer inside a folder, Animate indents the layer name.

2   Drag the layers photo2 and photo3 into the photos folder.

All three photo layers should be in the photos folder, in the same stacking order as they were outside the folder.

You can collapse the folder by clicking the arrow just to the left of the folder name. Expand the folder by clicking the arrow again. Be aware that if you delete a layer folder, you delete all the layers inside that folder as well.

Layer highlighting

Sometimes it's useful to highlight certain layers as you're working on a project to indicate that something is important in that layer.

Click the dot in the layer below the Highlight Layers indicator.

The selected layer becomes underlined in a highlighted color—the same color that is used for outlines and bounding boxes for the Show Layers As Outlines option.

Click the dot in the layer again to remove the highlight. You will not need it highlighted for the rest of this task.

Cut, copy, paste, and duplicate layers

When managing multiple layers and layer folders, you can rely on cut, copy, paste, and duplicate layer commands to make your workflow easier and more efficient. All the properties of the selected layer are copied and pasted, including its frames, its keyframes, any animation, and even the layer name and type. You can also copy and paste layer folders and their contents.

To cut or copy any layer or layer folder, simply select the layer, right-click the layer name, and choose Cut Layers or Copy Layers.

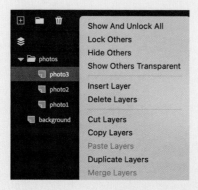

Right-click the timeline again and choose Paste Layers. The layer or layers that you cut or copied are pasted into the timeline. Use Duplicate Layers to copy and paste in one operation.

You can also cut, copy, paste, or duplicate layers from the application menu bar. Choose Edit > Timeline, and then choose Cut Layers, Copy Layers, Paste Layers, or Duplicate Layers.

Using the Properties panel

The Properties panel gives you quick access to the attributes you'll most likely need to modify as you create your animation. What appears in the Properties panel depends on what you've selected. For example, if nothing is selected, the Properties panel includes options for the general Animate document, including changing the Stage color or dimensions. If you've selected an object on the Stage, the Properties panel shows its x and y coordinates and its width and height, among other information. If you've selected a frame or keyframe on the timeline, as shown in the following figure, the Properties panel shows attributes of that keyframe, such as its label and whether it contains any sound. Different attributes are divided into sections that can be collapsed or expanded.

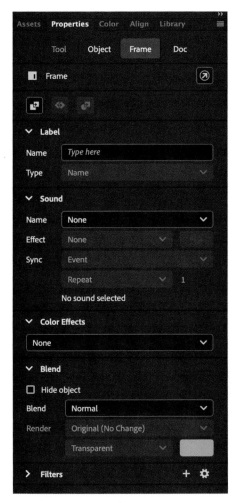

You can also quickly change the focus of the selection from the keyframe to objects on the Stage with the Properties panel. For example, selecting the Object tab at the top of the Properties panel switches the display from the attributes of the keyframe to the attributes of the selected item on the Stage in that keyframe.

You'll use the Properties panel to move your photos on the Stage.

Positioning an object on the Stage

▶ **Tip** If the Properties panel is not open, choose Window > Properties, or press Command+F3/Ctrl+F3.

You'll begin by using the Properties panel to move the photos. You'll also use the Transform panel to rotate the photos.

1   Move the playhead to frame 1 of the timeline, and select the photo1.jpg image that you dragged onto the Stage in the photo1 layer. A very narrow blue outline indicates that the object is selected.

2   In the Properties panel, type **50** for the X value and **50** for the Y value. Press Return (macOS) or Enter (Windows) to apply the values. You can also drag over the X and Y values to change them. The photo moves to the left side of the Stage.

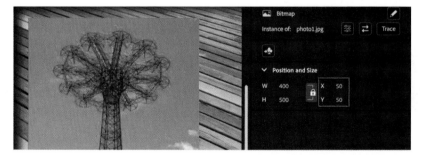

The X and Y values are measured on the Stage from the upper-left corner. X begins at 0 and increases to the right, and Y begins at 0 and increases downward. The registration point (the point from which Animate makes measurements) for imported photos is at the upper-left corner.

3   Choose Window > Transform to open the Transform panel. The Transform panel is also accessible from the column of icons on the side of the Properties panel.

4   In the Transform panel, select Rotate and type **−12** in the Rotate box, or drag over the value to change the rotation. Press Return/Enter to apply the value.

The selected photo on the Stage rotates 12 degrees counterclockwise.

5   Select frame 12 of the photo2 layer. Now click photo2.jpg on the Stage to select it.

6   Use the Properties panel and Transform panel to position and rotate the second photo in an interesting way. Use X=**200**, Y=**40**, and a Rotate value of **6** to give it some contrast with the first photo.

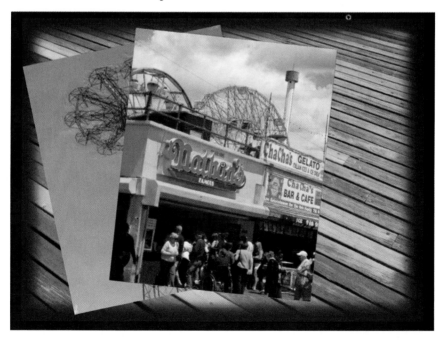

7   Select frame 24 in the photo3 layer. Now click photo3.jpg on the Stage to select it.

▶ Tip When images are scaled or rotated in Animate, they may appear jagged. You can use the Bitmap Properties dialog box to smooth each image. Double-click the bitmap icon or the image thumbnail in the Library panel to open the dialog box, and select the Allow Smoothing option.

8 Use the Properties panel and Transform panel to position and rotate the third photo in an interesting way. Use X=**360**, Y=**65**, and a Rotate value of −**2** so that all your photos have visual variety.

Working with panels

Just about everything you do in Animate involves a panel. In this lesson, you use the Library panel, Tools panel, Properties panel, Transform panel, History panel, and Timeline panel. In later lessons, you'll learn to use other panels to control various aspects of your project. Because panels are such an integral part of the Animate workspace, it pays to know how to manage them.

To open any panel in Animate, choose its name from the Window menu.

Individual panels float freely, and they can be combined in docks, groups, or stacks.

- A dock is a collection of panels or panel groups in a vertical column. Docks stick to the left or right edge of the user interface.

- A group is a collection of panels that can be placed within a dock or that can float freely.

- A stack is similar to a dock but can be placed anywhere in the interface.

In the Essentials workspace, most of the panels are organized in three docks on the right side of the screen. The Timeline and Output panels are grouped at the bottom, and the Stage is on the top. However, you can move a panel to any position that is convenient for you.

- To move a panel, drag it by its tab to a new location.

- To move a panel group or stack, drag it by the area next to the tabs.

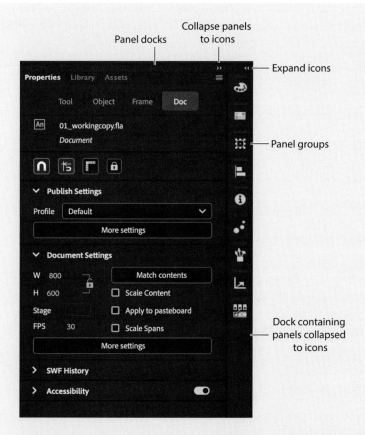

Panel docks

Collapse panels to icons

Expand icons

Panel groups

Dock containing panels collapsed to icons

As the panel, group, or stack passes over other panels, groups, docks, or stacks, a blue highlighted drop zone will appear. If you release the mouse button while a drop zone is visible, the panel will be added to the group, dock, or stack.

- To dock a panel, drag it by its tab into a new position at the left or right edge of the screen. If you drag it over the top or bottom of an existing dock, a horizontal drop zone will show you the panel's new location. If a vertical drop zone appears, dropping the panel will create a new dock.

- To group a panel, drag its tab onto the tab of another panel or the drop zone at the top of an existing group.

- To create a stack, drag a group out of a dock or an existing stack so that it floats freely. Alternatively, drag one free-floating panel onto the tab of another free-floating panel.

You also have the option of displaying most of the panels as icons to save space but still maintain quick access. Click the double arrowheads in the upper-right corner of a dock or stack to collapse the panels to icons. Click the double arrowheads again to expand the icons into panels.

Using the Tools panel

The Tools panel—the long, narrow panel on the far-left side of the Essentials work area—contains selection tools, drawing and type tools, painting and editing tools, navigation tools, and tool options. You'll use the Tools panel frequently to switch to tools designed for the task at hand. Most often you'll use the Selection tool, which is the black arrow tool at the top of the Tools panel, for selecting and clicking items on the Stage or the timeline.

Selecting and using a tool

When you select a tool, the options available at the bottom of the Tools panel and the Properties panel change. For example, when you select the Rectangle tool, the Object Drawing Mode option appears. When you select the Zoom tool, the Enlarge and Reduce options appear.

The Tools panel contains too many tools to display all at once. Some tools are arranged in hidden groups in the Tools panel; only the tool you last selected from a group is displayed. A small triangle in the lower-right corner of the tool's button indicates that there are other tools in the group. Press and hold the icon for the visible tool to see the other tools that are available, and then select one from the menu.

Tearing off tools

Many lesser-used tools are available, but they are stored away and you need to add them to your Tools panel to access them. You can customize the Tools panel to display only the tools you need or the tools you use most often. You can also arrange the tools to your liking.

● **Note** You cannot select a tool for use from the Drag And Drop Tools menu. You must add the tool to the Toolbar for it to become available for use.

1 Click the Edit Toolbar option at the bottom of the Tools panel.

2   Additional tools appear in an adjacent Drag And Drop Tools panel. Drag the tools that you want into the Tools panel.

You can add *spacers* (horizontal separators) to create groups of tools, which can be torn off from the main Tools panel to create a floating panel.

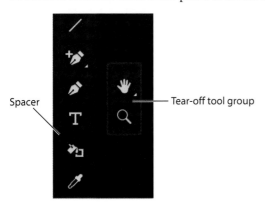

Spacer

Tear-off tool group

Tip If you're working with a smaller display, the bottom of the Tools panel may be cut off. That makes some of the tools and buttons invisible. But there's an easy way to fix the problem: drag the right edge of the Tools panel to widen it so that it can show multiple columns of tools.

3   Choose the options from the upper-right corner to reset the Toolbar to its default workspace configuration, select a different size icon for the tools, or close the Drag And Drop Tools menu.

Adding graphics

You'll use the PolyStar tool to add a little decoration to your short animation.

1   Select the folder in the timeline, and then click the New Layer button.

2   Name the new layer **stars**.

3   Lock the other layers below it so that you don't accidentally move anything into them.

4   In the timeline, move the playhead to frame 36 and select frame 36 in the stars layer.

5 Choose the Insert Keyframe button above the timeline, or choose Insert > Timeline > Keyframe (F6), to insert a new keyframe at frame 36 in the stars layer.

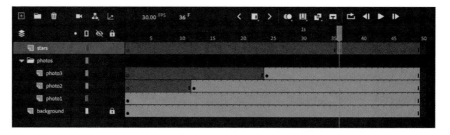

You will create star shapes to appear at frame 36 in this layer.

6 In the Tools panel, select the PolyStar tool, hidden under the Rectangle tool and indicated by the hexagon shape.

7 In the Properties panel, click the colored square next to the Stroke option, which indicates the color of the outline, and select the red diagonal line if it isn't selected already.

The red diagonal line represents a color of None for the stroke.

8 Click the colored square next to the Fill option, which indicates the color of the inside of the shape, and select a bright, cheery color such as yellow. You can click the color wheel at the upper right to access the Adobe Color Picker, or you can change the Alpha percentage, which determines the level of opacity, also at the upper right.

9 In the Properties panel, under the Tool Options section, choose Star from the Style menu. For Number Of Sides, enter **5**, and for Star Point Size, enter **0.5**. These options define the shape of your star.

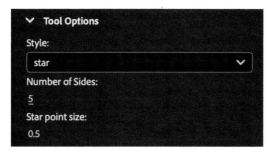

10 Make sure the empty keyframe in frame 36 of the stars layer is selected. Start dragging on the Stage where you want to add a star, and continue dragging to change the width of your star. Without releasing the drag, move your cursor around the center of the star to rotate it. Make multiple stars of different sizes and with different angles of rotation.

11 Exit the PolyStar tool by selecting the Selection tool.

12 Use the Properties panel or the Transform panel to reposition or rotate selected stars on the Stage, if desired. Or select the Selection tool and simply click to select a star and drag it to a new position on the Stage. The X and Y values in the Properties panel update as you drag the star around the Stage.

Adding layer effects

You can add interesting visual effects that change the appearance of objects in a particular layer. These layer effects include color effects and filters, both available in the Properties panel when a keyframe is selected.

The options on the Style menu in the Color Effects section include Brightness, Tint, and Alpha.

- Brightness controls the relative darkness or lightness of the layer.

- Tint controls how much color is added to the layer.

- Alpha controls the transparency of the layer.

- A fourth option, Advanced, allows you to vary brightness, tint, and alpha all at once.

Filters are special effects that change or distort the appearance in more dramatic ways, such as adding a drop shadow or adding a blur.

Adding layer effects to a keyframe

Layer effects are keyframe based. That is, a single layer can have different layer effects in different keyframes. You'll add a filter and a color effect to different keyframes in your layers to help add some depth to the slideshow and to help new images stand out as they're added.

1 Move the playhead to frame 12 on the timeline, and select frame 12 in both the photo1 layer and the background layer by pressing Shift as you click each frame. Frame 12 is the point at which photo2 appears in the slideshow.

2 Choose the Insert Keyframe button above the timeline (F6).

   A keyframe appears in frame 12 in both layers.

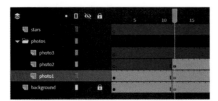

3 While the two keyframes are still selected, click the Add Filter button in the Properties panel and choose Blur to add a blur filter to the two selected keyframes.

4 Increase the Blur X and Blur Y values to **8** px.

The background photo and the first photo become blurry, which accentuates the new photo that appears in the photo2 layer.

The keyframes on your timeline become colored white, indicating that a layer effect is applied.

5 Select frame 24 in the photo2 layer; this is the moment when photo3 appears.

6 Choose Insert Keyframe from above the timeline (F6). This keyframe allows you to add a filter to the layer to change its appearance at that point in time.

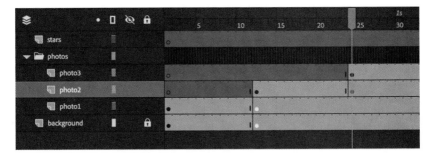

7 Click Add Filter in the Properties panel and choose Blur. Increase Blur X and Blur Y to **8** px.

The photo in the photo2 layer becomes blurry, helping your audience focus on the new photo that appears in the photo3 layer.

8 Select frame 36 in the photo1, photo2, photo3, and background layers and insert a keyframe (F6).

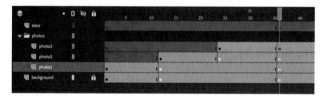

9 In the Color Effects section of the Properties panel, choose Brightness from the Style menu and drag the Bright value to −30%.

The selected layers become slightly darker, which adds drama to the bright yellow stars that appear at that moment in the stars layer.

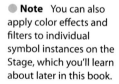
Note You can also apply color effects and filters to individual symbol instances on the Stage, which you'll learn about later in this book.

Undoing steps in Animate

In a perfect world, everything would go according to plan. But sometimes you need to move back a step or two and start over. You can undo steps in Animate using the Undo command or the History panel.

To undo a single step in Animate, choose Edit > Undo or press Command+Z/Ctrl+Z. To redo a step you've undone, choose Edit > Redo.

The easiest way to undo multiple steps in Animate is to use the History panel, which displays a list of the last 100 steps you've performed. Closing a document clears its history. To access the History panel, choose Window > History.

For example, if you aren't satisfied with the newly added stars, you can undo your work and return your Animate document to a previous state.

1   Choose Edit > Undo to undo the last action you made. You can choose the Undo command multiple times to move backward as many steps as are listed in the History panel. You can change the maximum number of Undo commands by choosing Animate > Settings (macOS) or Edit > Preferences (Windows).

● **Note** If you remove steps from the History panel and then perform additional steps, the removed steps will no longer be available.

2   Choose Window > History to open the History panel.

3   Drag the History panel slider up to the step just before your mistake. Steps below that point are dimmed in the History panel and are removed from the project.

    To add a step back, move the slider back down.

4   Finish by returning the History panel slider to its original position next to the bottom step in the panel.

Previewing and exporting your movie

As you work on a project, it's a good idea to preview it frequently to ensure that you're achieving the desired effect.

Testing your movie

To quickly see your animation, choose Control > Play, or simply press the Return/Enter key.

To see how an animation or movie will appear to a viewer, choose the Test Movie button at the upper-right corner of the Animate workspace, or choose Control > Test. You can also press Command+Return/Ctrl+Enter to preview your movie.

1   Choose Control > Test or the Test Movie button at the upper-right corner of the Animate workspace.

    Animate opens and plays the animation in a new panel.

    Animate automatically loops your movie in this preview mode.

2   Close the Test Movie panel.

Using Quick Share and Publish

When you are done with your project, you can export and share it quickly and easily to your favorite social media platforms. Adobe provides a seamless workflow from Animate straight to X (formerly Twitter), YouTube, video, and animated GIFs.

1   In the upper-right corner of Animate, click Quick Share And Publish, and choose Social Share.

2 Choose your target platform. In this lesson, we'll show you how Quick Share works with X, which may still be referred to as Twitter and by its bird logo in the user interface.

3 The preview window displays the first frame of your project to show how it would appear on X. Add a description. You can keep, edit, or remove the suggested hashtags.

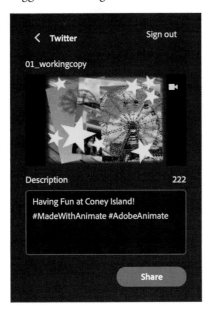

The number above the description indicates the number of characters left for your post.

4 Click Share.

5 Adobe Media Encoder automatically opens to convert your project to the compatible media format. If you're not signed in to X, Animate will ask for authorization to access X to post your exported animation. You will be required to sign in using your handle and password.

Note Keep an eye on the Quick Share and Publish options because Adobe will continue to add more social media channels.

Once authorized, you can post directly from Animate.

6 Navigate to X to check out your post and accompanying animation.

Modifying the content and Stage

When you first started this lesson, you created a new file with the Stage set at 800x600 pixels. However, your client may later tell you that they want the animation in several different sizes to accommodate different layouts. For example, they'd like to create a smaller version with a different aspect ratio for a banner ad. Or they may want to create a version that will run on AIR for Android devices, which require specific dimensions.

Fortunately, you can modify the Stage even after all your content is put in place. When you change the Stage dimensions, Animate provides the option of scaling the content with the Stage, automatically shrinking or enlarging all your content proportionally.

Stage resizing and content scaling

You'll create another version of this animated project with different Stage dimensions. Choose File > Save to save the work you've done so far.

1　In the Document Settings section of the Properties panel, note that the dimensions of the current Stage are set at 800x600 pixels. Click the More Settings button to open the Document Settings dialog box.

2　In the Width and Height boxes, enter new pixel dimensions. Enter **400** for Width and **300** for Height.

You can click the link icon between the Width and Height fields to constrain the proportions of the Stage. With the link icon selected, changing one dimension will automatically change the other proportionally.

3　Select the Scale Content option. Leave the Anchor option as is.

The Anchor option lets you choose the origin from which your content is resized, if the proportions of the new Stage are different.

4　Click OK.

Animate modifies the dimensions of the Stage and automatically resizes all the content. If your new dimensions are not proportional to the original size, Animate will resize everything to maximize the content to fit. This means that if your new Stage size is wider than the original, there'll be extra Stage space to the right. If your new Stage size is taller than the original, there'll be extra Stage space on the bottom.

5   Choose File > Save As.

6   In the Save dialog box, choose Animate Document (*.fla) from the File Format menu, and name the file **01_workingcopy_resized.fla**. Save the file.

    You now have two Animate files, identical in content but with different Stage dimensions. Close this file and reopen 01_workingcopy.fla to continue this lesson.

Saving your movie

● **Note** If you have unsaved changes in an open document, Animate adds an asterisk to the end of its filename at the top of the document window as a friendly reminder.

A mantra in multimedia production is "Save early, save often." Applications, operating systems, and hardware crash more often than anyone wants and at unexpected and inconvenient times. You should always save your movie at regular intervals to ensure that if a crash does happen, you will not have lost too much of your time.

Animate can help alleviate much of the worry over lost work. The Auto-Recovery feature creates a backup file in case of a crash.

Using Auto-Recovery to create a backup

The Auto-Recovery feature is a preference setting that applies to all Animate documents. It saves a backup file, so in case of a crash, you have an alternate file to return to.

1   Choose Animate > Settings > Edit Preferences (macOS) or Edit > Preferences (Windows).

    The Preferences dialog box appears.

2   Select the General category from the left column.

● **Note** To find out how to keep your copy of Animate up to date and to learn about the many sources of help available to you within Animate, see the Getting Started section at the beginning of this book.

3   Select the Auto-Recovery option, if it's not already selected, and enter a time (in minutes) for the interval at which Animate creates a backup file.

4   Click OK.

    If you make changes to your file but do not save it within the Auto-Recovery interval, Animate creates a new file in the same location as your FLA with RECOVER_ added to the beginning of the filename. The file remains as long as the document is open. When you close the document or when you quit Animate safely, the file is deleted.

Review questions

1 What is the Stage?

2 What is the difference between a frame and a keyframe?

3 How do you access hidden tools?

4 Name two methods to undo steps in Animate, and describe them.

5 What document type would be best for playing back animation in a modern browser?

6 What are layer effects, and how do you add them?

Review answers

1 The Stage is the rectangular area viewers see when a movie is playing. It contains the text, images, and video that appear on the screen. Objects that you store on the pasteboard outside the Stage do not appear in the movie.

2 A frame is used to measure time on the timeline. A keyframe is represented on the timeline with a circle and indicates a change in content on the Stage.

3 Because there are too many tools to display at once in the Tools panel, some tools are grouped, and only one tool in the group is displayed. (The tool you most recently used is the one shown.) Small triangles appear on tool icons to indicate that hidden tools are available. To select a hidden tool, press and hold the tool icon for the tool that is shown, and then select the hidden tool from the menu. Other tools are hidden in the drag-and-drop panel accessible from the Edit Toolbar button at the bottom of the Tools panel. Drag a tool into the Toolbar to make it available for use.

4 You can undo steps in Animate using the Undo command or the History panel. To undo a single step at a time, choose Edit > Undo. To undo multiple steps at once, drag the slider up in the History panel.

5 An HTML5 Canvas document targets modern browsers for playback of animation and interactive content. HTML5 Canvas exports HTML, JavaScript, and all the assets required to play in a browser.

6 Layer effects are filters or color effects that you can add to a keyframe on the timeline that change the appearance of the contents of the keyframe. Layer effects are added by selecting a keyframe and choosing a style or a filter from the Color Effects or Filters section of the Properties panel.

2 CREATING GRAPHICS AND TEXT

Lesson overview

In this lesson, you'll learn how to do the following:

• Draw rectangles, ovals, and other shapes.

• Modify the shape, color, and size of drawn objects.

• Understand fill and stroke settings.

• Create and edit curves and variable-width strokes.

• Apply gradients and transparencies.

• Use the different paintbrushes for expressive drawing.

• Create and edit text, and use web fonts.

• Distribute objects on the Stage.

• Create and edit symbols.

• Apply filters to symbol instances.

This lesson will take about 3 hours to complete.

 To get the lesson files used in this chapter, download them from the web page for this book at peachpit.com/AnimateCIB2024. For more information, see "Accessing the lesson files and Web Edition" in the Getting Started section at the beginning of this book.

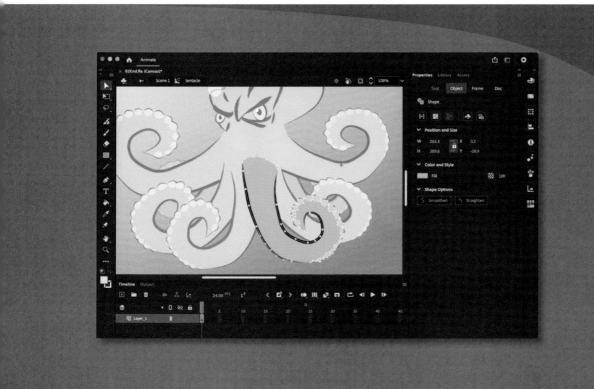

You can use rectangles, ovals, lines, and custom brushes to create interesting, complex graphics and save them as symbols, which will be displayed in your Library panel. Combine gradients, transparencies, text, and filters for even greater expressive possibilities.

Getting started

● **Note** If you have not already downloaded the project files for this lesson to your computer from your Account page, make sure to do so now. See Getting Started at the beginning of the book.

Start by viewing the finished project to see what you'll be creating in this lesson.

1 Double-click 02End.gif to view the image.

The project is a simple illustration consisting of an octopus character and a humorous caption. In this lesson, you'll draw the shapes, modify them, and learn to combine simple elements to create more complex visuals. You won't create any animation just yet. After all, you must learn to walk before you can run! And learning to create and modify graphics is an important step before doing any animation with Adobe Animate.

2 In the Animate Home screen, select More Presets or click Create New.

The New Document dialog box opens.

3 Choose Advanced from the top row of categories. In the Platforms section, choose HTML5 Canvas. In the Details section, make the Stage size **1200** pixels by **800** pixels, and click Create.

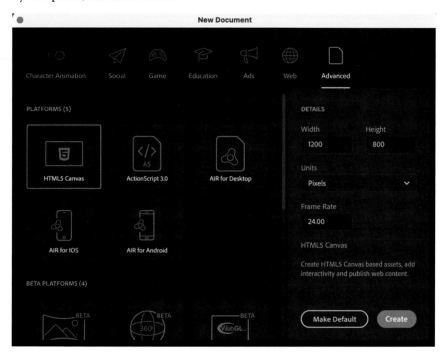

4 Choose File > Save. Name the file **02_workingcopy.fla,** and save it in the 02Start folder.

Saving your file right away is a good work habit (even if you've enabled the Auto-Recovery feature). It ensures that you won't lose your work if the application or your computer crashes.

Understanding strokes and fills

Every graphic created within Animate starts with a shape. A shape consists of two components: the *fill*, or the inside of the shape, and the *stroke*, or the outlines of the shape. If you always keep these two components in mind, you'll be well on your way to creating beautiful and complicated visuals.

The fill and the stroke function independently of each other, so you can modify or delete one without affecting the other. For example, you can create a rectangle with a blue fill and a red stroke and then later change the fill to purple and delete the red stroke entirely; you'll be left with a purple rectangle without an outline. You can also move the fill or stroke independently, so if you want to move the entire shape, make sure you select both its fill and its stroke.

Creating shapes

● **Note** In Animate, as well as in HTML documents and in web design and development in general, colors are often specified by hexadecimal numbers. The six digits after the # sign represent the red, green, and blue contributions to the color.

Animate includes several drawing tools, which work in different drawing modes. Many of your creations will begin with simple shapes such as rectangles and ovals, so it's important that you're comfortable drawing them, modifying their appearance, and applying fills and strokes.

You'll begin by drawing the face of the octopus.

Using the Oval tool

The eyes of the octopus are essentially a series of ovals overlapping one another. To make the eyes look angry, there is a diagonal line that cuts the largest oval at a slant. You'll start by drawing the ovals. It's useful to break down complicated objects into their component parts to make it easier to draw them.

1   Rename Layer_1 **octopus**.

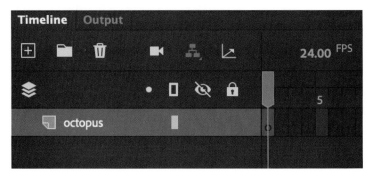

2   In the Tools panel, select the Oval tool, which is hidden under the Rectangle tool. Hold down the Rectangle tool to access the Oval tool underneath. Make sure the Object Drawing button at the bottom of the Tools panel or in the Properties panel is *not* selected.

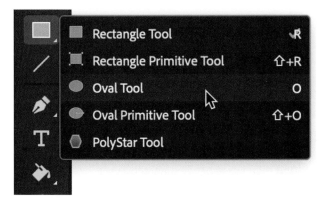

3 Choose a stroke color and a fill color from the bottom of the Tools panel or from the Properties panel. Enter **#CCCCCC** (light gray) for the fill and **#000000** (black) for the stroke.

4 On the Stage, draw an oval that is a little taller than it is wide.

5 Select the Selection tool.

6 Drag the Selection tool around the entire oval to select its stroke and its fill. When a shape is selected, Animate displays it with white dots. You can also double-click a shape, and Animate will select both the stroke and fill of the shape.

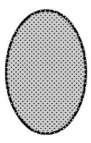

7 In the Properties panel, in the Position And Size section, enter **40** for the Width and **55** for the Height. Press Return (macOS) or Enter (Windows) to apply the values.

Adding the inside of the eye

 Note The last fill and stroke you used are applied to the next objects you create, unless you change the settings before you draw.

Now you'll create the inside of the eye and the white highlight.

1   In the Tools panel, select the Oval tool.

2   Choose a stroke color and a fill color from the bottom of the Tools panel. Enter **#000000** (black) for the fill and **#000000** (black) for the stroke.

3   Draw a smaller black oval inside the larger oval on the Stage.

 Tip Hold down the Shift key as you draw to constrain your shapes. Holding the Shift key when using the Oval tool creates perfect circles, much like holding the Shift key when using the Rectangle tool creates perfect squares.

4   Enter **#FFFFFF** (white) as the fill for your Oval tool.

5   Draw a third oval at the top of your black oval, which will be the highlight.

Animate drawing modes

Animate provides three drawing modes that determine how objects interact with one another on the Stage and how you can edit them. By default, Animate uses Merge Drawing mode, but you can enable Object Drawing mode or use the Rectangle Primitive or Oval Primitive tool to use Primitive Drawing mode.

Merge Drawing mode

In this mode, Animate merges drawn shapes, such as rectangles and ovals, where they overlap so that multiple shapes appear to be a single shape. If you move or delete a shape that has been merged with another shape, the overlapping portion is permanently removed.

Object Drawing mode

In this mode, Animate does not merge drawn objects; they remain distinct and separate, even when they overlap. To enable Object Drawing mode, select the drawing tool you want to use, and then click the Object Drawing button at the bottom of the Tools panel.

To convert an object to a shape (Merge Drawing mode), select the object and choose Modify > Break Apart (Command+B/Ctrl+B). To convert a shape to an object (Object Drawing mode), select the shape and choose Modify > Combine Objects > Union. The current shape becomes an object, but keep in mind that it doesn't restore the shape to how it was originally drawn.

Primitive Drawing mode

When you use the Rectangle Primitive tool or the Oval Primitive tool, Animate draws your rectangles or ovals as independent objects that maintain some editable features. Unlike with regular objects, you can modify the corner radius and the start and end angles of rectangle primitives as well as adjust the inner radius of oval primitives using the Properties panel.

Making selections

To modify an object, you must first be able to select different parts of it. In Animate, you can make selections using the Selection, Subselection, and Lasso tools. Typically, you use the Selection tool to select an entire object or a section of an object. The Subselection tool lets you select a specific point or line in an object. With the Lasso tool, you can make a free-form selection.

Selecting strokes and fills

Now you'll refine the ovals to look more like an eye. You'll use the Selection tool to delete unwanted strokes and fills.

1 In the Tools panel, select the Selection tool.

2 Double-click the stroke around the white oval.

The strokes around both the white oval and the black oval become selected.

3 Press the Delete/Backspace key.

The strokes are deleted, leaving behind a white oval as the highlight.

4 Choose the Line tool, and enter **#000000** (black) as the stroke color.

5 Draw a diagonal line that cuts through the top of the eyeball.

The straight line creates intersecting shapes in the eyeball so that they can be selected separately.

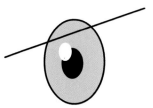

6 Choose the Selection tool and click the half-dome gray shape at the tip of the eye.

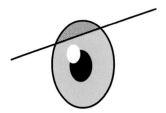

7 Press the Delete/Backspace key.

The gray fill is deleted.

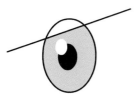

8 Choose the curved stroke above the straight line and delete it.

One eye is finished!

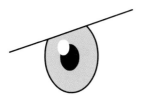

Editing shapes

When drawing in Animate, you'll often start with simple shapes such as rectangles, ovals, and lines. But to create more complex graphics, you'll use other tools to modify those base shapes. The Free Transform tool, the Copy and Paste commands, and the Selection tool can help speed up your workflow.

Using Copy and Paste

Use the Copy and Paste commands to easily duplicate shapes on the Stage. Your octopus needs two eyes, so copying and pasting will come in handy.

1 Select the Selection tool, and drag it around the entire drawing of your eye.

2 Choose Edit > Copy (Command+C/Ctrl+C).

The eye is copied.

3 Choose Edit > Paste (Command+V/Ctrl+V).

A duplicate eye appears on the Stage. The duplicate remains selected.

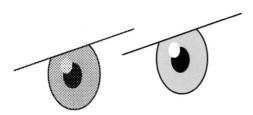

4 Move the duplicate eye close to your original eye.

▶ **Tip** Use Paste In Place (Shift+Command+V/ Shift+Ctrl+V) if you want to paste the copied graphic in the exact same place where you copied it from.

Using Free Transform

The duplicate eye needs to be flipped to make it look right. You'll use the Free Transform tool to make it a mirror image of itself. You can also use the Free Transform tool to change an object's scale, rotation, or *skew* (the way it is slanted), or to distort an object by dragging control points around a bounding box.

1 Choose Modify > Transform > Flip Horizontal.

   The object flips, and you now have a right eye and a left eye.

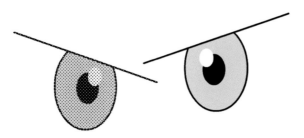

▶ **Tip** If you press the Option or Alt key while moving one of the control points, Animate scales the selected object relative to its transformation point, represented by the circle icon. You can move the transformation point anywhere, even outside the object. Press Shift to constrain the object proportions. Hold the Command/Ctrl key to distort the object from a single control point.

2 Choose the Free Transform tool from the Tools panel.

   Transformation handles appear on the eye.

3 Drag a corner point inward to make the left eye a little smaller. Hold down the Shift key while dragging to constrain the proportions so that the eye maintains the same aspect ratio.

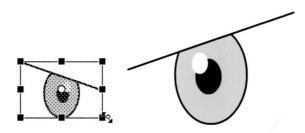

4 Have fun making the second eye a little crazy. You can drag the corner points to squash or stretch an object or to rotate the object. You can also drag the sides of the bounding box to skew the object so that it appears slanted.

▶ **Tip** Hold the Command/Ctrl key to drag a single control point to distort the eyeball. If you press and hold Shift+Command/ Shift+Ctrl as you drag a corner point, you can move both corners the same distance simultaneously.

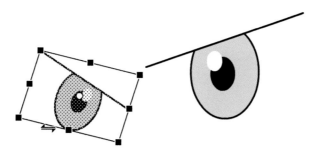

Changing shape contours

With the Selection tool, you can push and pull lines and corners to change the overall contours of any shape. It's a fast and intuitive way of working with shapes. You'll use this technique to create the organic shape of the octopus head and body.

1   Insert a new layer on the timeline and name it **body**. Drag it so that it is below the octopus layer, which currently contains the eyes.

2   In the Tools panel, select the Oval tool. Choose a green color for the fill (**#33CCCC**) and black for the stroke.

3   Create three overlapping ovals, similar to the following figure, off to the side of the eyes. You don't have to be exact here since you'll edit these shapes.

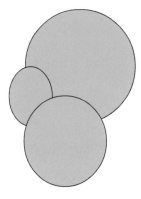

4   Select the black outlines and press the Delete key.

The black strokes are deleted.

5 Move your mouse cursor close to the side of one of the ovals.

A curved line appears near your cursor, indicating that you can change the curvature of the stroke.

6 Drag the stroke outward.

The side of the oval bends, giving the octopus head a slight bulge. Push and pull on the contours of the three ovals to create a more organic, bulbous head and natural-looking brow ridge for your octopus.

If you want to create a new corner point so that you can change the directions of a curve, hold down the Option/Alt key while you drag on the curve.

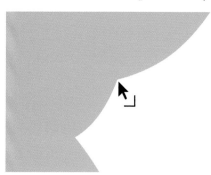

Changing strokes and fills

If you want to change the properties of any stroke or fill, you can use the Ink Bottle tool or the Paint Bucket tool. The Ink Bottle tool changes stroke colors; the Paint Bucket tool changes fill colors. The check mark next to the quick key indicates the currently selected tool that is displayed in the Tool panel.

▶ **Tip** If your Paint Bucket tool changes the fill in surrounding areas, there may be a small gap in the shape outline that allows the fill to spill over. Close the gap manually, or use the Gap Size menu at the bottom of the Tools panel to choose the gap size that Animate will close automatically.

- Select the Paint Bucket tool and choose a new fill color in the Properties panel. Click a fill to change its color.

- Select the Ink Bottle tool (hidden under the Paint Bucket tool) and choose a new stroke color in the Properties panel. You can also choose the thickness and style of the stroke. Click a stroke to change its properties.

- You can also simply select a stroke or a fill on the Stage and change its properties by using the Properties panel.

Using variable-width strokes

You can make many different styles of lines for your strokes. In addition to the basic solid line, you can choose a dotted, dashed, or ragged line, or even customize your own. You can also create lines with variable widths and edit the variations with the Width tool.

Adding thick and thin outlines

The variable width of strokes can help give your drawings more expressive character.

1 Select the Ink Bottle tool, and in the Properties panel, choose 6 for the Stroke Size and Width Profile 1 for the Width.

2 Click the large green octopus head.

Animate applies the thick-thin width profile to the outline of your green fill.

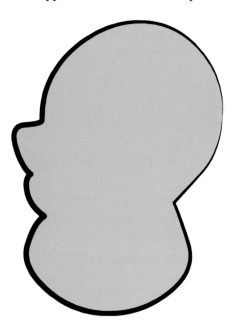

3 With the Selection tool, choose a single stroke segment around the green head, and then change the Stroke Size to 4.

Now you have two different stroke widths around your shape.

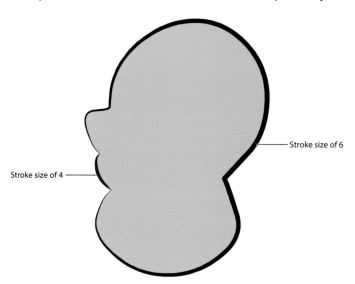

Stroke size of 6

Stroke size of 4

4   Delete the stroke around the bottom oval shape. You'll connect the octopus tentacles there, so you won't need the black outline.

Refining variable-width lines

In addition to applying different width profiles to a stroke, you can customize where the bulges appear and how wide the bulges are with the Width tool.

1   Hold down the Shift key and click the three line segments of one of the eyebrows.

2   In the Properties panel, change the Stroke Size to 10.

3   Change the Width to Width Profile 1.

▶ **Tip** Edit variable-width lines as you would any other stroke. Use the Selection or Subselection tool to bend the curves or move the anchor points.

The straight line turns into a thicker line that is skinny on the ends and fatter in the middle, giving it a little more personality.

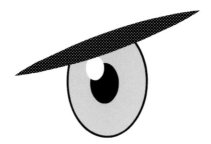

4   Click the three dots at the bottom of the Tools panel to edit the Toolbar.

5   Drag the Width tool from the Drag And Drop Tools panel to your Tools panel so that you can use it. Click off the Tools panel or press the Esc key to collapse it.

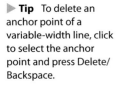

▶ Tip To delete an anchor point of a variable-width line, click to select the anchor point and press Delete/ Backspace.

6   Move your mouse pointer over one of your variable-width strokes.

Anchor points appear along the line to show you where the thick and thin portions of the line are located.

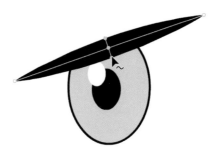

7   Drag the handles at any anchor point to change the width of the line. Exaggerate some of the restrictions and bulges.

▶ **Tip** Hold down Option/Alt when you want to modify only one side of a variable-width line.

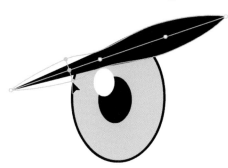

8   Drag an anchor point along the stroke to move its location.

9   Drag anywhere along the stroke to add a new anchor point and define the width at that location. Animate displays a small plus (+) sign next to your pointer to indicate that you can add an anchor point.

10 Modify both eyebrows of your octopus as you see fit, and apply a different width profile to the outline around the eyes as well.

Organizing your drawing

Now that you've finished creating the eyes and the head, you'll want to start organizing the different parts of the drawing. You've already organized different shapes by putting them in separate layers, but you can also use groups to keep them separated.

Grouping objects

A group holds together a collection of shapes and other graphics to preserve their integrity. When the elements that compose the eyes are grouped, you can move them as a unit without worrying that the eyes might merge and intersect with underlying shapes in the same layer.

1 Select the Selection tool.

2 Select all the shapes that make up one of the eyes, including the eyebrows.

3 Choose Modify > Group.

The eye becomes a single group. When you select it, a blue-green outline indicates its bounding box.

4 If you want to change any part of the eye, double-click the group to edit it.

Notice that all the other elements on the Stage dim, and the Edit bar above the Stage displays Scene 1 > Group. This indicates that you are now in a particular group and can edit its contents.

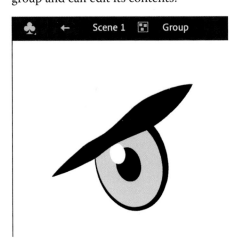

5 Click the Scene 1 icon in the Edit bar at the top of the Stage, or double-click an empty part of the Stage, and return to the main scene.

6 Group your other eye and move the two eyes on top of the head. Remember, you can resize the head or eyes with the Free Transform tool to get your graphics to fit just right.

▶ **Tip** To change a group back into its component shapes, choose Modify > Ungroup (Shift+Command+G/ Shift+Ctrl+G).

Using brushes

Although the Oval and Line tools (and related tools, such as the Rectangle tool) are useful for building complicated shapes from simpler ones, they are not that good for creating spontaneous, expressive marks.

For a more painterly approach, use the brush tools. There are three of them: the Fluid Brush tool, the Classic Brush tool, and the Paint Brush tool.

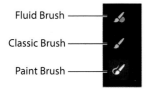

- The Fluid Brush tool is designed to respond to pressure from a graphics tablet or the speed at which you draw. The size of the brush can change as you draw, making it easy to create thick and thin marks.

- The Paint Brush tool allows you to use a brush shape that stretches or one that regularly repeats for borders and decorations. You can choose from dozens of different brushes, and if you don't find something you can use, you can customize the brushes or even create your own.

- The Classic Brush tool is the most basic of the three brushes, with limited controls over its size and shape.

Note The Fluid Brush and the Classic Brush produce fills, not strokes. The Paint Brush tool, by default, produces strokes, but you can enable the Draw As Fill option in the Properties panel for the Paint Brush to produce fills.

Using the Fluid Brush

You'll use the Fluid Brush to create the various furrows and wrinkles in the octopus's face.

1 Select the Fluid Brush tool.

2 In the Properties panel, under the Tool tab, choose the Velocity option, choose black for the Fill, and set the various parameters for the size and shape of the mark you want to make.

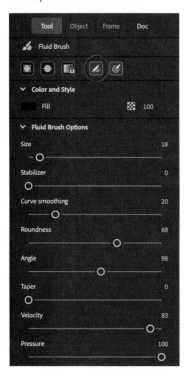

When you use the Velocity option, the size of your mark changes based on the speed of your pointer as you drag your brush on the Stage. If you choose the Pressure option, the size of your mark depends on the pressure of your pointer from a pressure-sensitive stylus and tablet.

Test out a few marks on the Stage and adjust the Velocity influence or the other parameters until you're comfortable with how your brush will behave.

3   Select the octopus layer.

4   Drag out a few marks on the octopus head with the Fluid Brush tool. Be bold!
    Make some angry brows and bulges as you see fit. You can use this example as
    a guide, but you don't have to copy all the marks exactly. Create an octopus face
    that reflects your personality.

● **Note** If you have
a drawing tablet, the
Fluid Brush tool can be
a source of endless fun,
as you can customize
the brush in countless
ways to respond to both
pressure and velocity.

Smoothing shapes

You may notice at this point that some of the lines you created are too wobbly. Fortunately, you can smooth out curves quickly and easily.

1   Select all the fills you made with the Fluid Brush tool.

2   At the bottom of the Tools panel, click the Smoothen option.

▶ **Tip** You can get finer control over smoothing curves by choosing Modify > Shape > Advanced Smooth or Modify > Shape > Optimize. These advanced options allow you to refine the number of curves and points that define your shapes.

The curves of the selected shapes simplify and appear smoother.

3   Click the Smoothen button repeatedly until you are satisfied with the level of smoothness.

Creating curves

You've used the Selection tool to push and pull on the edges of shapes to intuitively make curves. For more precise control, you can use the Pen tool.

Using the Pen tool

What would an octopus be without its arms? Now you'll create the curvy, sinewy tentacles for your octopus.

1   Insert a new layer called **tentacles**.

2   In the Tools panel, select the Pen tool. If it's not in the Tools panel, you must add it by choosing Edit Toolbar at the bottom of the panel and dragging it from the drag-and-drop panel.

3   Set the stroke color to black. Choose Hairline from the Style menu and Uniform from the Width menu.

4   Begin your shape by clicking your mouse button down on the Stage (away from the octopus head) to establish the first anchor point.

5   Move the mouse pointer to a new location and press—but don't release!—the mouse button to place the next anchor point. Keep holding the mouse button and dragging in the direction you want the line to continue. You will drag out a direction line from the new anchor point. When you release the mouse button, you will have created a smooth curve between the two anchor points.

To learn more about drawing with the Pen tool, see the sidebar "Creating paths with the Pen tool."

6 Continue to add curves to create a tentacle that appears as a J-like shape, pressing and dragging out direction lines to build the outline of the tentacle.

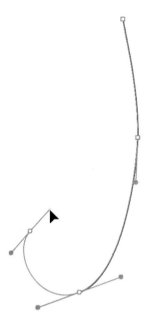

Don't worry if your curves aren't completely smooth. You can always edit them later.

7 When you get to the tip of the tentacle, click the anchor point itself.

One half of each pair of anchor-point handles disappears, creating a corner point and allowing you to change directions.

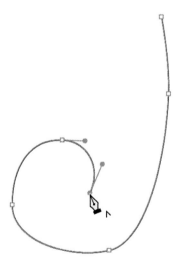

8 Continue drawing wavy lines parallel to the first curved line.

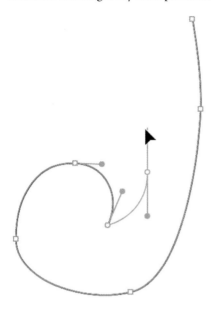

9 Close your shape by clicking the first anchor point.

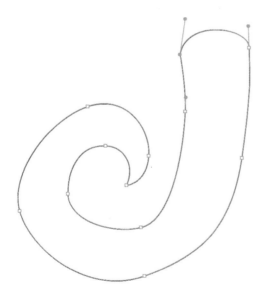

10 Select the Paint Bucket tool.

11 Set the fill color to the same color as your octopus head (you can use the Eyedropper tool to sample the fill of the octopus head and apply it to your tentacle).

12 Click inside the outline you just created to fill it with color.

13 Select the Selection tool, and double-click the outline to select all of it. Press the Delete key to remove the stroke.

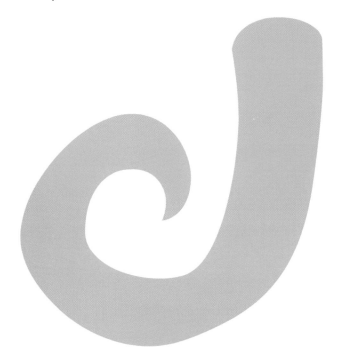

Editing curves with the Selection and Subselection tools

Your first try at creating smooth waves probably won't be very good. Use the Selection tool or the Subselection tool to refine your curves.

1 Select the Selection tool.

2 Hover your cursor over a line segment and look at the arced line segment that appears near your pointer. This indicates that you can edit the curve.

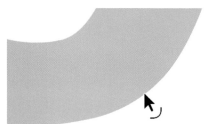

If a right-angle segment appears near your cursor, this indicates that you can edit the corner point.

3 Drag the curve to edit its shape.

4 In the Tools panel, select the Subselection tool (hidden under the Selection tool).

5 Click the outline of the shape.

6 Drag the anchor points to new locations, or move the handles to refine the overall shape. Lengthening the handles makes the curve flatter. Tilting the handles changes the direction of the curve.

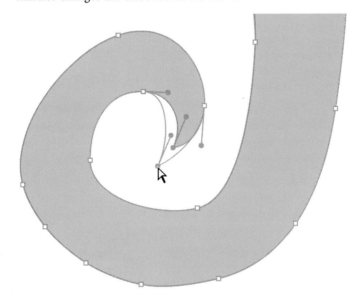

Deleting or adding anchor points

Use the hidden tools under the Pen tool to delete or add anchor points as needed.

- Click and hold the Pen tool to access the hidden tools under it.

- Use the Delete Anchor Point tool to delete an existing anchor point.

- Use the Add Anchor Point tool to add an anchor point to a curve.

- Use the Convert Anchor Point tool to drag out handlebars from an anchor point.

Creating paths with the Pen tool

You can use the Pen tool to create paths that are straight or curved, open or closed. If you're unfamiliar with the Pen tool, it can be confusing to use at first. Understanding the elements of a path and how to create those elements with the Pen tool makes paths much easier to draw.

To create a straight path, click the mouse button. The first time you click, you set the starting point. Each time you click thereafter, a straight line is drawn between the previous point and the current point. To draw complex straight-segment paths with the Pen tool, simply continue to add points.

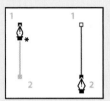

Creating a straight line.

To create a curved path, start by pressing the mouse button to place an anchor point; then drag to create a direction line for that point, and release the mouse button. Move the mouse to place the next anchor point, and drag out another set of direction lines. At the end of each direction line is a direction point; the positions of direction lines and points determine the size and shape of the curved segment. Moving the direction lines and points reshapes the curves in a path.

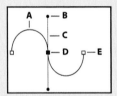

Creating a curved line.

A. *Curved line segment*
B. *Direction point*
C. *Direction line*
D. *Selected anchor point*
E. *Unselected anchor point*

Smooth curves are connected by anchor points called smooth points. Sharply curved paths are connected by corner points. When you move a direction line on a smooth point, the curved segments on both sides of the point adjust simultaneously, but when you move a direction line on a corner point, only the curve on the same side of the point as the direction line is adjusted.

Path segments and anchor points can be moved after they're drawn, either individually or as a group. When a path contains more than one segment, you can drag individual anchor points to adjust individual segments of the path, or select all of the anchor points in a path to edit the entire path. Use the Subselection tool to select and adjust an anchor point, a path segment, or an entire path.

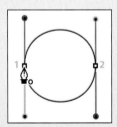

Creating a closed path.

Closed paths differ from open paths in the way that you end each one. To end an open path, select the Selection tool or press Escape. To create a closed path, position the Pen tool pointer over the starting point (a small ° will appear by the pointer) and click. Closing a path automatically ends the path. After the path closes, the Pen tool pointer appears with a small *, indicating that your next click will start a new path.

Excerpted with permission from Adobe Photoshop CC Classroom in a Book. © 2017 Adobe Systems Incorporated and its licensors. All rights reserved.

Using brush mode options

Choosing the right brush mode for your brush tool can make drawing in Animate much more efficient. Normally, you expect color wherever you drag your brush. But you can change that behavior. In the next task, you'll add suckers to your tentacle by using one of the brush modes.

Using Paint Fills Only

Choose the Paint Fills Only brush mode if you want to have your brush affect only existing fills on the Stage.

1   Select the Classic Brush tool.

2   In the Properties panel, choose a nice orange fill color. In the Classic Brush options section, change the Size to about 20 (or whatever size looks good depending on how big you've drawn your own tentacle).

3   At the top of the Properties panel, select the option for Brush Mode to Paint Fills Only.

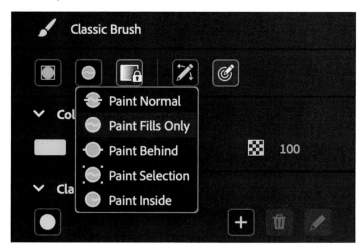

With this option enabled, the brush will affect only the fills of your shapes.

4 Begin painting a little circle at the bottom edge of the tentacle to represent a sucker. Don't worry about going over the outline of the tentacle. Release your mouse button.

The paint from the Fluid Brush tool affects only the inside fill of the tentacle.

5 Continue adding suckers along the bottom edge of your tentacle.

Your tentacle is finished!

Brush modes

There are five available brush modes for your paint brushes: Paint Normal, Paint Fills Only, Paint Behind, Paint Selection, and Paint Inside. Each one works slightly differently from the other, and mastering them can make drawing in Animate more efficient.

Paint Normal applies color over everything on the Stage in the active layer, covering strokes and fills.

Paint Fills Only applies color only in areas of fill.

Paint Behind affects only empty areas of the Stage, keeping existing strokes and fills intact on the active layer.

Paint Selection applies color only in selected fills or strokes.

Paint Inside applies color only in the fill of the shape in which you started.

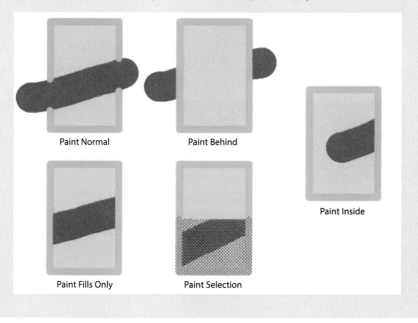

Paint Normal

Paint Behind

Paint Inside

Paint Fills Only

Paint Selection

Paint Brush tool and custom brushes

Animate has three brush tools: the Fluid Brush, which you used to create thick and thin expressive marks for the octopus face; the Classic Brush, which is a basic, no-frills brush; and the Paint Brush, which you have to add from the Drag and Drop Tools panel.

The Paint Brush tool provides a number of different brushes in the Brush Library, accessible from the Style options.

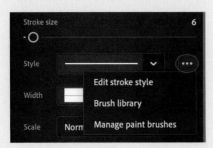

You can choose from arrows, decorative borders, and calligraphic and artistic brushes.

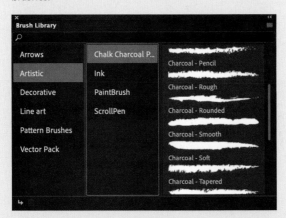

You might not find a brush to your liking in the Brush Library, or you may need something very specific for your project. In either case, you can edit an existing brush or create an entirely new one.

Pattern brushes repeat a shape over the length of a stroke, whereas Art brushes stretch the base art over the length of the stroke.

To edit a brush, click the Edit Stroke Style button next to the Style menu in the Properties panel.

The Paint Brush Options dialog box appears, and it shows multiple controls depending on what type of brush you have currently selected.

Art brushes and Pattern brushes have different options. Experiment with different spacing, how the shapes repeat or stretch to fit, and how corners and overlaps are handled. When you're satisfied with your new brush, click Add to add your customized brush to the Style menu.

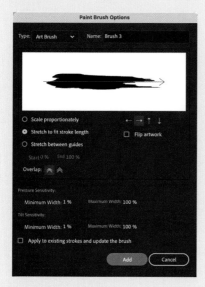
Options for Art brush.

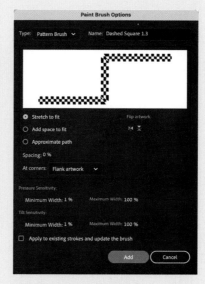
Options for Pattern brush.

To create an entirely new brush, first create some shapes on the Stage that you want to base your brush on. For example, if you want to create a train track, create the base art that repeats for a Pattern brush.

Select the artwork on the Stage, and then click the Create New Paint Brush icon at the top of the Properties panel.

The Paint Brush Options dialog box appears. From the Type menu, you can choose either Art Brush or Pattern Brush and then refine the brush options. The preview window shows you the results of your chosen options.

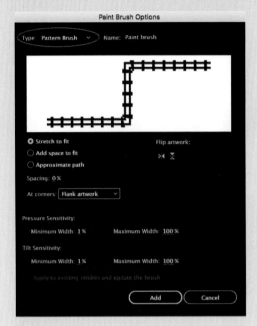

Enter a name for your new brush and click Add. Your new brush will be added to your Style menu and available for you to use.

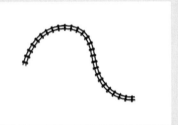

Rotating the Stage for easier drawing

When you draw on regular paper, it's often easier to rotate the page to get a better angle to draw or write something. In Animate, you can do the same thing with the Stage using the Rotation tool.

The Rotation tool is grouped under the Hand tool in the Tools panel and is also accessible above the Stage.

Select the Rotation tool and click the Stage to specify the pivot point, indicated by a crosshair. Once the pivot point has been established, drag the Stage to rotate it to your desired angle.

Click the Center Stage button at the top of the Stage to reset the Stage to its normal orientation.

About symbols

You might be wondering why your octopus has only one tentacle. You could create seven more, but there's an easier way—using *symbols*. Symbols are reusable assets that you create and store in the Library panel.

Symbols are also used for special effects, animation, and interactivity. Animate uses three kinds of symbols: *graphic*, *button*, and *movie clip*. You can use a symbol countless times in a project, but Animate includes its data only once. Symbols also make

Note In spite of its name, a movie clip symbol isn't necessarily animated.

editing easier. If you have eight tentacles on the Stage all based on a single symbol, you only have to make edits once.

Symbols are saved in the Library panel. When you drag a symbol to the Stage, Animate creates an *instance* of the symbol, leaving the original in the library. An instance is a copy of a symbol that has been placed on the Stage. You can think of the symbol as an original photographic negative and the instances on the Stage as prints of the negative. From a single negative, you can create multiple prints.

It's also helpful to think of symbols as containers for content. A symbol can contain a JPEG image, an imported Illustrator drawing, or a drawing that you created in Animate. At any time, you can go inside your symbol and edit it, which means editing or replacing its contents. Changing the contents of a symbol also causes all the symbol's instances to change.

Three types of symbols

Each of the three kinds of symbols in Animate is used for a specific purpose. You can tell whether a symbol is a graphic, button, or movie clip by looking at the icon next to it in the Library panel. Throughout this book, you'll encounter and learn to use all three symbols.

Movie clip symbols

The movie clip is one of the most versatile types of symbol. When you create animation, you will typically use movie clip symbols. You can apply filters, color settings, and blending modes to a movie clip instance to enhance its appearance with special effects.

A movie clip symbol also contains its own independent timeline. You can have an animation inside a movie clip symbol just as easily as you can have an animation on the main timeline. This makes very complex animations possible; for example, a butterfly flying across the Stage can move from left to right as well as have its wings flapping independently of its movement.

You can also control movie clips with code to make them respond to the user's input. For example, you can control a movie clip's position or rotation to create arcade-style games. Or a movie clip can have drag-and-drop behavior, which comes in handy when building a jigsaw puzzle.

Button symbols

Button symbols are used for interactivity. They contain four unique keyframes that describe how they appear when the mouse pointer is interacting with them. However, buttons need code to make them do something.

You can also apply filters, blending modes, and color settings to buttons. You'll learn more about buttons in Lesson 10, "Creating Interactive Media," when you create a nonlinear navigation scheme to allow the user to choose what an animation displays.

Graphic symbols

Often you use graphic symbols to build more complex movie clip symbols. They do not support interactivity, and you can't apply filters or blending modes to a graphic symbol.

Graphic symbols are useful when you have multiple versions of a drawing that you want to easily switch between—for example, when synchronizing lips to sound, keeping all the different mouth positions in individual keyframes of a graphic symbol makes voice syncing easy. Graphic symbols also are used when you need to synchronize an animation inside a symbol to the main timeline.

Creating symbols

There are two main ways to create a symbol. Both methods are valid; the one you use depends on your preferred way of working.

The first method is to start with nothing selected on the Stage and then to choose Insert > New Symbol. Animate will put you in symbol editing mode, where you can begin drawing or importing graphics for your symbol.

The second method is to select existing artwork on the Stage and then convert the artwork to symbols. Whatever is selected will automatically be placed inside your new symbol.

Many designers prefer to use the second method because they can create all their graphics on the Stage and see them together before converting the individual components into symbols.

● **Note** When you use the command Convert To Symbol, you aren't actually "converting" anything; rather, you're placing whatever you've selected inside a symbol.

Converting artwork on the Stage into a symbol

For this task, you'll select your tentacle and then convert it to a movie clip symbol.

1   On the Stage, select only the tentacle.

2   Choose Modify > Convert To Symbol (F8).

    The Convert To Symbol dialog box opens.

3   Name the symbol **tentacle** and choose Movie Clip from the Type menu.

4　Leave all the other settings as they are. The Registration grid indicates the registration point (x=0, y=0) of your symbol. This is the point around which all transformations (for example, rotations and scalings) are centered and the point that Animate uses to measure its position on the Stage. Leave the registration at the upper-left corner.

5　Click OK. The tentacle symbol appears in the Library panel.

You now have a symbol in your library, and an instance of that symbol is on the Stage.

Managing symbol instances

Having a symbol saved in your library allows you to use multiple copies, or *instances*, of that asset in your project without increasing your file size. More importantly, every instance doesn't have to be an exact duplicate of every other instance. Instances can vary slightly from their original master symbol—they can vary in position on the Stage, as well as in size, rotation, and even color, transparency, and applied filters.

Next, you'll add seven more instances of your tentacle symbol and change each of them slightly to give some variation to the octopus pose.

Adding another symbol instance

Additional symbol instances are added to the Stage by dragging them from the Library panel.

1 Select the tentacles layer.

2 Drag the tentacle movie clip symbol from the Library panel to the Stage.

 A duplicate of your tentacle graphic appears on the Stage. You now have two instances of the tentacle symbol on the Stage.

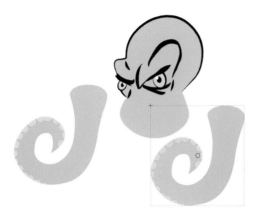

3 Drag six more tentacle symbols onto the Stage.

Changing the size, position, and overlapping of an instance

You'll now use the Free Transform tool to make the tentacles a little different from one another.

1 Arrange four tentacles on one side of the octopus.

2 Select the Free Transform tool, and rotate, skew, and scale the instances to make them fit the octopus body and to make them slightly different from one another.

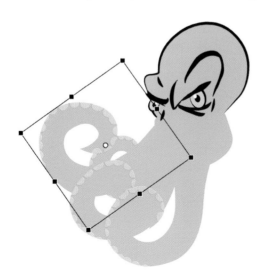

3 Arrange the other four tentacles on the opposite side of the octopus's body and flip them horizontally.

4 To change the stacking order of your tentacle instances (how they overlap each other), right-click an instance, choose Arrange, and select Bring To Front to move the instance to the top so that it overlaps all the other instances or select Bring Forward to move it one place higher in the stacking order. Select Send To Back to move the instance to the bottom so that all the other instances overlap it, or Send Backward to move it one place lower in the stacking order.

● **Note** When using the Free Transform tool on a symbol instance, you cannot make distortions by holding down the Command/Ctrl key to move only one corner point.

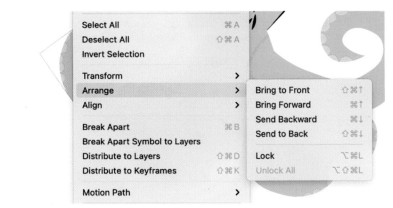

Editing a symbol from the library

You can also edit any symbol at any time. If you decide you want to change the shape of the tentacle, for example, you can easily go into symbol editing mode and make that change. You can edit symbols directly from the Library panel whether or not they've been used on the Stage.

What's important to remember is that when you edit a symbol, you're making changes to the "master," so those edits will be reflected in all the individual instances of that symbol on the Stage.

1 Double-click the tentacle movie clip symbol icon in the Library panel.

Animate puts you in symbol editing mode. In this mode, you can see the contents of your symbol—in this case, the tentacle on the Stage. Notice that the Edit bar at the top of the Stage tells you that you are no longer in Scene 1 but are inside the symbol called tentacle.

2 Using the Selection or Subselection tool, make bulges for each orange sucker on the tentacle. Recall that you can use the Selection tool to drag lines to change their curvature, or you can use the Subselection tool to move anchor points and drag their handlebars to change curvatures.

Tip You can quickly and easily duplicate symbols in the Library panel. Select the symbol, right-click, and choose Duplicate. Or choose Duplicate from the Library panel menu (in the upper-right corner of the panel). Animate will open a dialog box to give you an opportunity to create an exact copy of the selected symbol in your library.

3 Click the left-facing arrow on the Edit bar above the Stage to exit symbol editing mode and return to the main timeline.

The thumbnail of the movie clip symbol in the Library panel reflects the changes you made. The same is true of all instances on the Stage. All instances of a symbol change if you edit the symbol.

Editing a symbol in place

● **Note** When you edit a symbol in place with the Fluid Brush tool or the Classic Brush tool, note that there is an option in the Properties panel called Scale Size With Symbol Instance, which is selected by default. This option automatically adjusts the size of your brush so that edits are proportional to instances on the Stage that may have been shrunk or enlarged.

You may want to edit a symbol in context with the other objects on the Stage. You can do so by double-clicking an instance on the Stage. You'll enter symbol editing mode, but you'll also be able to see the symbol's surroundings. This editing mode is called *editing in place*.

1 Using the Selection tool, double-click a tentacle movie clip instance on the Stage.

All other objects on the Stage are dimmed and you are put into symbol editing mode. Notice that the Edit bar shows that you are no longer in Scene 1 but are inside the symbol called tentacle.

2 Apply a variable-width stroke to the sides of the tentacle and suckers.

▶ **Tip** To delete just the top outline of the tentacle, make sure that you have corner points on either side.

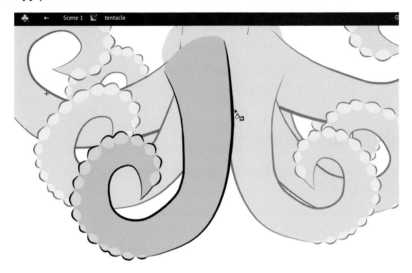

As you edit the symbol, notice that the changes ripple through all the instances of that symbol on the Stage.

3 Click Scene 1 on the Edit bar above the Stage to return to the main timeline. You can also just double-click any part of the Stage outside the graphic with the Selection tool to return to the next-highest group level.

Breaking apart a symbol instance

If you no longer want an object on the Stage to be a symbol instance, you can use the Break Apart command to return it to its original form.

Select the symbol instance and choose Modify > Break Apart.

Animate breaks apart the movie clip instance. What's left on the Stage are the contents of the movie clip symbol, which is the shape.

For this exercise, you'll keep all your tentacle instances, so if you used Break Apart, choose Edit > Undo to return your tentacle to a symbol instance.

Using gradient fills

So far, you have used solid colors as fills, but you can also use a gradient as a fill for a more interesting effect.

In a *gradient*, one color gradually changes into another. Animate can create *linear* gradients, which change color horizontally, vertically, or diagonally; and *radial* gradients, which change color moving outward from a central focal point.

For this lesson, you'll use a linear gradient fill to add an ocean background.

Creating gradient transitions

You'll use the Color panel to define the colors to use in your gradient. By default, a linear gradient moves from one color to a second color, but you can use up to 15 color transitions in a gradient in Animate. A *color pointer* determines where each color is defined, and smooth color changes happen between each pointer. Add color pointers beneath the gradient definition bar in the Color panel to add more colors and, hence, more gradients.

You'll create a gradient that moves from light blue to dark blue to create the appearance of the deep ocean.

1 Create a new layer and name it **background**. Move the layer to the bottom of the layers.

2 Open the Color panel (Window > Color). In the Color panel, click the Fill Color icon and choose Linear Gradient from the Color Type menu.

3 In the Color panel, select the color pointer at the left end of the color gradient definition bar (the triangle above it turns black when selected), and then type **66CCFF** in the hex value field to specify a light blue color. Press Return/Enter to apply the color. You can also select a color from the Color Picker, or double-click the color pointer to select a color from the color swatches.

4 Select the far-right color pointer, and then enter **000066** for a dark blue color. Press Return/Enter to apply the color.

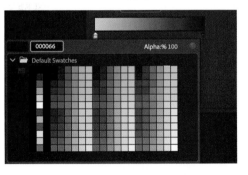

▶ **Tip** To delete a color pointer from the gradient definition bar, simply drag it off the bar.

5 Choose the Rectangle tool.

6 In the Properties panel, make sure the Fill has the gradient you defined in the Color panel. Choose no color for the stroke (the empty color chip with the red diagonal line through it).

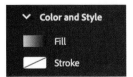

7 Draw a large rectangle that covers the entire Stage.

The large square is filled with a color that gradually blends from light blue to dark blue.

Using the Gradient Transform tool

In addition to choosing colors and positioning the color pointers for a gradient, you can adjust the size, direction, and center of a gradient fill. To change where the colors in your gradient begin to change in your ocean background, you'll use the Gradient Transform tool.

1 Select the Gradient Transform tool. (The Gradient Transform tool is grouped with the Free Transform tool.)

▶ **Tip** Move the center circle to change the center of the gradient, drag the round handle to rotate the gradient, and drag the square handle to stretch or compress the gradient.

2 Click the rectangle fill in your background layer. Transformation handles appear.

3 Drag the square handle on the right side of the bounding box inward to squeeze the gradient tighter. Drag the round handle in the corner to rotate the gradient so that the lighter blue appears at the upper-left corner and the darker blue appears at the lower-right corner.

Using transparency to create depth

Transparency is measured as a percentage and is referred to as *alpha*. An alpha value of 100% indicates that a color is totally opaque, whereas an alpha value of 0% indicates that a color is totally transparent.

Modifying the alpha value of a fill

You'll add small transparent bubbles to your scene to provide some interesting details. We know octopuses don't make bubbles, but they don't have angry eyes either, right?

1 Insert a new layer, name it **bubbles**, and move it to the top of all the other layers.

2 Choose the Oval tool.

3 In the Properties panel, choose white for the Fill and choose None for the Stroke.

4 Change the Alpha value for the Fill to 60%.

▶ **Tip** You can create gradients with different Alpha values as well.

▶ **Tip** You can also change the transparency of a shape from the Properties panel by clicking the Fill Color icon and changing the Alpha value in the color picker.

The color swatch in the Properties panel previews your newly selected color. Transparency is indicated by the gray grid that you can see through the transparent color swatch.

5 Hold down the Shift key and drag out circles of varying sizes across your octopus.

The bubbles are slightly transparent, allowing you to see the graphics in the layers behind them.

Using swatches and tagged swatches

Swatches are predefined samples of color. Access them via the Swatches panel (Window > Swatches, or Command+F9/ Ctrl+F9). You can save colors that you've used in your graphics as new swatches so that you always have them to refer to.

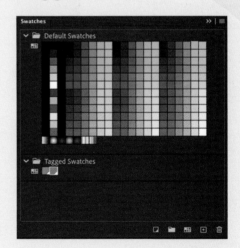

Tagged swatches are specially marked swatches that are linked to the graphics on your Stage that are using them. You can create a tagged swatch by choosing Convert To A Tagged Swatch at the bottom of the Swatches panel, and you can name your tagged swatch. A tagged swatch is indicated by the white triangle in the lower-right corner of the color.

The real power of tagged swatches is apparent when you have to make updates to your project. Suppose the art director or your client doesn't like the color of the white transparent bubbles. If you use a tagged swatch for the bubbles, you can simply update the color of the tagged swatch and all graphics using that tagged swatch will update.

Applying filters and color effects

In the previous lesson, you applied filters and color effects to keyframes on the timeline. You can also apply filters and color effects to symbol instances on the Stage. Use filters to create special effects such as blurs, glows, and drop shadows. Use color effects to brighten, darken, colorize, and make other changes to your transparencies.

Changing the color effect of an instance

Each instance can have its own value for transparency, color, tint, or brightness. The controls for these settings are in the Color Effects section of the Properties panel.

1   Using the Selection tool, select a few of the tentacles that are behind all the others.

2   In the Color Effects section of the Properties panel, choose Brightness from the Style menu.

3   Drag the Bright slider to –20%.

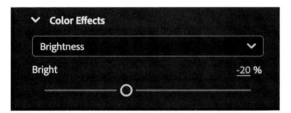

▶ **Tip** Choosing Advanced from the Style menu allows you to change the tint, transparency, and brightness of an instance at the same time by adjusting the individual color components (RGB) together with the Alpha percentage.

The selected tentacle instances on the Stage become darker and appear to recede into the distance.

▶ **Tip** To reset the color effect of any instance, choose None from the Style menu.

Applying the Blur filter

You can also apply a Blur filter to the farthest tentacle instances to help give the scene a greater sense of depth.

1 Select the instances of the tentacles that are already dimmed.

2 In the Properties panel, expand the Filters section.

3 Click Add Filter and choose Blur from the menu.

Properties and values for the Blur filter are displayed.

4 If the link icons next to the Blur X and Blur Y values aren't already selected, click one of them to constrain the blur effect in both directions.

5 Leave Blur X and Blur Y at their default values (4 pixels).

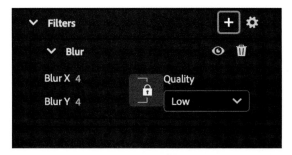

The instance on the Stage becomes blurry, helping to give an atmospheric perspective to the scene.

More filter options

The Options menu at the upper-right corner of the Filters section lists commands that help you manage and apply multiple filters.

- Save As Preset lets you save a particular filter and its settings so that you can apply it to another instance.
- Copy Selected Filter and Copy All Filters let you copy one or more filters.
- Paste Filters lets you paste the selected filter(s) to other instances.
- The Reset Filter command resets the values for the selected filter to the defaults.
- The Enable Or Disable Filter button (the eyeball icon at the head of the Value column) lets you see your instance with or without the filter applied.

Creating and editing text

Now let's add text to this illustration. Various options are available for text depending on what kind of document you're working on. For an HTML5 Canvas document like the one in this lesson, you can use static text or dynamic text.

Use static text for simple display text that uses fonts available on your (the designer's) computer. When you create static text on the Stage and publish to an HTML5 project, Animate automatically converts fonts into outlines. That means you don't have to worry about your audience having the required fonts to see the text as you intended it. The downside is that too much text can bloat your file size.

Use dynamic text to leverage web fonts available through either Adobe Fonts or Google Fonts. Thousands of high-quality fonts are available to you through your Creative Cloud subscription, and the fonts are hosted by Adobe and accessible directly through the Properties panel within Animate. High-quality open source fonts are available through Google Fonts, which is hosted on Google servers.

In the next task, you'll create the humorous caption accompanying your octopus illustration. You'll choose an appropriate web font and add the text.

Using the Text tool to add dynamic text

You'll create your text with the Text tool.

1 Select the top layer.

2 Choose Insert > Timeline > Layer, and name the new layer **text**.

3 Select the Text tool.

4 Choose Dynamic Text from the Text Type menu in the Properties panel.

5 Select a font, but don't worry too much about your choice because you will replace it with an Adobe font from the web. Your font choices may not match the ones in this book.

6 Choose the Align Center option for the paragraph.

7 Drag out a text box next to your octopus.

8 Enter the following text: **Why do octopuses make the best criminals?**

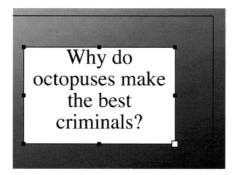

The text may not fit, or it might not be the size or font that you want. Don't worry—you'll select a web font for your text box in the next task.

9 Exit the Text tool by selecting the Selection tool.

10 Add the punchline on the Stage in the same layer below the first piece of text: **Because we're well armed**.

Adding a web font

Now you'll link a web font to your project. Make sure you have an internet connection because Animate retrieves the list of available fonts from the web. The processes for adding an Adobe font and a Google font are very similar. In this task, you'll add an Adobe font.

1 Select the first piece of text, and in the Character section of the Properties panel, click Add Web Fonts (its icon is a globe). Choose Adobe Fonts from the menu that appears.

Animate displays the Add Adobe Fonts dialog box. The list of fonts can be very slow to load. Be patient!

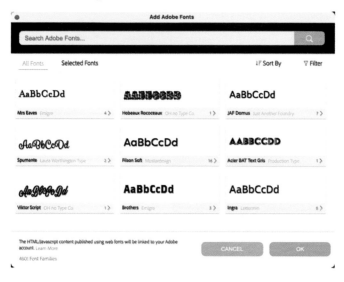

2 Choose Name from the Sort By menu.

The list of Adobe fonts on the right is displayed alphabetically. You can choose to sort by featured, by newest, or by other criteria in the Filter.

The Adobe fonts are listed with a sample AaBbCcDd string of characters. You can scroll through the font families with the scroll bar on the right. You can also search for specific fonts, or you can use the Category menu to narrow your search.

3 For now, peruse the range of typefaces and pick one that you think would suit this illustration. Click the box around the font to select it, then click OK.

**Tip** If you want more details on the font, click the name of the font under the sample text. Adobe Fonts displays the style variations of that font.

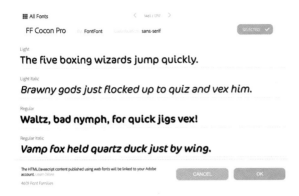

Your selected Adobe font is added to the list of fonts available. Web fonts appear at the top of the menu.

4   Select your text and apply the new Adobe font. Choose black for the color of the text. Adjust the font size and/or the line spacing (the space between lines) in the Properties panel (line spacing is in the Paragraph section) to get all the text to fit comfortably in the space.

5   Select the other piece of text and apply the same font.

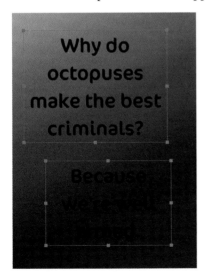

Don't worry if the text in your illustration looks a little different from the one printed in this book. Use your discretion to pick a font that appeals to you!

Removing a web font

If you change your mind, you can easily remove an Adobe web font and choose a different one.

1 Select all the text that uses the web font you want to remove.

2 Deselect the font by choosing a different one.

3 Click the Add Web Fonts button and choose Adobe Fonts to open the Add Adobe Fonts dialog box.

4 Click the Selected Fonts tab.

   Animate displays all the fonts, indicated by a blue check mark, that have been selected for your project.

   If the font has a gray check mark, that means you're still using it in some text on the Stage. You must deselect a font from every bit of text before removing it from your project.

5 Deselect the font by clicking it.

   Now, no fonts are displayed in the Selected Fonts area.

6 Click OK.

   The Add Adobe Fonts dialog box closes. The web font is removed from the Family menu in the Properties panel.

Adding speech balloons

Finally, add speech balloons to contain both the setup and punchline text.

1 Select the Oval tool and choose white for the Fill and black for the Stroke.

2 In the Properties panel, for the Stroke, choose a solid line for the Style and uniform thickness for the Width.

3 Draw an oval over the first text box and another one over the second text box.

4 Choose the Selection tool. Holding the Option/Alt key, drag on one side of each oval to pull out a point for the tail of the speech balloon to point to the octopus.

Holding the Option/Alt key creates a new anchor point on your shape.

5 Adjust the text over each speech balloon, if needed, and then group the text with its underlying speech balloon so that you can move the speech balloons as a single unit.

Aligning and distributing objects

You'll tidy up the text so that the layout is organized. Although you can use rulers (View > Rulers) and grids (View > Grid > Show Grid) to help position objects, here you'll use the Align panel, which is more effective when you're dealing with multiple objects. You'll also rely on the smart guides that appear when you move objects around the Stage.

Aligning objects

The Align panel, as you might guess, aligns any number of selected objects horizontally or vertically. It can also distribute objects evenly.

1 Select the Selection tool.

2 Shift-click both pieces of text to select them.

3 Open the Align panel (Window > Align).

4 Deselect the Align To Stage option, if it is selected. Click the Align Left Edge button.

Animate aligns the speech balloons along the left edge of their bounding boxes. If you want, you can try aligning them along their center line.

● **Note** You might have to lock the lower layers so that you don't accidentally select the shapes in those layers.

Using rulers and guides

You may want to be more precise in your placement of your graphics. In Lesson 1, you learned how to use the *x* and *y* coordinates in the Properties panel to position individual objects. Here, you've learned to use the Align panel to align several objects to each other.

Another way to position objects on the Stage is to use rulers and guides. Rulers appear on the top and left edges of the pasteboard to provide measurements along the horizontal and vertical axes. Guides are vertical or horizontal lines that appear on the Stage but do not appear in the final published movie.

To use rulers, choose View > Rulers (Option+Shift+Command+R/Alt+Shift+Ctrl+R). Horizontal and vertical rulers measured in pixels appear along the top and left edges of the pasteboard. As you move objects on the Stage, tick marks indicate the positions of their bounding boxes on the rulers. The x=0 and y=0 points begin at the upper-left corner of the Stage, with the X values increasing to the right and the Y values increasing downward. Move your mouse pointer over the top horizontal ruler or the left vertical ruler and drag a guide onto the Stage. A colored line appears on the Stage that you can use as a guide for alignment.

Double-click any guide with the Selection tool to call up the Move Guide dialog box to enter pixel values for precise guide positioning.

Choose View > Snapping and make sure Snap To Guides is selected. Objects will now snap to any guides on the Stage.

Choose View > Guides > Lock Guides to lock your guides. This prevents you from accidentally moving them. Remove all guides by choosing View > Guides > Clear Guides. Change the color of the guides and the snapping accuracy by choosing View > Guides > Edit Guides.

Sharing your final project

There are many different ways you can share your final illustration. Animate exports to several different formats and platforms. In addition to the Quick Share And Publish option you learned about in Lesson 1, Animate has options for virtually every graphic file format.

Exporting art as PNG, JPEG, or GIF

If you want a simple image file in a format such as PNG, JPEG, or GIF, use the Export Image panel to choose your format and fine-tune the compression for optimal web download performance.

1   Choose File > Export > Export Image.

▶ **Tip** Vector art—
especially art with
complex curves and
many different shapes
and line styles—can
put heavy demands
on CPU resources. This
can be a problem on
mobile devices, whose
less powerful processors
struggle to render
complex artwork. Use
the Modify > Convert
To Bitmap command to
turn selected artwork on
the Stage into a single
bitmap, which can
be less taxing on the
processor. Once you've
converted the object to
a bitmap, you can move
it without worrying
about it merging with
underlying shapes.
However, the graphics
are no longer editable
with Animate's editing
tools.

The Export Image dialog box opens.

The figure shows the dialog box with a menu showing the graphic formats you can choose. The dialog box will look different with other settings.

2 Choose the appropriate file format, select the amount of compression, select a color palette, and even compare different settings to weigh image quality and file size. You can also resize the image.

Exporting as HTML Canvas

If you wish, you can also export your project as an HTML Canvas document, although the simpler graphic file formats (JPEG, GIF, PNG, and SVG) are more appropriate for an illustration.

To do so, choose File > Publish, or choose Control > Test Movie > in Browser, or click the Test Movie button at the top corner of the Animate application.

Animate publishes the required files to display your project in a browser. The files are a combination of HTML, JavaScript, and asset support files.

If you chose the Test Movie option, your browser will automatically open with your completed project.

● **Note** If your
Animate document
contains multiple
frames, you can also
choose to export it as
an animated GIF.

● **Note** To learn more
about optimization
options for images and
different image file
formats, check out the
Animate User Guide
under Workspace and
Workflow, "Optimization
Options for Images
and Animated GIFs."
Instructions for
accessing the User
Guide are provided in
the Getting Started
section near the start
of this book, under
"Additional resources."

Collaborating via the Assets panel

You may be working with many other designers and animators on large projects, and sharing art and other assets can be essential for collaboration. Animate's Assets panel can make those collaborations easy. Save static or animated assets, use keywords for efficient searching, and export assets as an ANA file for others to use.

Saving art to the Assets panel

The Assets panel has two tabs: a Default tab for Adobe-provided animated and static assets for you to examine and use in your projects, and a Custom tab where you can store your own assets.

1. In the Library panel, right-click your tentacle movie clip symbol and choose Save As Asset.

The Save As dialog box opens.

2. Enter a name for your asset. In this case, **tentacle** would be an apt description.

3. In the Tags field, enter keywords separated by commas. Keywords will help you search for the asset in the Assets panel. You can use descriptive terms, project names, author names, or any other identifiers.

4. Click Save.

The asset is saved to the Custom tab of the Assets panel. Click the arrow to the left of Static to expand the category and view the asset. Your assets will be available to you across different Animate files.

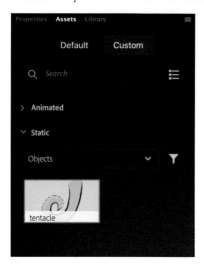

Exporting and importing assets

If you want to share an asset with another user, export an ANA file.

1 In the Library panel, right-click your tentacle movie clip symbol and choose Export Asset.

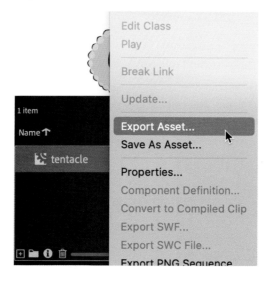

The Export Asset dialog box opens.

2   In the Tags field, enter (optional) keywords, separated by commas.

3   Click Export.

Animate asks you where to save the ANA file. Save it to your computer.

4   To import an asset, click the options menu in the upper-right corner of the Assets panel and choose Import.

5   Navigate to the ANA file you wish to import and choose Open.

The asset is imported into the Custom tab of your Assets panel. To use the asset in your Animate file, drag it to your Stage, and it will be added as a symbol in your Library panel.

Review questions

1 What are the three drawing modes in Animate, and how do they differ?

2 When would you use each of the selection tools in Animate?

3 What can you do with the Width tool?

4 What is the difference between the Fluid Brush and the Classic Brush?

5 What are web fonts, and how are they used in HTML5 Canvas documents?

6 What is a symbol, and how does it differ from an instance?

7 What are the two ways to edit symbols?

8 How can you change the transparency of an instance in Animate?

Review answers

1   The three drawing modes are Merge Drawing mode, Object Drawing mode, and Primitive Drawing mode.

- In Merge Drawing mode, shapes drawn on the Stage merge to become a single shape.
- In Object Drawing mode, each object is distinct and remains separate, even when it overlaps another object.
- In Primitive Drawing mode, you can modify the angles, radius, or corner radius of an object.

2   Animate includes three selection tools: the Selection tool, the Subselection tool, and the Lasso tool.

- Use the Selection tool to select an entire shape or object.
- Use the Subselection tool to select a specific point or line in an object.
- Use the Lasso tool to draw a free-form selection area.

3   Use the Width tool to edit the variable widths of a stroke. You can drag the handlebars of any anchor point to expand or narrow the width, add or delete anchor points, or move anchor points along the stroke.

4   The Fluid Brush provides controls for pressure and velocity sensitivity. The Classic Brush is a basic brush with more limited options.

5   Web fonts are fonts that are specifically created for online viewing and are hosted on a server. Animate offers two kinds of web fonts for inclusion in HTML5 Canvas documents: Adobe Fonts and Google Fonts.

6   A symbol is a graphic, button, or movie clip that you create once in Animate and can then reuse throughout your document or in other documents. All symbols are stored in your Library panel. An instance is a copy of a symbol located on the Stage.

7   To edit a symbol, either double-click the symbol in the library to enter symbol editing mode, or double-click the instance on the Stage to edit it in place. Editing a symbol in place lets you see the other objects around the instance.

8   The transparency of an instance is determined by its alpha value. To change the transparency, select Alpha from the Color Effects menu in the Properties panel and then change the alpha percentage.

3 ANIMATING SYMBOLS WITH CLASSIC TWEENS

Lesson overview

In this lesson, you'll learn how to do the following:

- Animate the position, scale, and rotation of objects using classic tweening.
- Adjust the pacing and timing of your animation.
- Animate transparency and filters.
- Create a nested animation.
- Animate an object on a path.
- Swap a symbol instance on the Stage.
- Edit multiple keyframes at once.
- Change the easing of an object's motion.
- Position an object in 3D space.

 This lesson will take about 2 hours to complete.

To get the lesson files used in this chapter, download them from the web page for this book at peachpit.com/AnimateCIB2024. For more information, see "Accessing the lesson files and Web Edition" in the Getting Started section at the beginning of this book.

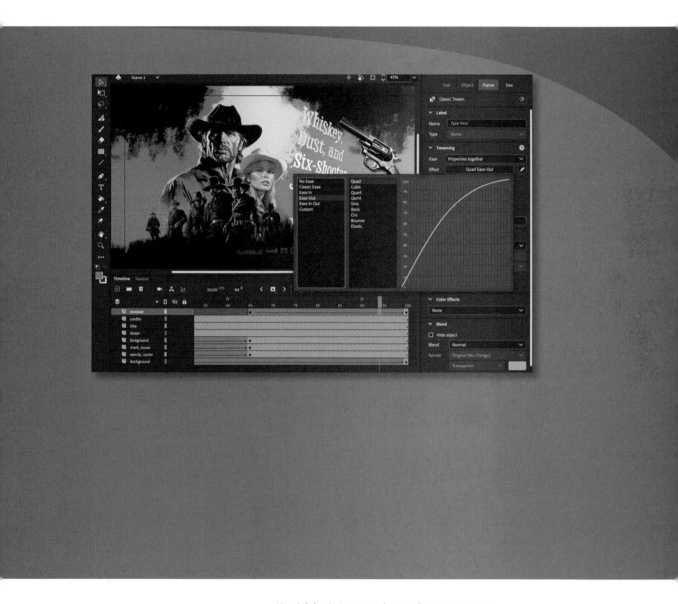

Use Adobe Animate to change almost any aspect of an object—position, color, transparency, size, rotation, and more—over time. Classic tweening is a foundational technique for creating animation with symbol instances.

Getting started

● **Note** If you have not already downloaded the project files for this lesson to your computer from your Account page, make sure to do so now. See Getting Started at the beginning of the book.

Start by viewing the finished movie file to see the animated title page that you'll create in this lesson.

1 Double-click the 03End.mp4 file in the 03/03End folder to play the final animation, which was exported as a high-definition video file.

The project is an animated opener that can be placed on a website for an imaginary, soon-to-be-released motion picture. In this lesson, you'll use motion tweens to animate several components on the page: the background, the bandits, the main (male) character, the secondary (female) character, and the revolver that slides across the page.

2 Close the 03End.mp4 file.

3 In Animate, choose File > New.

The New Document dialog box appears.

4 Choose the first category, Character Animation, and in the details section on the right, enter **1800** for Width and **1024** for Height. Keep the Frame Rate at 30.00 and the Platform Type to ActionScript 3.0. Click Create.

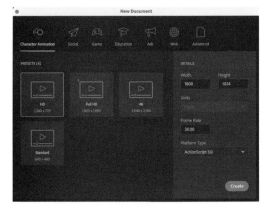

You'll use all the animation functionality available to an ActionScript 3.0 document and then export an MP4 video file.

5 From the view options above the Stage, choose Fit In Window, or choose View > Magnification > Fit In Window, so that you can see the entire Stage on your computer screen.

6 Choose File > Save As. Name the file **03_workingcopy.fla**, and save it in the 03Start folder. Saving a working copy ensures that the original start file will be available if you want to start over.

About animation

Animation is the change of an object's appearance over time. Animation can be as simple as moving a ball across the Stage, which is a change in the object's position. It can also be much more complex. As you'll see in this lesson, you can animate many different properties of an object. In addition to an object's position, you can change its color or transparency, change its size or rotation, and even animate the filters that you saw in the previous lesson. You also have control over an object's path of motion as well as its *easing*, which is the way an object accelerates or decelerates its property changes.

Classic tweens can create animation for changes in:

- Position

- Rotation

- Size

- Color or transparency

- Filters

Classic tweens require you to use a symbol instance. If the object you've selected is not a symbol instance, Animate will automatically ask to convert the selection to a symbol.

In Animate, the basic workflow for animation with classic tweens goes like this: Begin with a symbol instance on the Stage. Establish a beginning keyframe and an ending keyframe on the timeline and change the symbol instance's properties in one of those keyframes. Select one of the frames between the beginning and ending keyframes, and choose Create Classic Tween. Animate takes care of the rest by smoothly interpolating the changes between the two points in time.

There are just two simple rules to follow. One, there can be only one tween per layer; and two, no element other than your symbol instance can be on that layer.

Note The term "tween" comes from the world of classic animation. Senior animators would be responsible for drawing the beginning and ending poses for their characters. The beginning and ending poses were the keyframes of the animation. Junior animators would then come in and draw the "in-between" frames, or do the "in-betweening." Hence, "tweening" refers to the smooth transitions between keyframes.

Importing Photoshop assets

Sometimes you'll create your graphics directly in Animate, as you did in the previous lesson. Other times, you'll create graphics in applications such as Adobe Photoshop or Illustrator, or you'll be provided with graphics to use in an animation.

No worries. Animate provides a seamless process to import graphic assets, with numerous options to preserve layers, transparencies, and other key information.

Importing Photoshop layers

In the 03Start folder, you'll find a Photoshop file named 03_assets.psd that contains all the images you'll need for the animation in this lesson.

1 In Animate, choose File > Import > Import To Stage (Command+R/Ctrl+R).

2 Choose 03_assets.psd in the 03Start folder. Click Open.

The Import To Stage dialog box appears. On the left side, Animate shows previews of each layer of the Photoshop file.

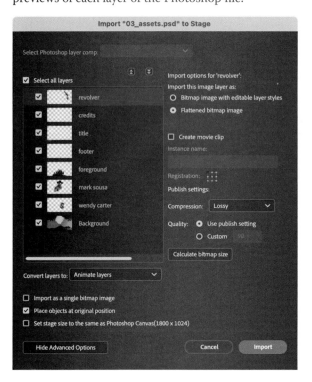

On the right side, you can set import options for each individually selected layer.

At the bottom, you can choose how the Photoshop layers will be arranged in Animate.

3 Shift-select all the layers and choose the Bitmap Image With Editable Layer Styles option.

This option preserves the transparency in the layers. The bottom layer does not contain transparency, so you can import that layer as a flattened bitmap.

4 At the bottom of the dialog box, make sure Convert Layers To: is set to Animate Layers, and select Place Objects At Original Position. Click Import.

Animate imports each Photoshop layer as an individual bitmap and separates them in new Animate layers with the same name. The images in the layers maintain their relative positioning.

In the Library panel, the bitmap assets are stored in a folder called 03_asset.psd Asset. Each bitmap is also converted to a movie clip symbol.

5   Delete the original layer in the Timeline panel, called Layer_1, which is empty.

Animating position

You'll start this project by animating the colorful background. You will make the background slightly larger than the Stage so that you'll have room to animate it, slowly scrolling from left to right.

1   Select frame 100 for all layers, and add frames (F5) so that you have room to play with all your moving elements.

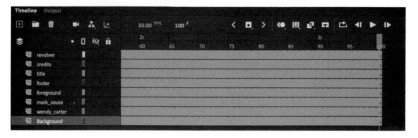

2 Lock all the layers except the background layer so that you don't accidentally modify them.

3 Select the background instance and change its dimensions in the Properties panel. Enter **2000** for the Width. Keep the lock icon intact so that the Height will change proportionally.

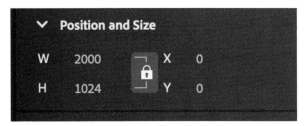

The background graphic becomes slightly larger than the Stage.

4 Insert a new keyframe (F6) at frame 100. You'll recall from Lesson 1 that there is an Auto Keyframe mode, but while doing the tasks in this book, you should disable it.

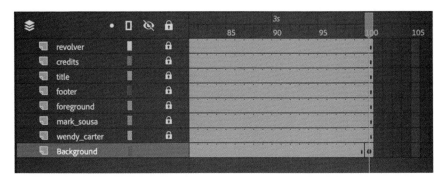

You now have two keyframes in the background layer: a beginning keyframe at frame 1 and an ending keyframe at frame 100.

5 In frame 100, select the instance of the background on the Stage. Holding down the Shift key, move the instance to the left so that its right edge aligns with the right edge of the Stage.

The two keyframes now contain the same symbol instance at different positions on the Stage.

6 Select any frame between the two keyframes and choose Create Classic Tween above the timeline, or right-click and choose Create Classic Tween.

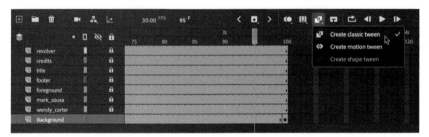

A classic tween is applied between the two keyframes, indicated by a black arrow over a purple background.

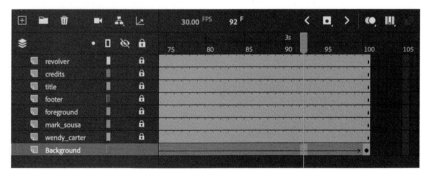

Animate smoothly interpolates the change in position from frame 1 to frame 100. The background slowly rolls by, providing a dramatic setting for your foreground characters.

Your tween satisfies all the criteria for success: it uses a symbol instance, it is on its own layer, and it is placed between two keyframes.

7   Drag the playhead back and forth at the top of the timeline to see the smooth motion. You can also choose Control > Play, or press Return (macOS) or Enter (Windows), to make Animate play the animation.

Previewing the animation

Integrated into the Timeline panel is a set of playback controls. These controls allow you to play, rewind, loop, or go step by step backward or forward through your timeline to review your animation in a controlled manner. You can also use the playback commands on the Control menu.

1   Click any of the playback buttons on the controller above the timeline to play, stop, or step forward or backward one frame. Hold the Step Forward or Step Backward button to move the playhead to the last or first frame.

Tip Remove a motion tween by selecting the tween and clicking Remove Tween in the Frame tab of the Properties panel. You can also right-click the tween on the timeline or the Stage and choose Remove Classic Tween.

▶ **Tip** You can also
use the Time Scrub tool
(hidden under the Hand
tool) to move back and
forth on the timeline to
preview your animation.
Select the Time Scrub
tool (or hold down
Spacebar+T) and drag
left and right on the
Stage.

2 Select the Loop button (to the left of the controller), and then click the Play
button.

The playhead loops, allowing you to see the animation over and over for careful
analysis.

3 Move the start or end marker in the timeline header to define the range of
frames that you want to see looped.

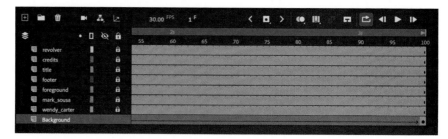

The playhead loops within the marked frames. Click the Loop button again to
turn it off.

Animating scale

Next, you'll animate the bandits in the foreground getting larger, suggesting a loom-
ing threat.

1 Lock the background layer and unlock the foreground layer.

2 Insert a new keyframe (F6) at frame 100 in the foreground layer.

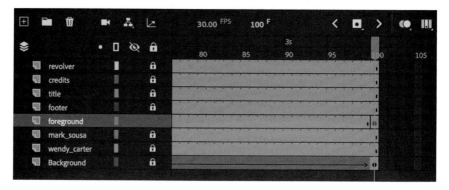

You now have your beginning keyframe at frame 1 and your ending keyframe at frame 100.

3   In frame 100, select the instance of the bandits on the Stage, and choose the Free Transform tool.

The transform control handles appear around the instance.

4   While holding the Shift key to constrain the proportions of the bandits instance, drag the corner control point to make the graphic larger.

You don't have to be exact, but aim for a new Width of about **1320**. You can use the Properties panel and enter the width value instead, if you wish.

5   Select any frame between the two keyframes and choose Create Classic Tween above the timeline.

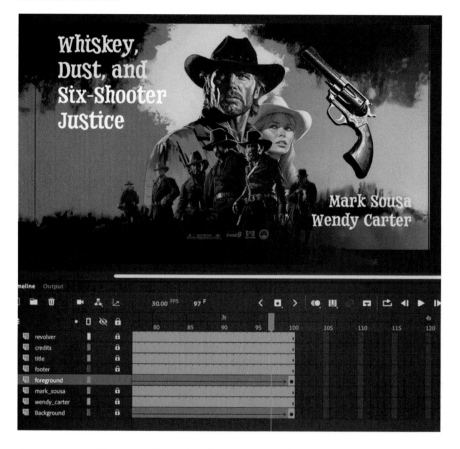

Animate smoothly interpolates the change in scale from frame 1 to frame 100. As the background slowly rolls by in the background layer, the foreground image of the bandits looms larger.

Animating multiple properties

In the previous tasks, you animated single properties: position and scale. But you can just as easily animate multiple properties, and you don't have to retween the animation. If you change the properties of the instance in either keyframe, Animate will automatically incorporate those changes in the animation.

1   Select frame 1 in the foreground layer.

2 With the Selection tool, move the bandits instance on the Stage slightly to the left. In this example, the instance is positioned at X=270.

3 Preview your animation by pressing Return/Enter.

The bandits in the foreground grow larger and move on the Stage slightly from left to right. The opposing motion of the background sky accentuates the motion of the foreground figures.

Changing the pacing and timing

You can change the duration of the entire tween span or change the timing of the animation by dragging keyframes on the timeline.

Changing the animation duration

If you want the animation to proceed at a slower pace (and thus lengthen the animation), you need to lengthen the entire tween between the beginning and ending keyframes. If you want to shorten the animation, you need to decrease the number of frames in between the keyframes.

1 Drag the last keyframe from frame 100 to frame 65.

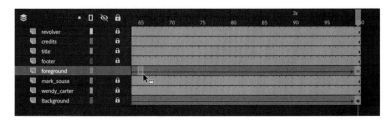

Your tween shortens to 65 frames, reducing the time it takes the bandits to move and resulting in faster motion.

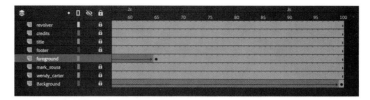

2 Drag the beginning keyframe forward from frame 1 to frame 10.

Your motion tween begins at a later time, so now it only plays from frame 10 to frame 65. However, since you moved the keyframe, frame 1 now has an empty keyframe.

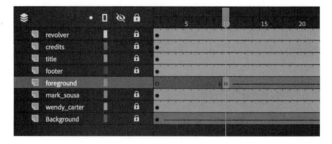

3 Copy (Command+C/Ctrl+C) the bandits instance in frame 10, and then, in frame 1, click Paste In Place (Command+Shift+V/Ctrl+Shift+V).

Paste In Place puts the copied instance in the exact position where it was copied from. Now your Stage shows the bandits static from frames 1 to 9. At frame 10, they begin their animation.

Understanding frame rate

The speed of your animation is tied to the frame rate of your document (shown in the Properties section of the Properties panel with the Document tab selected). But you should not modify the frame rate to change the speed or duration of your animation.

The frame rate determines how many frames on the timeline make up 1 second of time. The default is either 30 or 24 frames per second (fps). The seconds are marked on the timeline. Frame rate is a measure of how smooth an animation appears—the higher the frame rate, the more frames there are to show the action. Animations at slower frame rates appear choppy because there are fewer frames to show the action. Slow-motion videography depends on very high frame rates to capture action that happens very quickly, such as a speeding bullet or a falling water droplet.

If you want to modify the overall duration or speed of your animation, don't change the frame rate. Instead, add frames to or delete frames from your timeline.

If you want to change the frame rate but keep the overall duration constant, select the Scale Spans option in the Properties panel before you modify the frame rate.

Animating the main character

Now you'll animate the main character—played by fictional actor Mark Sousa—so that he rises prominently above the foreground bandits.

1 Lock all layers except for the mark_sousa layer.

2 Insert a new keyframe (F6) at frame 65.

3 In the keyframe at frame 1, move the sousa instance down to about X=501 and Y=150.

4 Insert a new keyframe at frame 30.

You now have two keyframes where the main character is lower on the Stage (at frame 1 and at frame 30), and you have a third keyframe where he is higher on the Stage at his original position (at frame 65).

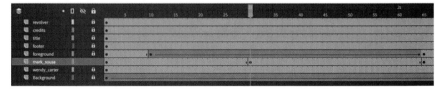

5 Select any frame between the two keyframes and choose Create Classic Tween above the timeline.

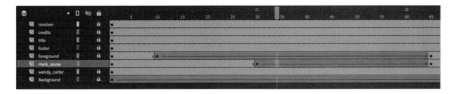

Animate creates the smooth motion of the main character rising confidently in the center of the Stage. Feel free to experiment with the timing, pacing, or even positioning of the various moving elements in the composition so far.

Animating transparency

In the previous lesson, you learned how to change the color effect of any symbol instance to change the transparency, tint, or brightness. You can change the color effect of an instance in one keyframe and change the value of the color effect in another keyframe, and Animate will automatically display a smooth change, just as it does with changes in position or scale.

You'll change the transparency of the secondary character, played by the fictional Wendy Carter, who is behind the main character. She will start out transparent, and as she emerges, she will become opaque. Animate will create a smooth fade-in effect.

1 Lock all layers except for the wendy_carter layer.

2 Select the carter instance, and in the Color Effects section of the Properties panel within the Object tab, choose Alpha from the Style menu.

3 Set the Alpha value to **0**%.

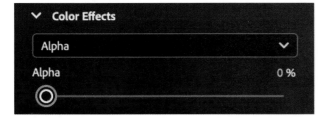

The secondary character becomes transparent, disappearing from view on the Stage. The blue bounding box around the instance remains, and it is still selectable.

4 Insert a new keyframe (F6) at frame 50 and in frame 65. The secondary character will begin her animation after the main character starts his, but both will finish their tweens at the same time.

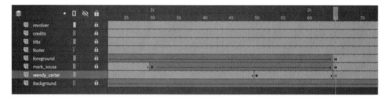

5 In the keyframe at frame 50, move the transparent carter instance to the left so that the secondary character is partially hidden by the main character at about X=740.

6 In the keyframe at frame 65, select the carter instance.

7 In the Color Effects section of the Properties panel, choose Alpha from the Style menu.

8 Set the Alpha value to **100**%.

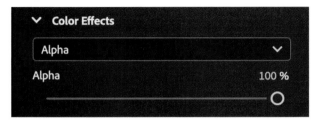

The secondary character becomes opaque. You now have two keyframes: one at frame 50 where the secondary character is transparent and behind the main character, and another at frame 65 where she is opaque and to the right of him.

9 Select any frame between the two keyframes and choose Create Classic Tween above the timeline.

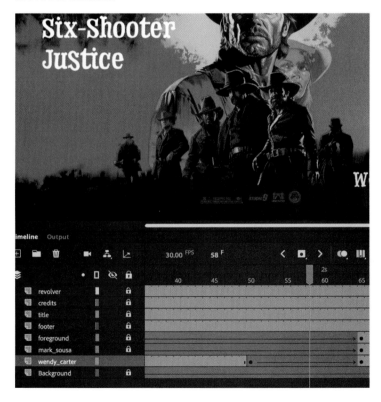

Animate tweens the secondary character fading in as she slides into view.

Easing

So far, you've created motion for four elements: the background, the foreground bandits, the main character, and the secondary character. However, their motions appear rather mechanical in the way they begin and end their animation. To incorporate a more organic, realistic sense to the motion, you can add easing.

Easing refers to the way in which a motion tween proceeds. You can think of easing for changes in position as acceleration or deceleration. An object that moves from one side of the Stage to the other side can start off slowly, build up speed, and then stop suddenly. Or the object can start off quickly and then gradually slow to a halt. Your keyframes indicate the beginning and ending points of the motion, but the easing determines how your object gets from one keyframe to the next.

Easing helps give your objects a sense of weight, which adds realism.

To apply easing to a motion tween, use the Effect menu under the Tweening section of the Properties panel. You can choose a Classic ease, which provides easing values that range from –100 to 100. A negative value creates a gradual increase in speed from the starting position (known as an *ease-in*). A positive value creates a gradual decrease in speed (known as an *ease-out*). Or you can choose more complex ease effects that alter both the ease-in and ease-out.

Adding eases to motion

You will add an ease to your main and secondary characters' movements in this task, but eases can be applied to any property change, including scale, transparency, and color.

1   Select any of the tweened frames between the first and last keyframes of the animation in the mark_sousa layer.

2   In the Properties panel, under the Tweening section, choose the Classic Ease button next to Effect.

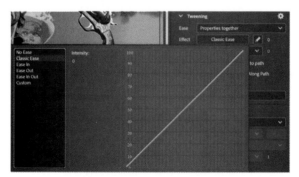

Different types of eases appear in the pop-up menu. The ease curve on the graph on the right shows on the vertical axis how the property (in this case, the position) changes for every interval of time, which is on the horizontal axis.

3 Choose Ease In Out in the first menu and Cubic in the second menu.

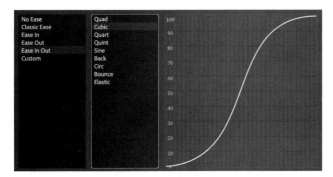

For an Ease In Out, your instance begins its motion slowly and ends its motion slowly. There is very little change at the beginning and end of the tween, which is why the curve is very shallow at the front and back, creating an "S" shape.

The second menu determines the intensity of the ease and includes some more interesting optional effects at the bottom (Elastic and Bounce).

4 Double-click the Cubic option to apply the ease and dismiss the panel.

5 Press Return/Enter to preview your animation.

The animation of the main character now gradually rises (ease-in) and then slows at the end (ease-out).

6 Add an Ease In Out for the tween of the secondary character and for the tween of the foreground bandits to complete the animations.

Adding more complex eases

The Effect menu in the Tweening section of the Properties panel contains many other ease options you can explore.

Choose Custom, and then double-click New to create a new ease. Enter a name in the Name field for your custom ease. You can design your own ease profile by using Bezier curves to control the ease curve.

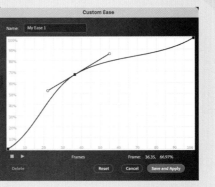

Simply click the ease curve to add an anchor point. Drag the anchor point to move it, or drag the handlebars to change the curvature at that point.

Choose Save and Apply to save your custom ease.

Note When you copy and paste the frames of a tween, the ease that is applied to it is also copied and pasted.

Tip To remove an ease, choose No Ease from the Effects menu in the Tweening section of the Properties panel.

Animating filters

● **Note** Filters can be applied, but not animated, in an HTML5 Canvas document.

Filters, which give instances special effects such as blurs and drop shadows, can also be animated. Animating filters is no different from animating changes in position or changes in color effects. You simply set the values for a filter at one keyframe and set different values for the filter at another keyframe, and Animate creates a smooth transition.

1 Lock all layers except for the revolver layer.

2 Insert a new keyframe (F6) at frame 65 and in frame 100. The revolver will slide across the screen just as all the motions of the characters end.

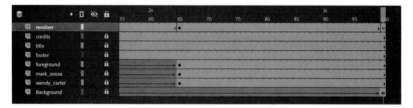

3 Select the revolver in frame 1 and press Delete to remove it from the Stage.

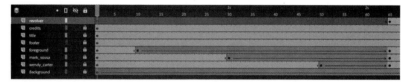

The keyframe in frame 1 is empty. At frame 65, the revolver appears.

4 Select the revolver in frame 65 and move it off the left edge of the Stage.

5 Insert a classic tween in between frames 65 and 100.

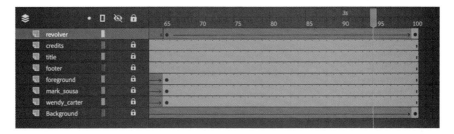

The revolver moves smoothly from the left to the right.

6 Add an Ease Out > Quad to the tween so that the revolver gradually comes to a stop and there is a more realistic sense of inertia.

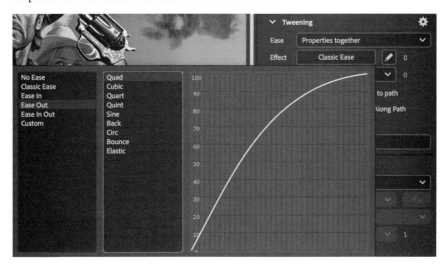

7 To add the filter, select the revolver in the last keyframe. In the Properties panel, click the Add Filter (+) button in the Filters section, and choose Drop Shadow from the menu to add a drop shadow to the instance.

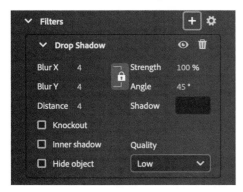

8 In the Filters section of the Properties panel, select the link icon, if it isn't already selected, to apply equal values to the Blur X and Blur Y directions. Set the Blur X value to **10** pixels.

The Blur Y value also changes to 10 pixels.

9 Change the Distance to **12** and the Strength to **60**%.

The Distance determines how far the shadow is from the object, the Strength is the intensity (opacity) of the shadow, and the Blur value changes the sharpness of the edges of the shadow. You can also change the color and angle of the shadow.

10 After all your filter options are set, choose the gear icon in the upper-right corner and then choose Copy All Filters.

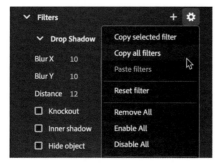

The copied Drop Shadow filter settings from this instance will be pasted to the instance in frame 65.

11 Select the revolver instance at frame 65.

12 In the Filter section of the Properties panel, choose the gear icon and then choose Paste Filters.

Your settings from the copied filter are applied to this instance.

13 Preview your animation (Return/Enter).

As the revolver slides into view, the drop shadow under it provides a sense of three-dimensionality as if it is sitting on top of the screen.

Note Recall that you can also apply filters to the keyframe itself (represented by a white keyframe dot), rather than instances in a keyframe. Make sure you select the revolver instance before you paste your filter. If you merely select the keyframe, the filter will be applied to the keyframe and not the instance.

Tip Click the Enable Or Disable Filter button in the Filters section of the Properties panel to toggle the visibility of the filter effect on your animation to make your work easier. The Enable Or Disable Filter option doesn't affect the final exported animation.

Tip You can add more than one filter to an animation. Drag the filters to rearrange the order in which they appear in the Properties panel, or collapse each filter to save space in the panel.

Automatic rotations

You'll add a little more excitement to the revolver sliding into view by giving it a bit of a spin. In Animate, you can manually rotate an instance at the beginning or ending keyframe, or you can use the Rotate option, which automatically rotates your instances during a tween.

1 Select the tween in the revolver layer.

2 In the Tweening section of the Properties panel, select the Rotate option and choose Clockwise. Leave the number of rotations at 1.

3 Preview your animation (Return/Enter).

The revolver now spins clockwise as it slides across the Stage.

Creating a path for motion

In the previous task, the revolver moved in a straight line from off the Stage. In some cases, you'll want to make your symbol instance travel along a particular path. For example, a car travels along a racetrack, or a leaf makes a zigzag descent from a tree to the ground.

To move an object along a specific path, classic tweens require that you draw the path in a separate layer called a motion guide.

A *motion guide* tells an object in a classic tween how to move from its position in the first keyframe to its position in the last keyframe. Without a motion guide, a classic tween will animate an object's position in a straight line from the first to the last keyframe. You draw the path in the motion guide. The path can curve, zigzag, or make all sorts of detours as long as it doesn't cross itself. The path itself should be a stroke (and not a fill).

To better demonstrate how you can create the path of the motion, open the sample file 03MotionGuide_Start.fla in the 03/03Start folder. The file contains a single classic tween with a leaf moving from the top of the Stage to the bottom.

1 Open 03MotionGuide_Start.fla from the 03/03Start folder.

The leaf tweens from the top to the bottom, rotating and becoming slanted as it does so. You'll create a more interesting path for the leaf to take as it falls.

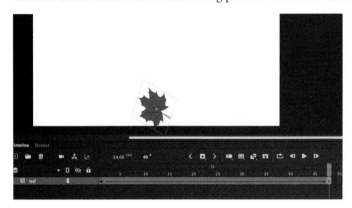

2 Right-click near the layer name containing the classic tween of the falling leaf, and choose Add Classic Motion Guide.

A new layer, called a classic motion guide, is added above the layer containing your classic tween. The classic tween layer becomes indented under the classic motion guide, indicating that it will follow any path drawn in the classic motion guide layer.

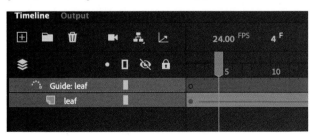

3 Select the Pencil tool, and choose the Smooth option in the Tool tab of the Properties panel or from the bottom of the Tools panel. You may need to add the Pencil tool to the Tools panel if it's not there already.

4 Select the motion guide layer and then start drawing on the Stage. Draw a path for the leaf to move on that starts from the top of the Stage and curves gracefully downward in an s-shape. Make sure the path does *not* cross itself. End the path near the leaf position at the last keyframe.

5 Switch to the Selection tool, and make sure that Snap To Objects is selected (the magnet icon is depressed) in the Properties panel.

The Snap To Objects option makes sure that objects align with each other, and it will help position the leaf's registration point on the path.

6 Move the playhead to the first keyframe (frame 1). Drag the leaf so that it snaps to the starting point of the path.

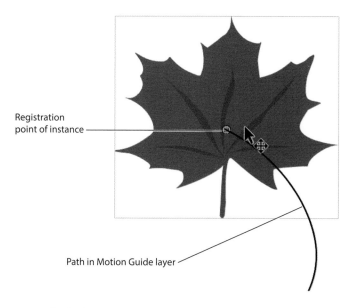

Registration point of instance

Path in Motion Guide layer

7 Move the leaf in the last keyframe so that it snaps to the end of the path.

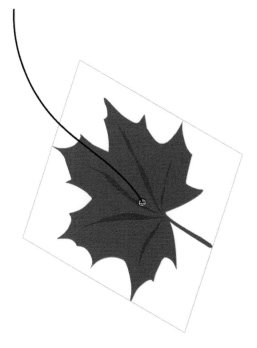

8 Press Return/Enter to test the effect of the motion guide on the classic tween.

The leaf makes a graceful curved descent down the Stage, following the path that is drawn in the classic motion guide.

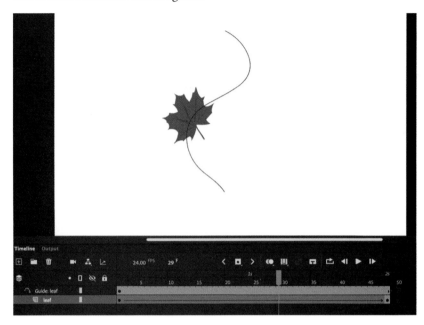

When you export or publish the final animation, the path in the motion guide layer will not be visible. Choose Control > Test Movie to see the animation without the motion guide path.

Orienting objects to the path

Sometimes the orientation of an object traveling along a path is important. In the previous task, the orientation of the leaf doesn't matter since it tumbles as it falls. However, if you are animating a rocket ship moving along a path, its nose should always point in the direction in which it is heading. Orient To Path in the Properties panel gives you this option.

1 Select the leaf instance in the first keyframe of the classic tween layer.

2 In the Object tab of the Properties panel, select the Swap Symbol option.

The Swap Symbol dialog box appears.

3 Choose the rocket symbol and click OK.

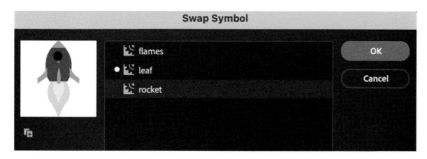

The leaf instance is replaced by a rocket.

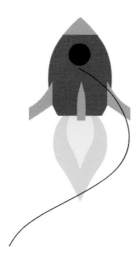

4 Select the leaf instance in the last keyframe of the classic tween layer and use the Swap Symbol option to swap the leaf for the rocket.

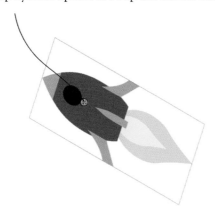

Your leaf in both the first and last keyframes of the classic tween has now been replaced by a rocket.

5 Select the rocket on the Stage in the last keyframe of the classic tween layer, and choose the Transform panel option.

6 Choose the Remove Transform option at the bottom of the Transform panel.

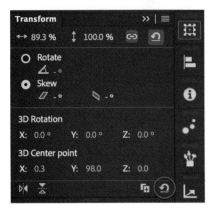

The transformations that were applied to the original leaf are reset so that the rocket is in its original size and orientation.

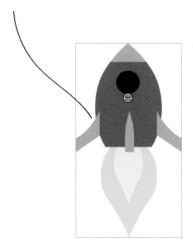

7 Use the Free Transform tool to rotate the rocket so that its nose is pointing in the same direction as the path.

8 Use the Selection tool to move the rocket to make sure that its registration point snaps to the end of the Motion Guide path.

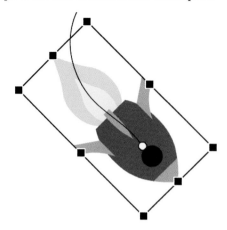

9 Select the rocket in the first keyframe, and with the Free Transform and Selection tools, make similar adjustments so that the rocket is on the path and rotated in the direction of the path.

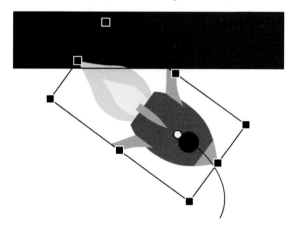

10 Select any frame in the classic tween. In the Frame tab of the Properties panel, under the Tweening section, enable the Orient To Path option.

Animate maintains the rocket orientation so that its nose always points in the direction of the path.

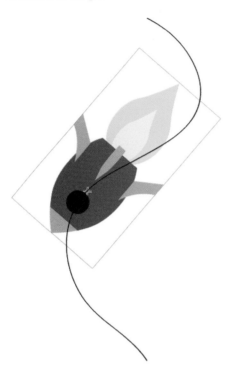

Creating nested animations

Often, an object that is animated on the Stage will have its own internal animation. For example, the wings of a butterfly may flap as the butterfly moves across the Stage. Or the rocket you worked with previously could have animated flames coming out of its fuselage as it flies. These kinds of animations are called *nested animations* because they are contained inside their movie clip symbols. Movie clip symbols have their own timeline capable of displaying animation that is independent of the main timeline.

In this task, you'll create an animation of flames flickering out of the tail of the rocket inside the rocket movie clip. When the movie clip loops, the animation will play as it moves along its path on the Stage.

Creating animations inside movie clip symbols

You will be editing the rocket movie clip symbol to insert a tween of the flames.

1 In the Library panel, double-click the rocket movie clip symbol.

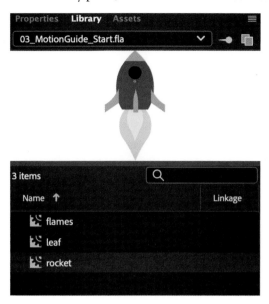

This brings you to symbol-editing mode for the rocket symbol.

There are two layers in the movie clip symbol. One layer contains the rocket ship and the other contains the flames.

2 Add 15 frames (F5) to both layers.

3 Insert a keyframe (F6) in frames 5, 10, and 15 within the flames layer.

You now have four keyframes in the flames layer. You'll keep the instance in frames 1 and 15 (the first and last frames) identical so that the animation will loop smoothly, but you'll change the shape of the flames in frames 5 and 10.

4 In frame 5, select the flame instance on the Stage and choose the Free Transform tool.

5 Holding the Option/Alt key, drag the tip of the flame to change its length to be shorter while maintaining its position at the base.

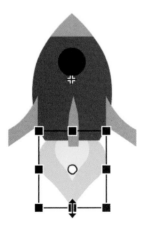

6 In frame 10, modify the shape of the flame. Holding the Option/Alt key, drag the tip of the flame to lengthen it, and drag the sides of the flame to make it fatter or skinnier.

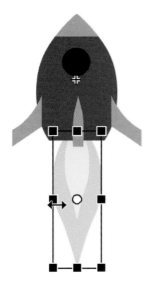

7 Select all the frames between frames 1 and 15 and insert a classic tween.

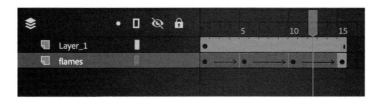

8 Using the Loop playback option above the timeline, drag the beginning and ending frame markers to include all 15 frames. Preview your looping animation.

Tip You can quickly build nested animations with a workflow shortcut, Convert Layers To Symbols. If you have an animation on the main timeline, simply select the layers, right-click, and choose Convert Layers To Symbol. Animate will put the selected layers into a symbol of your choosing and leave an instance of the symbol on the Stage.

Note In order to view nested animations, you must use the Test Movie playback option. If you simply play the animation on the main timeline, you will see tweens only on the main timeline and no internal tweens inside movie clip symbols.

Note Animations inside movie clip symbols will loop automatically. To prevent the looping, you need to add code to tell the movie clip timeline to stop on its last frame. You'll learn to control those timelines with ActionScript or JavaScript in later lessons.

The flames flicker back and forth out of the rocket's fuselage.

9 Select the left-facing arrow at the top corner of the Stage to return to the main timeline.

10 Test your movie (Test Movie > In Animate) or Command/Ctrl+Return/Enter.

As your rocket moves along its path, notice the animated flames coming out of it. The animation continues, independent of the rocket's motion on the Stage. In fact, even if the rocket is not moving, the animation will continue.

Editing multiple frames

Return to your cinematic animation in 03_workingcopy.fla to continue this lesson.

If you need to make changes across multiple keyframes, you can use the Edit Multiple Frames option above the timeline. This option allows you to make edits that affect many keyframes in the same layer or even across many different layers.

For example, imagine that you like the motion of the main and secondary characters and foreground bandits, but you want to move all of them to a different location on the Stage. Instead of moving every instance at each keyframe of the animation, you can use the Edit Multiple Frames option to do one move for all of them at once.

Moving multiple keyframes

You will move the animation of the characters and the bandits so that they are on the left of the Stage.

1 Lock all the layers except the ones you want to edit: the foreground, mark_sousa, and wendy_carter layers.

2   Select and hold the Edit Multiple Frames option above the timeline and choose All Frames.

Brackets appear on the timeline indicating the span of frames that will be editable. The All Frames option automatically puts the brackets at the beginning and end to encompass all the frames of the timeline.

Choose Selected Range if you want to select only a span of frames. With the Selected Range option, you can move the beginning or ending bracket.

3   Choose Edit > Select All (Command+A/Ctrl+A).

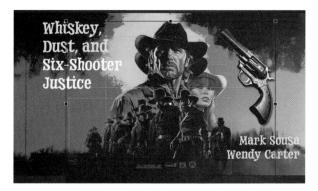

All the instances in all the keyframes in the unlocked layers become selected. You can see multiple instances of the main character and the foreground bandits.

4   While holding down the Shift key, drag the selection of multiple instances to the left on the Stage. The title will crash into the main character's head, but you'll move that later.

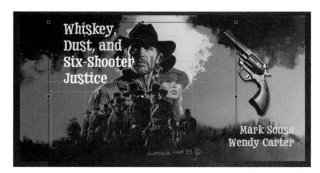

You are actually moving multiple instances in multiple keyframes across all three layers at the same time.

5 Deselect Edit Multiple Frames.

6 Scrub the timeline to play the new animation.

The main character and the bandits maintain their animation, but they have been moved to the left side of the Stage.

7 Unlock the title and revolver layers and, in the last keyframe, move the title and revolver elements to the right on the Stage in the newly created empty space.

Adding a 3D title

Finally, you'll position the title in 3D space for added visual interest. The 3D Rotation tool and 3D Translation tool allow you to move symbol instances in 3D space to give your projects more depth. Both tools are provided in the additional Drag And Drop Tools panel and must be added to your Tools panel.

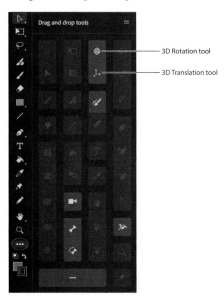

Moving objects in 3D presents the added complication of a third axis (z). When you choose the 3D Rotation or 3D Translation tool, you need to be aware of the Global Transform option at the bottom of the Tools panel (see the sidebar "Global versus local transformations"). Global Transform toggles between a Global option (when you select the button) and a Local option (when you deselect the button). Moving an object in Global mode makes the transformation relative to the global coordinate system, whereas moving an object in Local mode makes the transformation relative to itself.

The 3D title will add more drama to the composition, but it will not be animated. Three-dimensional objects cannot be animated with classic tweens. In order to animate symbol instances with the 3D Rotation tool or 3D Translation tool, you must use a motion tween, which we'll cover in Lesson 6, "Animating Symbols with Motion Tweens."

Global versus local transformations

When you select the 3D Rotation or 3D Translation tool, be aware of the Global Transform toggle button found at the bottom of the Tools panel when one of the 3D tools is selected.

When the button is toggled on (and highlighted), Global mode is engaged and the rotation and positioning of 3D objects are relative to the global, or Stage, coordinate system. The 3D display over the object that you're moving shows the three axes in constant position, no matter how the object is rotated or moved. Notice in the following image how the 3D display is perpendicular to the Stage.

However, when the Global Transform option is turned off (the button is not highlighted), Local mode is in force and rotation and positioning are relative to the object. The 3D display shows the three axes oriented relative to the object, not to the Stage. For example, in the following image, notice that the 3D Rotation tool shows the rotation relative to the object, not to the Stage.

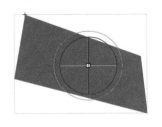 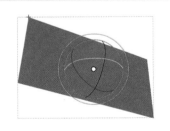

1 Lock all the layers except the title layer and select the title layer and select the title layer.

2 Select the 3D Rotation tool. The 3D Rotation tool is hidden in the additional tear-off tools at the bottom of the Toolbar (you'll have to add it to your Toolbar to use it).

The 3D rotation control appears on the selected movie clip.

3 Deselect the Global Transform button at the bottom of the Tools panel to put the 3D Rotation tool into Local mode.

4 Drag the left arm of the green Y control to rotate the title around the y axis to angle it so that it seems to recede into the distance. If you have trouble with the 3D controls on the Stage, just change the 3D Rotation values in the Transform panel (Window > Transform). Use the following 3D Rotation values: X=**6** degrees, Y=**−24** degrees, and Z=**8** degrees.

You can move the title with the Selection tool to better fit the space. The title appears to recede in the distance because of its tilted angle in 3D space.

5 Unlock the credits layer and rotate the credits with the 3D Rotation tool to create a similar effect. You can follow the example in the screenshot here or try a different design.

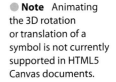 **Note** Animating the 3D rotation or translation of a symbol is not currently supported in HTML5 Canvas documents.

Congratulations! This concludes the composition of the animated opener.

Exporting your final movie

You can quickly preview your animation by "scrubbing" the playhead back and forth on the timeline, by choosing Control > Play, or by using the Time Scrub tool from the Tools panel. You can also use the integrated controller at the top of the Timeline panel. But to create a final project as a movie and to see any nested animations inside movie clip symbols, you must export it.

Use the Quick Share And Publish option to create an MP4 movie file. Your animation is converted in Adobe Media Encoder, a freestanding application that is part of Adobe Creative Cloud.

1 Choose Quick Share And Publish > Publish > Video (.mp4). Click Publish.

Animate exports a video from Adobe Media Encoder, which automatically launches. Your project is added to the Queue panel for processing.

2   The encoding process will begin automatically. If it doesn't, click the Start Queue button (the green triangle) or press Return/Enter to begin the encoding process.

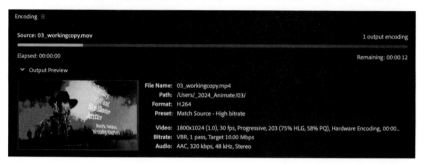

Media Encoder converts your project file into an H.264-formatted video with the standard .mp4 extension and notifies you when the process is finished.

Congratulations—you're done! The final file can be uploaded to your favorite video-sharing sites or put on a promotional website for the fictional cinematic release.

● **Note**   You can also publish an MP4 movie by choosing File > Export > Export Video/ Media. If you choose this route, you will have an opportunity to tinker with the options in Adobe Media Encoder and change audio/video encodings, cropping, trimming, and other properties of your video.

Review questions

1 What are two requirements of a classic tween?

2 What kinds of properties can a classic tween change in an ActionScript 3.0 document?

3 What does the Edit Multiple Frames option do?

4 How do you animate an object on a path?

5 What does easing do to a classic tween?

Review answers

1 A classic tween requires a symbol instance on the Stage and its own layer. No other tween, graphic, or asset can exist on the tween layer.

2 A classic tween creates smooth transitions of an object's location, scale, rotation, transparency, brightness, tint, and filter values.

3 The Edit Multiple Frames option provides a way for you to edit many different keyframes across a span of frames and across multiple layers at once. For example, use the Edit Multiple Frames option to apply the same operation on both the first and last keyframes of a tween.

4 To animate an object's motion on a path, add a Motion Guide layer to the classic tween. Create a stroke on the Motion Guide and make sure that the instances in the first and last keyframes are snapped to the path.

5 Easing alters the rate of change in a tween. Without easing, a tween proceeds linearly, where the same amount of change happens over time. An ease-in makes an object begin its animation slowly, and an ease-out makes an object end its animation slowly.

4 LAYER PARENTING AND CHARACTER ANIMATION

Lesson overview

In this lesson, you'll learn how to do the following:

- Animate characters with classic tweening.

- Create and edit object hierarchies with layer parenting.

- Swap symbol instances.

- Understand graphic symbol playback options.

- Add sound, and understand sound sync options.

- Automatically synchronize dialogue with graphic symbols.

- Use the Frame Picker for graphic symbols.

 This lesson will take about 90 minutes to complete.

To get the lesson files used in this chapter, download them from the web page for this book at peachpit.com/AnimateCIB2024. For more information, see "Accessing the lesson files and Web Edition" in the Getting Started section at the beginning of this book.

Layer parenting creates hierarchies for your animation to make character animation easy. Add sound and automatic lip-syncing with graphic symbols to bring your characters to life.

Getting started

● **Note** If you
have not already
downloaded the project
files for this lesson to
your computer from
your Account page,
make sure to do so now.
See Getting Started at
the beginning of the
book.

● **Note** Monkey
character design by
Chris Georgenes (www.
keyframer.com) used
with permission.

Start by viewing the finished project to see the short animation that you'll create in this lesson.

1 Double-click the 04End.mp4 file in the 04/04End folder to play the finished video.

The project is an animation of a monkey who waves to you and then recites some of Hamlet's famous "To be, or not to be" soliloquy while holding a skull.

2 Close the 04End.mp4 file.

As you complete this project, you'll learn how to create object hierarchies with layer parenting and synchronize dialogue for character animation.

Layer parenting

Animating characters depends a lot on object hierarchies, which describe how one object is connected to another object. For example, your hand is connected to your forearm, which is connected to your upper arm, which in turn is connected to your torso. When you move your upper arm, your forearm and hand must follow. When you move your torso, all the pieces connected to your torso also move.

Defining how objects are linked creates a hierarchy, which we often describe in terms of relationships: the torso is the *parent* to the upper arm, and the upper arm is the *child* of the torso.

In Adobe Animate, you create hierarchies for your layers using the Parenting View option in the timeline. In Parenting View, you connect the child layer to the parent layer. A colored line in between the layers shows the relationship. When the objects in the parent layer move, rotate, or grow smaller or larger, so do the objects in the child layer.

The following figure shows the Parenting View option in the timeline for this finished project. The colored lines connecting the layers indicate the various relationships between the objects in those layers.

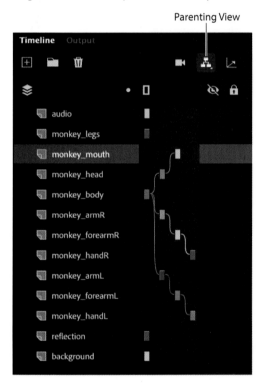

Connecting the monkey parts in Parenting View

To begin animating the monkey character, you need to establish the relationships between the various parts of his body.

1   Open the 04Start.fla file and then save it as **04_workingcopy.fla**.

The file contains all the completed graphics and symbols saved in the library. Symbol instances have been placed and arranged on the Stage. Each instance is separated on its own layer so that you can apply a tween to any individual part.

2   On the main timeline, click the Show Parenting View button. If you click and hold, you will be able to deselect options for the kinds of tweening changes affected.

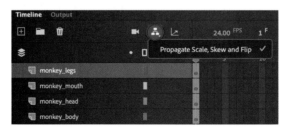

The button remains depressed, indicating that Parenting View is enabled. The space after the layer names expands.

3 Drag from the colored rectangle in the monkey_mouth layer to the colored rectangle in the monkey_head layer.

A curvy line connects the monkey_mouth layer to the monkey_head layer. The monkey_mouth is now the child of the monkey_head.

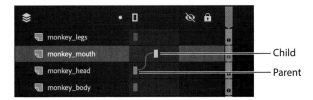

4 Drag from the colored rectangle in the monkey_head layer to the monkey_body layer.

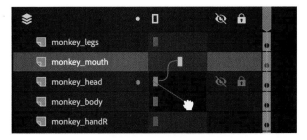

A curvy line connects the monkey_head layer to the monkey_body layer. You now have three layers that are connected: the body is connected to the head, which is connected to the mouth. It's important that your layer names are accurate so that you can easily understand the object relationships on the Stage.

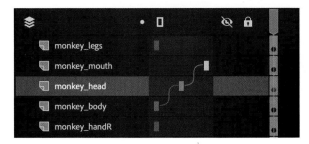

5   Connect the parts of the right arm by dragging from monkey_handR to monkey_forearmR, then from monkey_forearmR to monkey_armR, and then finally from monkey_armR to monkey_body.

You're always connecting child to parent (not the other way around).

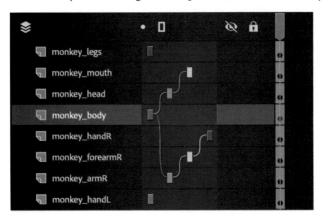

The monkey's right arm is now connected to his body. Notice that a single layer—in this case, monkey_body—can have more than one child. However, a child layer cannot have more than one parent.

6   Connect the parts of the left arm by dragging from monkey_handL to monkey_forearmL, then from monkey_forearmL to monkey_armL, and then finally from monkey_armL to monkey_body.

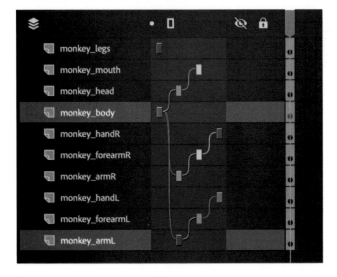

Your Parenting View diagram should look similar to this figure. All layers are connected to the monkey_body layer except for the monkey_legs layer.

Editing layer parenting

If you make a mistake, you can easily change a layer's parent or remove a parent.

- To remove a layer's parent, click the dark gray area to the right of the layer's name in Parenting View and choose Remove Parent.

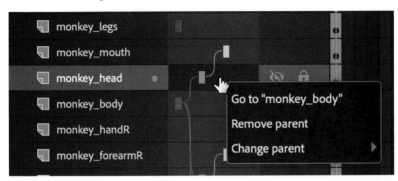

● **Note** The connections between layers in Parenting View are keyframe based, which means they can be broken and changed in new keyframes.

- To change a layer's parent, click the layer in the Parenting View section of the timeline and choose Change Parent, and then select a different layer.

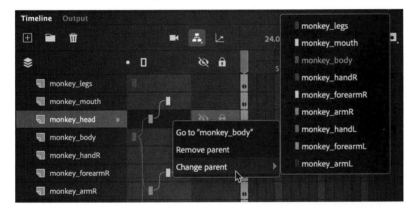

● **Note** When you change a layer's parent, that layer's children will follow.

- To change a layer's parent, you can also simply drag from a layer's colored rectangle to a new layer.

Editing layer stacking

Keep in mind that connecting layers in Parenting View is independent from how your layers overlap each other. The order in which your layers appear in the timeline determines how the objects in your layers overlap each other on the Stage.

You can reorder layers to change how objects overlap and still maintain the parent–child connections.

1 Drag the monkey_forearmL layer below monkey_armL, and then drag the monkey_handL layer below monkey_forearmL.

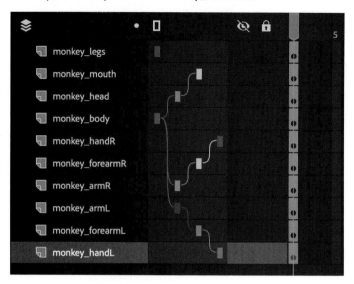

The stacking order of the monkey's left arm changes so that the hair at the monkey's wrist more naturally overlaps the monkey's hand. The parent–child relationships do not change, however.

2 Rearrange the monkey's right arm parts so that his hand is below his forearm, and his forearm is below his arm.

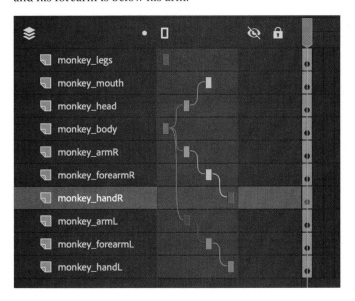

Tweening instances in connected layers

Now we're ready to animate our monkey. We'll start by making him wave to us. When we animate the arm (the parent layer), we'll see that the hand (the child layer) automatically moves with it.

Creating beginning and ending keyframes

Classic tweens require a beginning and an ending keyframe. Regardless of whether your Auto Keyframe mode is enabled or disabled, you will manually create your keyframes (F6) in these tasks.

1 Select frame 72 in all your layers, and add frames (F5) so that you have about 3 seconds in your timeline to work with this animation.

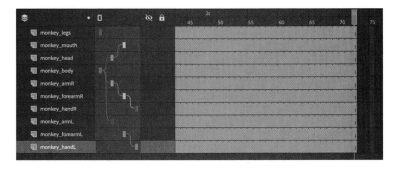

2 Select frame 8 in the monkey_forearmR layer.

3 Choose the Insert Keyframe option from above the timeline (F6).

A new keyframe appears in frame 8. This will establish the start of the motion to raise the monkey's arm.

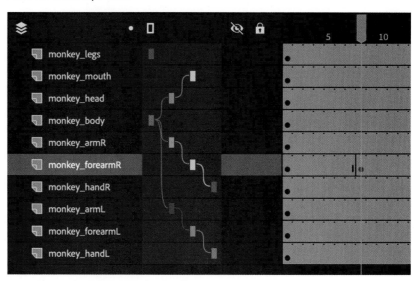

4 Select frame 15 in the monkey_forearmR layer and insert another keyframe.

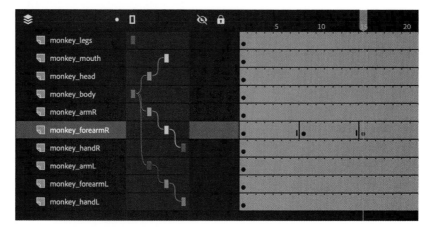

You now have an ending keyframe.

5 Select the monkey's right forearm on the Stage.

6 Select the Free Transform tool, and drag a corner point to rotate the monkey's forearm upward as if to wave.

As you rotate the forearm, the hand that's connected to it automatically follows. You now have a beginning keyframe where the forearm is at the monkey's hips and an ending keyframe where the forearm is raised.

Applying a classic tween

A classic tween interpolates the changes in a symbol instance between two keyframes.

1 Select any frame in between the beginning keyframe (frame 8) and the frame just before the last keyframe.

2 Choose Create Classic Tween from the Create Tween menu above the timeline.

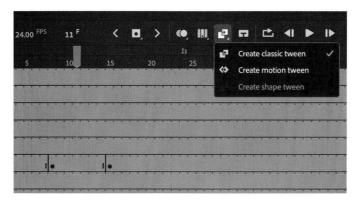

Animate creates a classic tween between your two keyframes, resulting in the monkey raising his arm and the arm's child (the hand). Even though only the forearm layer contains keyframes and a tween, the child layer also moves.

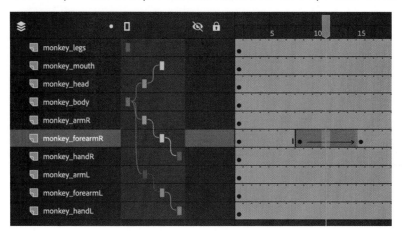

Finishing the arm wave

You'll insert additional tweens to complete the animation.

1 In the monkey_handR layer, insert keyframes (F6) at frames 15, 18, 22, 25, and 29.

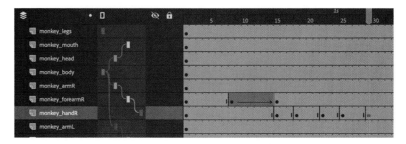

These keyframes will represent the different up and down positions of the hand for the waving motion.

2 At frame 18, select the hand on the Stage and choose the Free Transform tool to swivel the monkey's hand downward.

3 At frame 25, do the same to lower the monkey's hand.

The resulting keyframes show the hand in alternating up and down positions.

4 Select the span of frames between the first keyframe up to a frame before the last keyframe.

5 Choose Create Classic Tween above the timeline.

Tweens are applied across all the keyframes. The monkey raises his arm and waves. Notice that moving a child layer does not affect the parent layer.

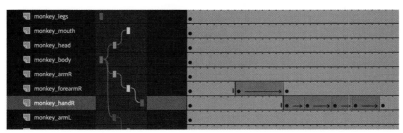

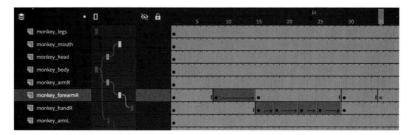

6 Insert keyframes (F6) at frames 29 and 35 in the monkey_forearmR layer.

7 At frame 35, select the forearm and then select the Free Transform tool. Rotate the forearm downward to bring the attached hand back to the monkey's hip.

8 Select the first keyframe (or any frame between the two keyframes) and choose Create Classic Tween.

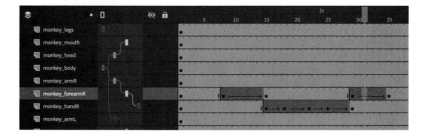

After the monkey waves, his arm lowers to the original position.

Tweening the parent layer

When you tween parent layers, all their child layers are affected as well. Next, you'll bend the monkey's body slightly, and all the connected parts—even those that are animated—will follow.

1   In the monkey_body layer, insert keyframes at frames 20 and 35.

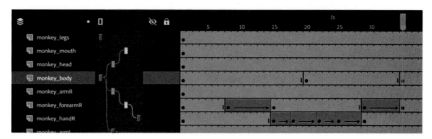

2   At frame 20, select the monkey's body on the Stage, and then select the Free Transform tool if it isn't already selected.

3   Rotate the body counterclockwise slightly to give some overall sway.

4   Select the span of frames between frame 1 and frame 34.

5 Choose Create Classic Tween above the timeline.

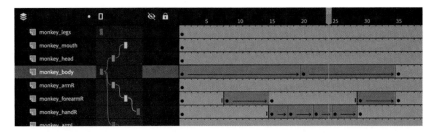

As the monkey slowly sways back and forth between frames 1 and 34, all the connected parts, including his waving right arm, move along with the rotation, maintaining the integrity of the whole character.

Swapping instances

For the animation to be complete, the monkey needs to reach behind his back and pull out a skull to ponder life and death before his soliloquy. You'll animate his left arm for the motion and then swap his hand instance with another that includes a skull.

1 In the monkey_armL layer, insert keyframes at frames 35, 45, and 55.

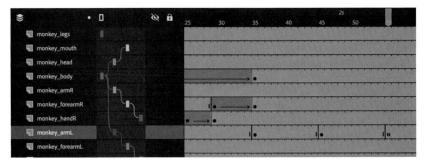

2 At frame 45 (the middle keyframe), select the monkey's left upper arm on the Stage if it isn't already selected.

3 Use the Free Transform tool and rotate the upper arm clockwise so that his hand disappears behind his back.

4   Select the span of frames between frames 35 and 54 and click Create Classic Tween above the timeline.

5   In the monkey_forearmL layer, insert keyframes at frames 55 and 59.

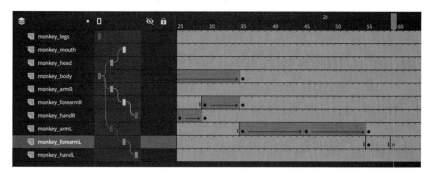

6   At frame 59, select the monkey's left forearm on the Stage if it isn't already selected.

7   Use the Free Transform tool to rotate the forearm counterclockwise so that his arm is fully extended horizontally.

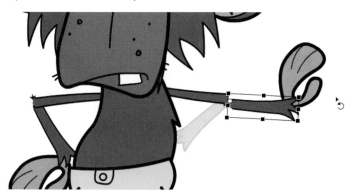

8   Select the span of frames between frames 55 and 58 and choose Create Classic Tween above the timeline.

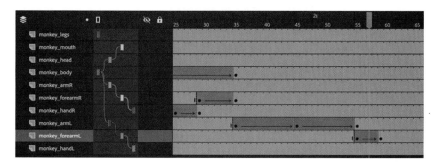

9   Insert a keyframe in the monkey_handL layer at frame 45, where his hand is behind his back.

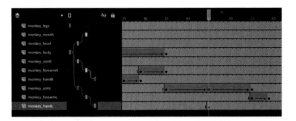

10 Now you'll need to swap the hand instances so that when the monkey pulls his hand from behind his back, a skull appears. At frame 45, select the hand on the Stage. You'll have to hide or lock all the layers above the monkey_handL layer to select it if it isn't already selected.

11 In the Object tab of the Properties panel, click the Swap Symbol icon.

The Swap Symbol dialog box appears, showing you all the symbols in your library. The current symbol has a dot in front of it.

12 Select the "monkey_hand skull down" symbol and click OK.

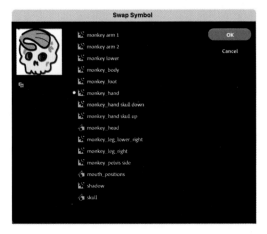

The instance of the plain hand is swapped with one that shows a hand holding a skull.

13 Unlock or unhide all the layers.

14 Insert keyframes at 55 and 59 in the monkey_handL layer, and rotate the monkey's hand in the last keyframe so that it is level with his arm.

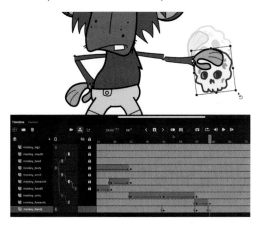

15 Apply a classic tween between the keyframes at frames 55 and 59.

As the monkey pulls the skull from behind his back, his hand rotates so that his arm, forearm, and hand are all level.

16 Insert a keyframe at frame 60 in the monkey_handL layer.

17 Select the hand instance on the Stage and swap it with the "monkey_hand skull up" symbol.

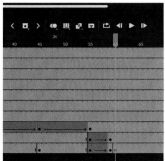

> **Tip** Any classic tween can have an ease applied to it. In the Properties panel, choose Classic Ease for a simple ease-in or ease-out, or choose the options under Classic Ease to create complex and even customized ease curves.

The swapped instances work with the tweens to create a smooth, integrated animation.

Advanced easing for classic tweens

For advanced control over easing for classic tweens, choose a different ease in the Effect menu. Animate provides several easing profiles with varying intensities of ease-ins and ease-outs. You can even apply Bounce and Elastic eases that simulate physics-based motion.

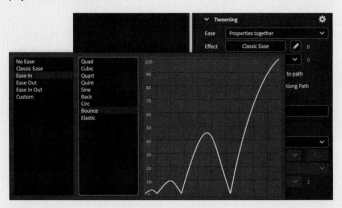

To customize the eases, click the Edit Easing button in the Properties panel. The Custom Ease dialog box will appear, showing you the ease profile for the animation.

The graph shows you how a property value changes from the first keyframe to the last keyframe. In this example, the curved line means that, in the beginning, the changes in value occur quickly, but near the end, the changes in value slow down. You can edit the ease profile in any frame by simply clicking the graph to add an anchor point. Move the handles to change the curve of the graph to change the ease.

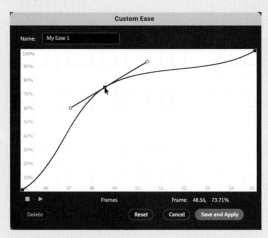

Graphic symbols for lip-syncing dialogue

In Lesson 3, you used movie clip symbols to create a nested animation of the fiery exhaust of a moving rocket ship. Movie clip symbols allow for animations that proceed independent of the main timeline.

You can also have nested animations and graphics inside *graphic symbols*, although they work a little differently.

An animation inside a graphic symbol doesn't play independently the same way it does in a movie clip symbol. It will play only if there are sufficient frames on the main timeline where the instance is placed. In other words, the two timelines are synchronized. And while you can control the internal playhead of a movie clip timeline with code, you can control the playhead of a graphic symbol only from the Properties panel (see the sidebar "Looping options for graphic symbols"). Because of the ease with which you can choose which frames appear inside graphic symbols, they are ideal for lip-syncing or other projects that require character variations.

Looping options for graphic symbols

The Looping section of the Properties panel provides many powerful options for playback control of graphic symbols.

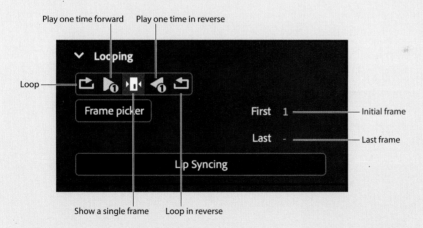

By default, a graphic symbol will play from its first frame to its last and then repeat as often as there are frames on the main timeline. You can change this behavior, however, if you want only a single frame of the graphic symbol's timeline to show (as demonstrated with the Frame Picker in the next task). You can also play the graphic symbol's timeline only once, pick the first frame and last frame to play, play it in reverse, or even loop it in reverse. Select the graphic symbol instance on the Stage, and choose the option for the desired looping behavior.

Using the Frame Picker and lip-syncing

When animated characters talk, their mouths should be synchronized with their words. Each sound, or *phoneme*, is produced by a different mouth shape. For example, an explosive "p" or "b" sound is made by closing the lips, and an "o" sound is made by a rounded open mouth. Animators draw a collection of these mouth positions, called *visemes*, to synchronize to the soundtrack.

You can store each mouth position as a keyframe in a graphic symbol. The Frame Picker panel (accessed from the Properties panel) lets you choose the frame on graphic symbols' timelines that matches each sound.

Animate also includes a powerful feature that analyzes any imported voice recording to detect individual phonemes and then automatically applies the correct viseme from a graphic symbol to create lip-syncing animation.

In this exercise, you'll use the Frame Picker panel and the Lip Syncing feature to animate the mouth of the monkey to match imported dialogue.

1 Create a new layer at the top of all the other layers and rename it **audio**.

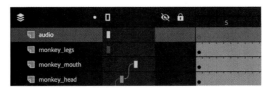

2 Insert a new keyframe (F6) at frame 72, 3 seconds into the animation and just after the animation of the monkey holding the skull finishes.

3 Drag the sound file called To_Be_or_Not.wav from the Library panel onto the Stage. The audio file is a recording of Hamlet's famous soliloquy pondering life and death.

The sound file gets added to the audio layer in the keyframe at frame 72. A tiny waveform representing the audio file is displayed in the keyframe.

4   With frame 72 selected, in the Sound area of the Properties panel in the Frame tab, choose Stream from the Sync menu.

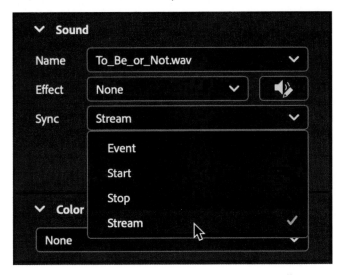

The Stream option ties the audio to the timeline so that you can synchronize animation to it.

5   Extend the timeline for all your layers to frame 938—enough frames so that the entire audio file can play to the end. When you've added the frames, you'll see the end of the sound file represented in the audio layer.

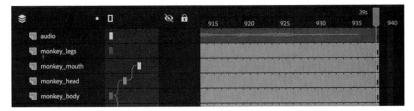

6 In the Library panel, double-click the graphic symbol mouth_positions to examine it.

Animate takes you to symbol-editing mode for the mouth_positions symbol. Notice that in the bottom layer, there are 12 individual keyframes, each containing a different graphic corresponding to a mouth position for a specific sound.

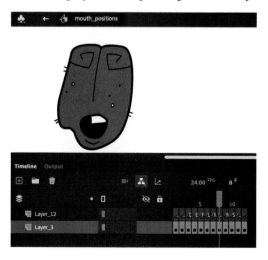

In the top layer, individual keyframes are labeled (indicated by red flags). In the Properties panel, each label has a different name corresponding to the phoneme.

The first keyframe is labeled Neutral because the mouth position is closed in a resting state. The second keyframe is labeled Ah because the mouth position is open in a way that produces that particular sound.

When you create your own lip-synced animation, you'll want to set up a graphic symbol similar to this one, where you draw 12 different mouth positions in 12 different keyframes.

7   Exit symbol-editing mode.

8   Select the mouth_positions symbol instance on the Stage in the monkey_mouth layer.

9 In the Properties panel, click the Lip Syncing button.

The Lip Syncing dialog box opens. The first step is to set up the visemes. A grid of 12 visemes is displayed, each associated with a specific phoneme. At first, all the visemes are set to the same graphic. You'll change that next.

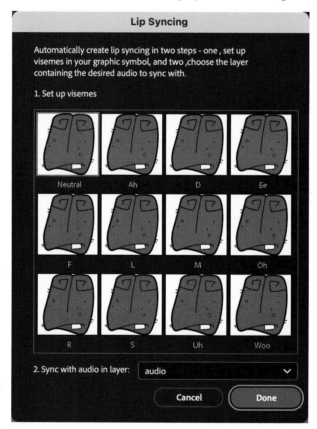

10 Click the first viseme, marked Neutral.

A menu opens, allowing you to choose one of your frames from the mouth_ positions graphic symbol. The labeled keyframes from your graphic symbol correspond to the required visemes, making the matching process simple. Select the 1 neutral keyframe.

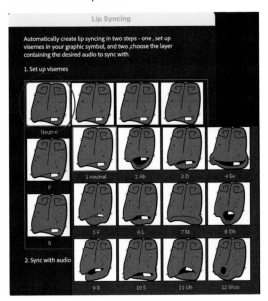

11 Click the second viseme, marked Ah, and in the menu that opens, select the second keyframe from your graphic symbol labeled 2 Ah.

Animate matches the second keyframe from your graphic symbol to the Ah viseme.

12 Continue setting all 12 visemes by matching them with the corresponding keyframes from your graphic symbol.

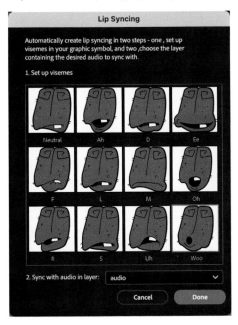

13 Now move on to step 2 in the Lip Syncing dialog box. Choose the layer named audio from the menu, if it is not already chosen. This is the sound file that Animate will use to match the visemes.

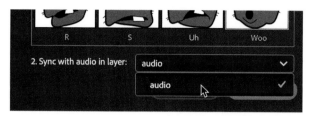

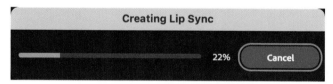

14 Click Done.

Now sit back and watch the magic happen!

Animate will process the selected audio file and then automatically create labeled keyframes in the monkey_mouth layer with the correct keyframe from your graphic symbol to synchronize the dialogue.

15 Press Return (macOS) or Enter (Windows) to play the animation.

As the sound file plays, the graphic symbol switches from one of its keyframes to another, matching the sound to the correct mouth position.

16 If you want to make any adjustments to a particular mouth position at any keyframe, select the instance on the Stage and choose Frame Picker in the Properties panel.

In the Frame Picker panel that appears, you can manually choose a different keyframe from your graphic symbol.

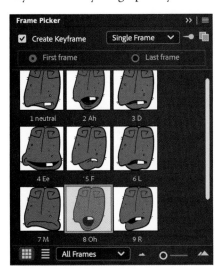 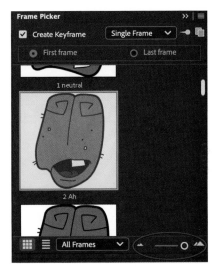

▶ **Tip** If you need to examine each frame more carefully and in more detail, you can adjust the preview size of the frame at the bottom of the Frame Picker panel. Animate will maintain your preview settings even after you close the panel.

Adding head motion

Whenever characters talk, there is usually other motion besides their mouths opening and closing. There may be times when the head may tilt or shake, the nose may wrinkle, or an eyebrow may rise. These are all important movements that contribute to an animation's overall naturalness. The monkey_head movie clip symbol already includes a few keyframes to make occasional blinks and eye movements, but you'll add slight head tilts as well.

1 Insert keyframes in the monkey_head layer at frames 89, 94, 102, and 109.

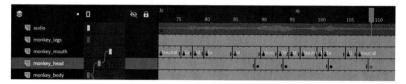

2 In the keyframe at frame 94, select the monkey head instance and choose the Free Transform tool.

3 Rotate the head clockwise about 9 degrees to give some head tilt just as the monkey begins to speak. Make the same rotation in frame 102.

Since the monkey_head layer is the parent to the monkey_mouth layer, the rotation also affects the monkey's mouth.

4 Select any frame between frames 89 and 94, and choose Create Classic Tween above the timeline.

The slight head tilt is animated.

5 Select any frame between frames 102 and 109, and choose Create Classic Tween above the timeline.

The monkey's head animates back to its normal position.

6 Experiment with adding little head bobs and tilts along the timeline for emphasis to the dialogue and to give some visual variety to the animation. Have fun giving your character some attitude and making him come to life!

Providing a background

For the final touch, your character needs a setting for his profound soliloquy.

1 Add a new layer at the bottom of all your current layers and name it **background**.

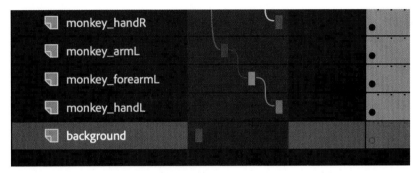

2 In the Library panel, drag the Bitmap 3 onto the Stage and align it at X=0, Y=0.

3 Drag the shadow movie clip from the Library panel onto the Stage, and position it so that its top edge aligns with the bottom of the monkey's shoes.

Adding a shadow helps anchor our character on the scene.

4 In the Blend section of the Property panel, change the Blend mode to Multiply.

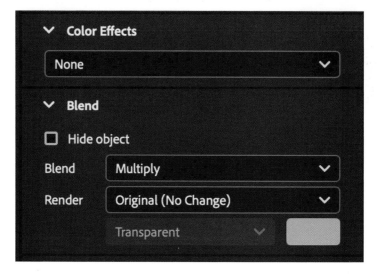

The Multiply Blend mode layers the colors of the movie clip over the background scene.

Exporting the movie

As you did in Lesson 3, you'll export your finished project as an MP4 video. As an MP4 video, the nested animations that were included in the movie clip symbols will be rendered and will appear, so you'll be able to see your monkey blink and narrow his eyes occasionally.

Choose File > Export > Export Video/Media, or use the QuickShare And Publish button to publish to video via Adobe Media Encoder.

Review questions

1 How do you create a parent–child relationship between objects for tweening?
2 What are three ways in which you can edit a parent–child relationship between layers?
3 How do you prevent scale transformations in the parent layer from affecting the child layer?
4 How is a graphic symbol different from a movie clip symbol?
5 What are the 12 visemes, and what is required for lip-syncing animation to dialogue?

Review answers

1   To create a parent–child relationship between objects for tweening, the objects must be symbol instances in different layers. Activate the Parenting view from the timeline, and then drag from the colored rectangle in the child layer to the colored rectangle in the parent layer.

2   You can edit a parent–child relationship between layers by dragging the child layer to a new parent; clicking the child layer and choosing Remove Parent; or clicking the child layer, choosing Change Parent, and selecting a new layer for its parent.

3   To prevent scale transformations in the parent layer from affecting the child layer, disable the Propagate Scale, Skew, And Flip option in the Parenting View button on the timeline.

4   A graphic symbol plays an animation on its timeline only if there are sufficient frames on the main timeline where the instance is placed. A movie clip symbol, on the other hand, contains an independent timeline, so it will play its animation regardless of how long the main timeline lasts, as long as an instance remains on the Stage.

5   The 12 visemes are graphical representations of 12 positions of a character's mouth that correspond to individual sounds, called phonemes. To lip-sync dialogue in an animation, you create 12 visemes in separate keyframes of a graphic symbol. Click the Lip Syncing button in the Properties panel to automatically have Animate analyze an audio file on the timeline and create synchronized keyframes containing the correct frame of your graphic symbol along the main timeline.

5 ANIMATING WITH MODERN RIGGING

Lesson overview

In this lesson, you'll learn how to do the following:

- Use the Asset Warp tool on a bitmap or a vector shape for modern rigging.

- Create and edit rigs with the Asset Warp tool.

- Animate rigs with classic tweening.

- Freeze or rotate joints for precise and easier rig positioning.

- Understand and apply different bone types in your rig, such as hard, soft, and Flexi bones.

- Distort the contours of a graphic with the envelope deformer.

- Organize and manage your warped assets in the Library panel.

- Apply single joints to your rig.

 This lesson will take about 90 minutes to complete.

To get the lesson files used in this chapter, download them from the web page for this book at peachpit.com/AnimateCIB2024. For more information, see "Accessing the lesson files and Web Edition" in the Getting Started section at the beginning of this book.

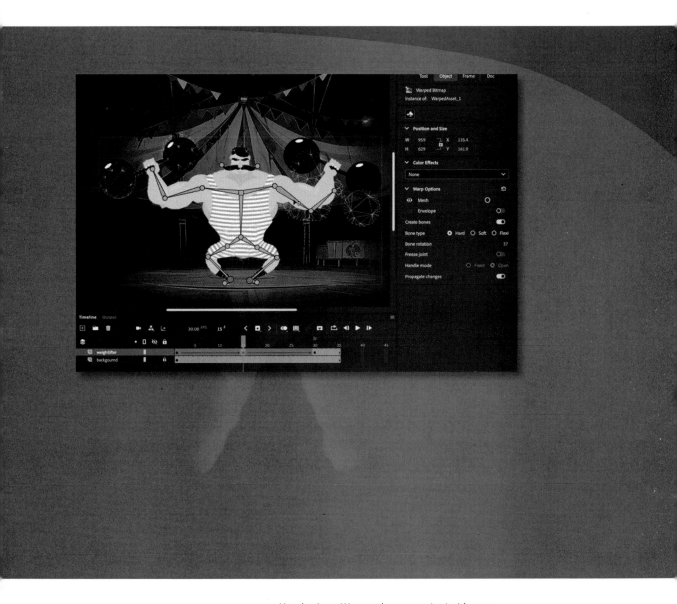

Use the Asset Warp tool to create rigs inside your graphics for modern rigging, Animate's powerfully intuitive approach to animation. Rigs allow you to stretch, rotate, deform, and move vector shapes and bitmap images fluidly with classic tweening.

Getting started

Start by viewing the finished projects to see the three short animations that you'll create in this lesson.

1   In a browser, open the 05End.gif file from the 05/05End folder to play the finished animation.

● **Note** If you have not already downloaded the project files for this lesson to your computer from your Account page, make sure to do so now. See Getting Started at the beginning of the book.

This project is an animation of a child lying flat on his back in the snow and moving his arms and legs to make a snow angel.

2   Close the 05End.gif file.

3 Open the 05End_weightlifter.gif file from the 05/05End folder to play the finished animation.

This project is an animation of a cartoon weightlifter holding weights over his head. He does small squats to exercise.

4 Close the 05End_weightlifter.gif file.

5 Open the 05End_snakedancing.gif file from the 05/05End folder to play the finished animation.

The project is an animation of a snake dancing to music coming from a boom box.

6 Close the 05End_snakedancing.gif file.

As you complete these projects, you'll learn how to animate bitmaps and vector shapes with the Asset Warp tool in an approach called modern rigging.

What is modern rigging?

Modern rigging is an animation technique in which you create a structure inside a graphic to animate with classic tweening. The structure can have multiple joints and branches, much like a skeleton in a body. The bones of the rig can be straight or curved, and they can stretch or shrink. Manipulating this structure—which is referred to as a *rig* in Animate—moves and deforms a mesh that is superimposed on the graphic. Moving the mesh makes the graphic move and deform accordingly.

The outlines of the mesh, known as the *envelope*, can also be modified, which lets you alter the contours of your graphic.

Modern rigging is a powerful yet intuitive way of working. Once you've established the internal rig for your graphics, adding animation is very much like controlling a puppet.

Characters are natural targets for modern rigging since they have limbs that can be controlled with the bones of a rig. But any graphic—even those that don't have limbs—can be animated with modern rigging.

Using the Asset Warp tool

You use the Asset Warp tool to create, edit, and move your rig. A rig is similar to an armature that you'll learn to create with the Bone tool in Lesson 9, "Inverse Kinematics with Bones." A rig can be created inside a bitmap or inside a vector shape. Animate converts the graphic associated with a rig to a special Library item known as a warped asset.

The rig can be a series of connected bones, branching bones, or even single points.

You'll start by animating the child lying in the snow and creating a snow angel.

Creating your first rig

You'll establish your first rig inside a bitmap image.

1 Create a new file from the Character Animation category with a Width of **796** and a Height of **900**. Leave the Platform Type as ActionScript 3.0, and click Create.

2 Save your new file as **05_workingcopy.fla**.

3 Choose File > Import > Import To Stage (Command+R/Ctrl+R).

In the Import To Stage dialog box, choose the Photoshop layered file in the 05Start folder called snow-angel.psd.

4 In the Import To Stage dialog box, choose the Flattened Bitmap Image option for both layers. Click Import.

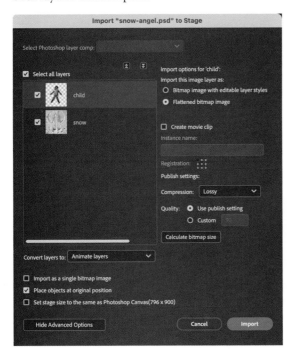

The Photoshop layers are imported into separate layers in Animate. The top layer is an image of a child that has its background removed. The bottom layer is an image of snow.

5 Delete the original Layer_1 layer that remains empty.

6 Select the Asset Warp tool .

7 In the Properties panel, under the Tool tab, make sure the Envelope option is turned off, the Create Bones option is turned on, and the Bone Type is set to Hard.

8 Click the child to select him, then click his left shoulder.

Animate creates a mesh over the bitmap and creates a single joint. Your rig is established.

If you use the Selection tool to select the child, you'll notice that the mesh goes away, and the object on the Stage is no longer a bitmap and is now called a Warped Bitmap in the Properties panel.

The Warped Bitmap object is stored in the Library as WarpedAsset_1. You'll learn to rename and organize warped assets later in this lesson.

9 Select the Asset Warp tool again and click your first joint to select it. Move your cursor over the child's elbow.

Animate shows a preview of where a bone will be created, based on the position of the cursor.

10 Click the child's elbow. Animate creates another joint at his elbow, and a bone appears, connecting the first point at his shoulder to the second point at his elbow. Hard bones are shown as elongated triangles, with the fatter base at their origin and the narrower tip at the farthest joint. The first joint becomes a square, indicating that it is the root joint.

11 Finally, click the child's left wrist.

Animate creates a third joint with another bone connecting to it. You've just completed the first rig for your bitmap.

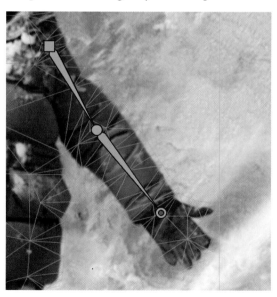

Creating additional bones

Your first set of bones and joints will control the child's left arm. Now you'll create additional bones for your rig for his other limbs.

1   With the Asset Warp tool selected, click an area outside the mesh.

The last joint of your rig becomes deselected.

2   Click the child's right shoulder.

A new joint is created.

In step 1, you needed to click an area outside the mesh to ensure that in step 2, Animate creates a new joint that is not connected to a previously selected joint. If you were to click the child's right shoulder when the joint of his left wrist was still selected, you would create a connecting bone as in the following screenshot (which is something that you do not want!).

3 As you did with his left arm, continue creating bones down his right arm by clicking his elbow and his wrist.

4 Click an area outside the mesh and build bones inside each of the child's legs, with joints at the hips, knees, and ankles.

Your rig is complete! Notice that your bitmap can have multiple bones that are not connected to one another.

Moving your rig

Now for the fun part. With the Asset Warp tool, you get to move the individual joints around to position your graphic for animation.

1 Drag the child's left upper arm upward by dragging on the bone between the shoulder and elbow joints.

His arm rotates upward. The bone is highlighted in orange, and the joint at the elbow is highlighted in red.

2 Drag the child's left lower arm (his forearm) upward.

His forearm rotates upward. The bone is highlighted in orange, and the joint at the wrist is highlighted in red.

3 Now try dragging the joint at the child's left wrist.

▶ **Tip** As you'll notice, moving the bones of your rig too much will likely result in unnatural distortions as the bitmap gets stretched too far from its original position. When working with bitmaps, the Asset Warp tool is most effective when used with less dramatic or extreme motions.

When you move a joint, you can reposition the attached bone by stretching or shortening the bone as well as rotating it. Dragging a bone, as you did in steps 1 and 2, allows only for rotation.

If you've elongated his forearm, then move the joint at the wrist back so that his forearm is back to normal.

Note that when you move a joint, any attached joint and bone farther down the chain also move. So when you move the upper arm bone and elbow joint, the forearm bone and wrist joint follow. Another way to describe this relationship is to call the first joint the parent and the connecting one the child. Moving the parent also moves the child.

Using rotation angles

Sometimes you'll want precise control over the angle of a joint. You can enter numerical values for the rotation angle in the Properties panel.

1 Select either the bone in the child's other upper arm or the joint at the child's right elbow.

2 In the Properties panel, under Warp Options, enter the value **150** as the new rotation angle.

His right arm moves upward at the new angle.

3 Select the bone in his right forearm or the joint at his wrist.

4 In the Properties panel, under Warp Options, enter the value **−180** as the new rotation angle.

His right forearm moves upward at the new angle.

Feel free to adjust either of his arms to establish the first position in the animation of the snow angel.

Mesh options

When you're working with your rig, you may want to see your bitmap more clearly, without the superimposed mesh. You can hide the mesh by deselecting the Mesh option (the eye icon) in the Warp Options section of the Properties panel.

Hiding the mesh allows you to see only the joints and bones of your rig.

The slider to the right of the Mesh option allows you to change the resolution of the mesh over the bitmap. Move the slider to the right to increase the mesh density, or move the slider to the left to decrease the mesh density.

Low mesh density

High mesh density

The mesh density determines how coarse or refined the warping of the bitmap over your rig is. For most purposes, you can leave the slider at its default middle position.

Editing your rig

If you make a mistake in placing your joints, you can easily move them into a better position, or remove them entirely to start over.

Repositioning joints and bones

Use the Edit Rig mode to move joints within a rig without affecting the mesh.

1   With the Selection tool or the Asset Warp tool, right-click your rig and choose Edit Rig.

Animate puts you in rig editing mode. The rig appears in a different color, indicating that you can reposition it without affecting the underlying mesh or graphic.

2 Drag the elbow joint to a new position within your mesh.

The joint and connecting bones move to a new position but do not modify the bitmap.

Make sure you drag the joint back to its original (correct) position before moving on (or use Undo [Command+Z/Ctrl+Z]).

3 Exit rig editing mode by clicking the left-facing arrow at the top of the Stage.

You return to Scene 1.

Removing joints and bones

Use the Delete/Backspace key to remove joints and connecting bones.

1 Select the last joint (in the wrist).

2 Press the Delete/Backspace key.

The selected joint and its connecting bone are removed from the rig.

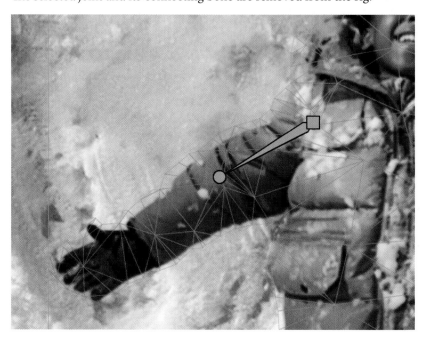

3 Press Command+Z/Ctrl+Z to undo your edit to the rig.

4 Select just the bone in the forearm.

5 Press the Delete/Backspace key.

The selected bone is removed from the rig, but the joint in the wrist remains.

Pressing the Delete/Backspace key on a selected pin deletes the pin as well as the bone associated with it. Pressing it on just a selected bone deletes the bone, leaving the pin as it is.

Reconnecting joints and bones

Use the Option/Alt key to reconnect joints with bones.

1 Select the child's right elbow joint with the Asset Warp tool.

2 Hold down the Option/Alt key and click the joint in his right wrist.

Animate creates a bone between the two joints.

Animating your rig

Animating your rig involves positioning it in different keyframes and using classic tweening to interpolate the changes between keyframes.

Creating your keyframes

Each keyframe shows your rig in different positions.

1   On the timeline, select frame 40 in both layers, and add frames (F5) to extend the amount of time that you see the child and the background snow.

2   Insert a keyframe (F6) in the child layer at frame 16 and at frame 40.

3   Select the keyframe at frame 16.

4   Move the bones of your rig to position the child's arms downward so that the arc of his arms traces the depression in the snow.

You won't be able to move his arms all the way down to his sides without making major distortions to the rest of his body since all the joints are connected, so keep the motion modest.

5 Move the joints in his legs so that they are close together.

Applying a classic tween

A classic tween between the first and second keyframes and between the second and third keyframes will interpolate the rig positions.

1 Select any frame between the first and second keyframes.

2 Right-click and choose Create Classic Tween.

3 A classic tween is created from the first keyframe to the second keyframe.

As Animate is making the calculations to create the tween, you may see light blue squares appearing briefly above the tween on the timeline. This is just a progress indicator for the calculations.

4 Select any frame between the second and last keyframes.

5 Right-click and choose Create Classic Tween.

▶ **Tip** As with any classic tween, you can also make changes to the scale, rotation, position, or color effect of your warped object, and Animate will interpolate those changes between keyframes. If you want to move your entire rig, for example, use the Selection tool to move the warped object to a new location on the Stage. To change the scale or rotation, use the Free Transform tool.

▶ Tip You can modify your rig even after a tween has been added so long as the Propagate option is enabled for the Asset Warp tool. If, for example, you add or remove a joint from your rig in one keyframe, that change will be reflected, or propagated, in all the keyframes for the integrity of the tween to be maintained.

A classic tween is created from the second keyframe to the last keyframe.

Animate creates a smooth motion between keyframes to move your rig and the bitmap image.

6 Choose the Loop Playback option and extend the brackets to include all frames, from 1 to 40. Play the animation to see the looping snow angel being created by the child's arm and leg motions.

Adding a drop shadow effect

To make the animation look more integrated into the snowy background, you'll add a drop shadow filter.

1 Select the first keyframe at frame 1 of the child layer.

2 In the Properties panel, in the Filters section, click the Add Filter button and choose Drop Shadow.

A Drop Shadow filter is added to the objects in the child layer.

3 Change the settings for the Drop Shadow filter. For Blur X and Blur Y, enter **20**. For Distance, enter **10**. For Strength, enter **75%**.

The settings create a softer shadow under the child for a greater sense of depth and make him appear to be on top of the snow.

On the timeline, the keyframe appears white, indicating that a filter has been applied.

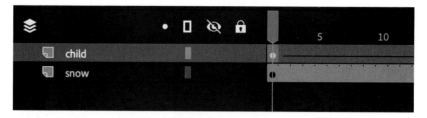

4   In the Filters section of the Properties panel, click the options in the upper-right corner and choose Copy All Filters.

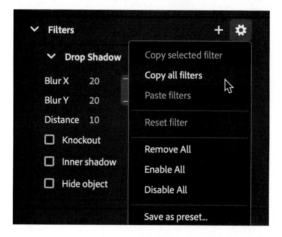

The Drop Shadow filter and all its settings are copied.

5   Select the second keyframe at frame 16.

6   In the Filters section of the Properties panel, click the options in the upper-right corner and choose Paste Filters.

The Drop Shadow filter, including all its settings from the first keyframe, is pasted into the second keyframe.

7 Select the third keyframe at frame 40 and paste the filter into the third keyframe.

All three keyframes contain the same Drop Shadow filter.

Organizing warped assets

Currently you have only one warped asset in your Library panel. However, as your animation project grows in complexity, you'll need ways to keep track of your graphics.

Renaming and grouping warped assets

In the Library panel, you can manage your warped assets by renaming them and by organizing them in folders, just as you can with symbols and imported assets.

1 In the Library panel, double-click the warped asset named WarpedAsset_1, or right-click and choose Rename.

2 Enter **snow_angel** as the new name. Press Return (macOS) or Enter (Windows) to accept the modification.

3 Click the New Folder symbol at the bottom of the Library panel.

A new folder is created in the Library panel.

4   Enter **warped_assets** as the name of the new folder. Press Return/Enter to accept the modification.

5   Drag the snow_angel warped object into the new folder.

Keeping your Library panel organized will keep your workflow efficient and save you future headaches.

Editing warped assets

Warped assets can be edited through the Library. However, limit those edits to minor changes, as more substantial changes can produce unpredictable results in how the current rig is associated with the graphic.

Editing the snow_angel warped object

The child's jacket and pants are currently monochromatic and rather dull. Imagine that the creative director wants you to change the color of the child's pants even though all the animation work has been completed. Fortunately, you can make minor changes to a warped object without having to redo the rigging or tweening process.

1   In the Library panel, double-click the snow_angel warped object, or right-click and choose Edit.

Animate warns you to limit your modifications to minor changes that don't alter the image's dimensions or position.

2 Click OK.

You enter asset warp editing mode. The graphic appears on the Stage, but the rig is absent.

This mode is different from rig editing mode, which you learned about previously. In this editing mode (accessed through the Library), you make modifications to the graphic. In rig editing mode (accessed by right-clicking the rig itself on the Stage), you make modifications to the rig without altering the graphic.

3 Right-click the graphic on the Stage and choose Edit With Adobe Photoshop 2024, or choose Edit With and choose Photoshop in the dialog box that appears.

Photoshop opens, and opens the bitmap file of the child.

4   Make simple changes to the photo color (Image > Adjustments > Hue/Saturation Or Color Balance). Depending on your skill with Photoshop, you can first make a selection to just target the child's snow pants.

5   Save the changes to the image in Photoshop (Command+S/Ctrl+S).

6   Return to Animate. In Animate, click the left-pointing arrow above the Stage to exit editing mode and return to Scene 1.

The warped asset in Animate reflects all the changes you made to it in Photoshop. You may have to save the file, close it, and open it again in Animate.

The creative director should be happy with your revision. (You don't need to let them know how easy it was to make in Animate!)

Rigs with branching joints

● **Note** When you create a rig on a vector shape, Animate converts it to a bitmap by default to maintain high-quality warping and tweening. However, you can change this setting in Animate > Preferences if you want to maintain the vector shape.

Now you'll create something a little more complicated. The snow angel animation you just completed contained bones in each of the child's limbs that were connected in a straight line, but in the next animation, you'll create a rig that branches. You'll also explore some of the other warp options.

Creating a branching rig

A branching rig is one in which a single joint can connect to multiple joints and bones, much like a human pelvis branches into two legs. Moving the pelvis (the parent) moves the joints and bones in the legs (the children). In this task, you'll create a branching rig in a vector shape of a weightlifter.

1   Save your 05_workingcopy.fla file and close it. You will not need it for the remainder of this lesson.

2   Open the 05Start_weightlifter.fla file in the 05Start folder and save it as **05_workingcopy_weightlifter**.

The file contains a drawing of a weightlifter, composed of different colored fills. The shapes are in frame 1 of a single layer called weightlifter.

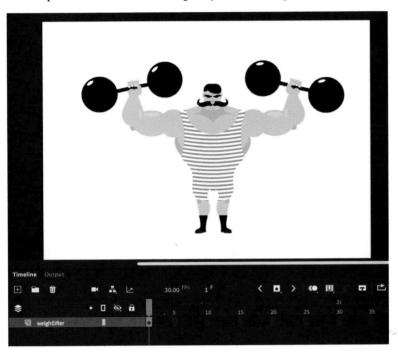

3   Select the Asset Warp tool, and click the weightlifter graphic on the Stage.

The whole shape becomes selected.

4 Click the top of the weightlifter's chest.

A mesh is applied to the selected shape, and a single joint is created.

5 Click the weightlifter's abdomen, just below his belt, to create a second joint with a bone connecting the two joints.

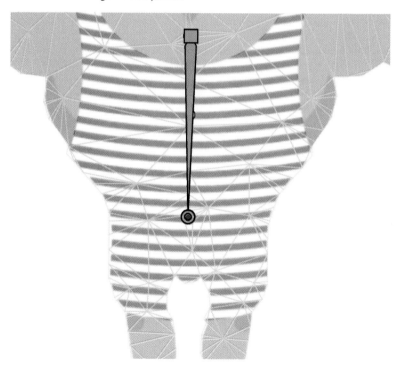

6 Continue building the bones down the weightlifter's right leg with joints in his hip, knee, ankle, and foot.

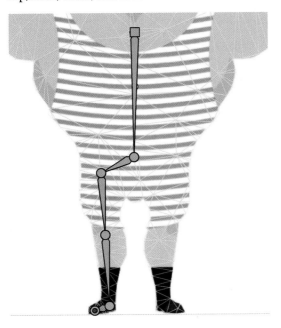

Note A joint can have multiple children but only one parent.

7 Click the joint in the abdomen to select it.

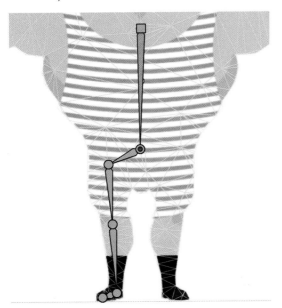

New bones will be created from the currently selected joint.

8 Click the weightlifter's left hip, knee, ankle, and foot.

Animate creates bones that branch from the hip.

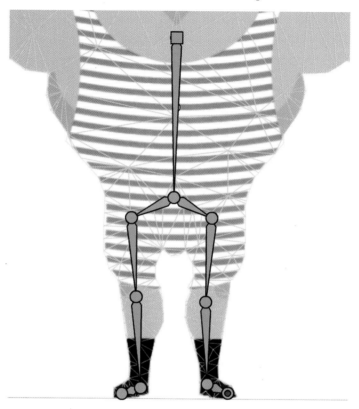

9 Click your first joint at the top of his chest. This parent joint is square and is also known as the root joint.

10 Click the weightlifter's outstretched left arm to create joints and connecting bones. Create joints at the shoulder, elbow, and fist.

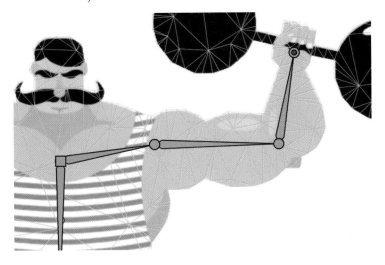

Your finished rig should look similar to the following screenshot. Don't worry about adding joints to his other arm. You'll do that later.

Warp options

You'll animate the weightlifter doing squats to help bulk up his skinny legs. Animating that motion would mean moving his body up and down, flexing his legs, and keeping his feet planted firmly in place. To facilitate the animation process and to keep certain joints (such as his ankles and feet) frozen in position, you can turn to the different warp options in the Properties panel.

Freezing joints

To prevent a joint from moving from its position on the Stage, use the Freeze Joint option in the Warp Options section of the Properties panel.

1   If you drag the rig in the weightlifter from the root joint (the square joint in his chest), the entire rig, and therefore the entire mesh, moves.

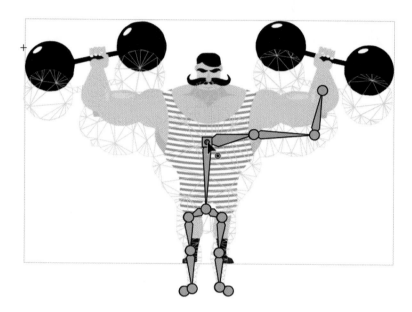

2   Move the rig back to its original position.

3   Select the joint in one of his ankles.

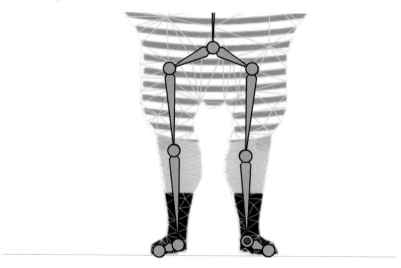

4 In the Warp Options section of the Properties panel, turn on the Freeze Joint option.

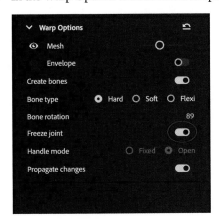

The selected joint becomes a large blue circle to indicate it is a frozen joint.

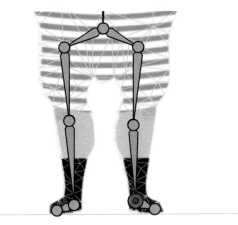

5 Select the other ankle joint and toggle on Freeze Joint.

Both joints are frozen and are fixed to the Stage.

● **Note** You cannot select multiple joints to change their warp option preferences. Only single selections are possible.

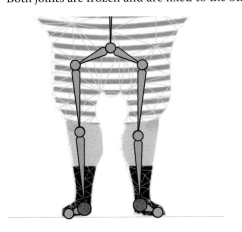

Now when you drag the root joint of the rig, the entire mesh moves *except* the two ankle joints, keeping the weightlifter's feet in place.

Frozen joints

Using soft bones for flexible connections

In the previous task, you froze the weightlifter's ankle joints so that as his body moved downward, his legs became compressed. That effect happens when you use hard bones, the default bone type in the Asset Warp tool. Hard bones allow you to elongate and compress the mesh. An alternative option, soft bones, keeps the mesh from being compressed. See the sidebar "Hard, soft, and Flexi bones" for additional details.

In this task, you'll modify the bones in the weightlifter's legs from hard to soft bones.

1 Select the weightlifter's right ankle joint.

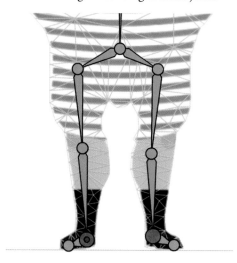

2 In the Warp Options section of the Properties panel, change the Bone Type from Hard to Soft.

The connecting bone becomes a soft bone, indicated by its shape. Soft bones are thin and rod-like, while hard bones appear as triangles.

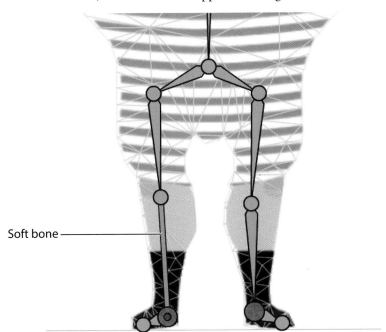

Soft bone

3 Select the other ankle joint and change the Bone Type from Hard to Soft.

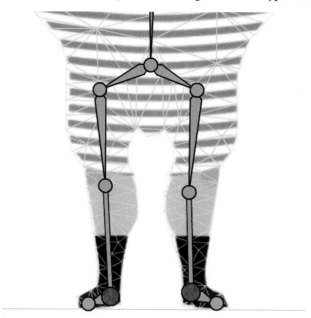

4 Move the parent joint of the mesh downward.

Because the ankle joints are frozen, the mesh has nowhere to go as you move the rig downward. Rather than being compressed, the mesh bends in a flexible manner. It's not entirely natural, but in the next series of tasks to animate the weightlifter, you'll move the rig into a more natural position by dragging the other joints.

5 Move the rig back to its original position before moving on to the next task.

Hard, soft, and Flexi bones

Which one do you pick? Rigs can be made of hard, soft, or Flexi bones, and you can mix and match them within the same warped asset, depending on the needs of your rig. You can also change them at any time.

What's the difference between these bones? Hard bones appear as triangles that are thicker at their parent joint and thinner at their child joint. Soft bones appear as straight rods of uniform thickness, and Flexi bones can appear as curved rods.

Different bone types change the mesh of the warped asset differently. In a hard bone, if you were to move two joints closer together, the mesh would squash and shorten.

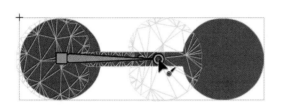

Hard bone.

On the other hand, soft bones will attempt to preserve the volume of the mesh as you move the joints of the rig. If you were to move the two joints closer together, the mesh would compensate and bulge outward. Soft bones have the potential to distort the mesh more naturally, but their behavior can also be less predictable.

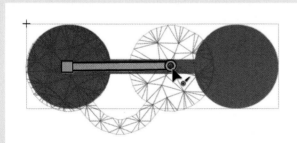

Soft bone.

Flexi bones are the latest addition to Animate. Flexi bones allow you to create curved bones with Bezier handles. Instead of clicking to position each joint in a rig, you drag to pull out handles to create your curves. You can not only move and rotate joints, but also change the curvature of each bone for more precise control.

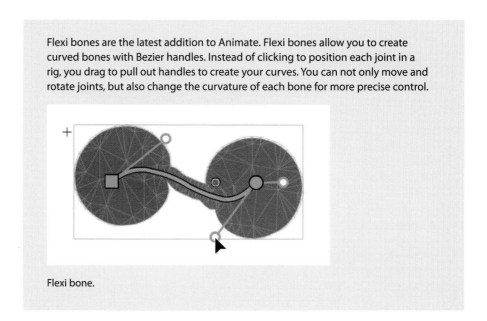

Flexi bone.

Animating your weightlifter

With the modifications to your rig for soft bones and frozen joints, you're now ready to animate your character.

1 Create new keyframes at frame 15 and frame 30 on your timeline.

The first and last keyframes (frames 1 and 30) will remain identical, with the weightlifter in his full upright position. You will modify the rig in the middle keyframe, at frame 15.

2 Move your playhead on the timeline to frame 15.

3 With the Asset Warp tool, move the root joint downward.

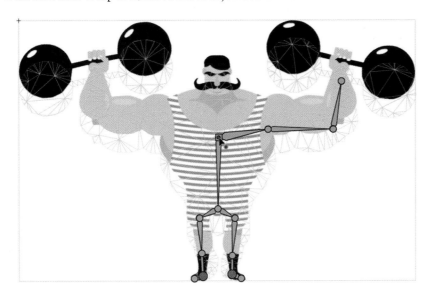

4 Move the knee joints outward so that the weightlifter's legs bend naturally.

5 On the timeline, insert a classic tween in between frames 1 and 15 and in between frames 15 and 30.

6 Select the Loop option for playback on the timeline, and move the first and last brackets to encompass all your frames. Play the animation to see your weightlifter in action!

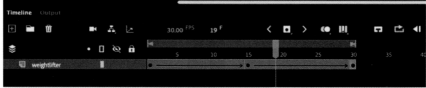

Isolating joints

Fine-tuning your animation means positioning your rig exactly how you want it. Double-clicking a joint isolates the positioning of only that selected joint without affecting its child bones.

1 Turn off the Loop Playback option.

2 Move your playhead on the timeline to frame 15.

3 With the Asset Warp tool, select the joint in the weightlifter's left hip.

4 Move the joint slightly outward.

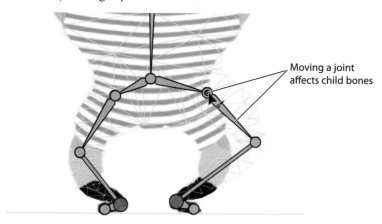

Moving a joint affects child bones

The joint moves and all its child bones follow. Undo (Command+Z/Ctrl+Z) any alterations to the joint.

5 Double-click the joint.

The child bone of the selected joint becomes pale orange, indicating that the selected joint is now isolated. You can move the joint without affecting any of its child bones.

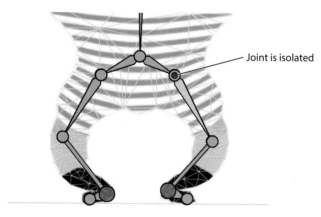

Joint is isolated

6 Move the left hip joint.

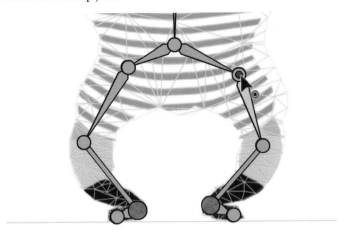

Moving the isolated joint repositions that joint alone.

Propagating rig edits

You'll notice that you created only one branch of bones in the weightlifter's left arm. You can add more bones to your rig, even after you've applied a tween to multiple keyframes, as Animate propagates changes to your rig to preserve the integrity of the tween.

Adding more bones

You'll add bones to the weightlifter's right arm and see how those changes propagate to all the keyframes.

1 Select the first keyframe on your timeline.

2 Choose the Asset Warp tool, and in the Tool tab of the Properties panel, make sure the Propagate Changes option is turned on.

3 Select the root joint, and create additional joints in the weightlifter's shoulder, elbow, and fist, just as you did with his other arm. Make sure the Bone type is turned back to the Hard option.

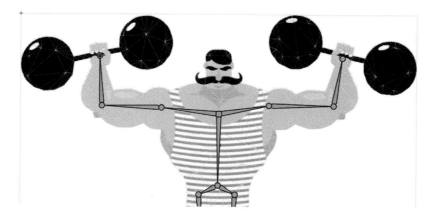

4 Move your playhead on the timeline to the middle keyframe, at frame 15.

The additions you made to your rig in the first keyframe propagate to the other keyframes to keep the tweens intact.

● **Note** Animate
propagates both
deletions and additions
of bones and joints
across keyframes.

5 Feel free to move the weightlifter's arms around in the middle keyframe so that his elbows dip down a little as he squats. The additional motion can help provide a sense of weight and realism.

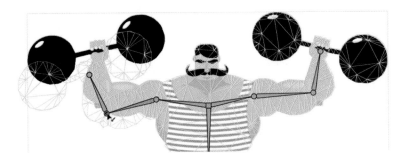

Single joints

Your rig can also contain single joints that are not connected by bones. With these independent joints, you can deform the mesh in more organic ways without being tied to a hierarchical structure.

Adding single joints

You'll add an unconnected joint in the mustache of your weightlifter. As he does his squat, his mustache unfurls.

1 Select the middle keyframe, at frame 15.

2 Choose the Asset Warp tool. Click off the rig to deselect any selection, and then click the tip of one side of his mustache.

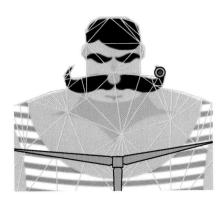

A single joint is created at the tip of his mustache, and the change is propagated across the other keyframes.

3 Click off the mesh to deselect the joint, and then click the tip of the other side of his mustache.

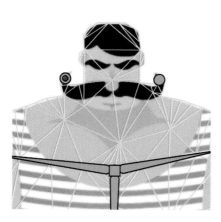

Another joint is created at the tip of the other side of his mustache. The rigs in your other keyframes also get the additional joint.

If you are creating multiple joints without connecting bones and you do not want to keep deselecting joints, you can change the options in the Tool tab of the Properties panel. Turn off the Create Bones option to create joints only.

4 Move the joints away from the weightlifter's face to straighten out his mustache.

Animate animates the changes so that his mustache unfurls as he squats with his weights.

5 Add an ease-out to your first tween and an ease-in to your second tween to give your motion a little more realism. (You'll learn more about applying eases in Lesson 6, "Animating Symbols with Motion Tweens.") Feel free to experiment to make the motion your own!

6 Finally, add a new layer below the weightlifter layer, and drag the background bitmap from the Library onto the Stage.

A strongman needs a circus tent to show off his talents, after all.

7   Choose Quick Share And Publish > Publish > Animated GIF to export an animated GIF to share on social media.

Fixed and Open Handle modes

When you create single joints in a rig, you can choose whether those joints are Fixed or Open for the Handle mode in the Warp Options section of the Properties panel. This determines how they behave and how they affect the mesh.

For Open Handle mode, which is the default option, you can move the joints to different positions to warp the mesh. In this example, there are three joints in a long rectangle. Moving the middle Open joint upward deforms the rectangle so that it bends.

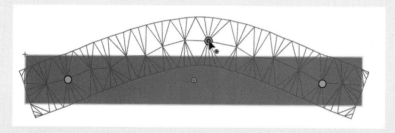

For the Fixed Handle mode option, you can move the joint position as well as rotate the mesh around the joint. Move your cursor close to the dotted circle around the joint, and drag to rotate the mesh.

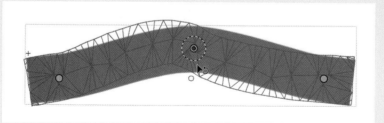

Using Flexi bones

Flexi bones, the third option in the Asset Warp tool's Bone Type option, lets you deform your bones with Bezier curves for more fluid, organic shapes and motions.

Adding Flexi bones

Close the **05_workingcopy_weightlifter** file and open the **05_Start_snakedancing.fla** file to explore the animation potential of Flexi bones. Save the file as **05_workingcopy_snakedancing.fla.**

1 Examine the project timeline.

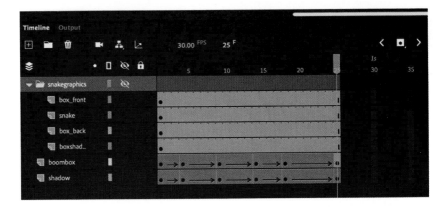

The timeline contains multiple layers. Inside the snakegraphics folder are four layers that contain graphics that show a snake inside a cardboard box.

The other layers outside the snakegraphics folder contain completed classic tweens of a boom box bouncing up and down.

You will use the Asset Warp tool with Flexi bones to animate the snake.

2 Make sure all the layers are locked except for the snake layer. Hide the box_front layer so that you can see the snake's entire body.

3 Choose Animate > Settings > Edit Preferences (Command+U/Ctrl+U).

4 Select the Drawing section on the left menu, and for Asset Warp Tool, deselect the Auto Convert Vector To Bitmap For Better Warping And Tweening option. Click OK.

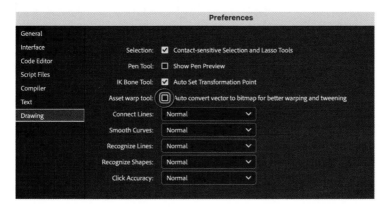

The option, which is selected by default, allows you to choose whether to keep your warped assets as a bitmap or a vector. If your starting graphic is already a bitmap (like the snow angel child), then the option really doesn't matter. If your starting graphic is a vector graphic (like the snake), then consider these trade-offs: bitmaps are easier for the mesh to handle, but converting vectors to bitmaps can often result in a loss of the sharp, high-resolution appearance characteristic of vectors.

In this task, since the vector shapes of the snake are relatively simple, you will deselect the option to maintain the vectors.

5 Select the Asset Warp tool.

6 In the Tool tab of the Properties panel, make sure Envelope is disabled, Create Bones is enabled, and Bone Type is set to Flexi.

7 Click the snake's body near its base to select it, and then click it again.

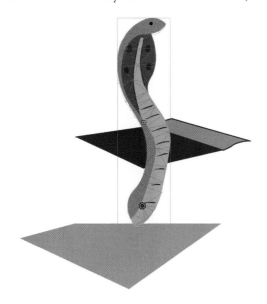

A mesh appears over the graphic, and your first joint is created.

8 Move your pointer up the snake's body and drag to create the next joint.

As you drag your pointer, handles appear from the joint, and the bone curves in the same direction as the Bezier handles.

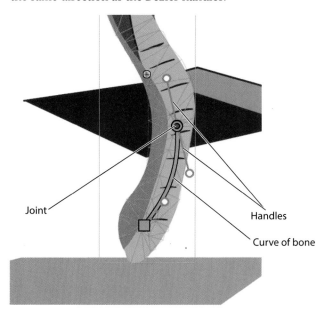

Joint

Handles

Curve of bone

9 Release your pointer and create the next joint farther up the snake's body in the same manner, creating curved Flexi bones that follow the curves of the snake.

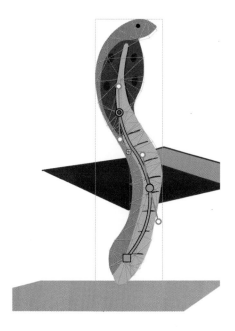

10 Create the last joint, in the snake's head.

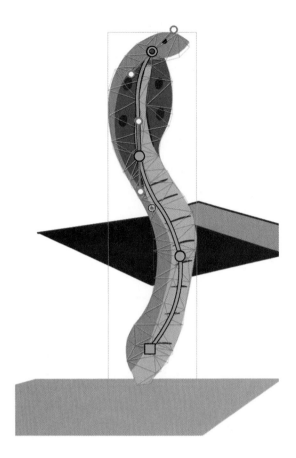

Animating the snake

The snake will dance to the boom box's music. You'll animate its slinky movements by changing the curvature of the Flexi bones in the rig.

1   On the timeline, create a keyframe (F6) at frame 25.

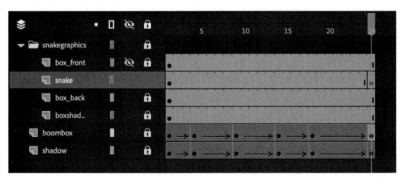

The first keyframe and the last keyframe will be identical so that the animation can loop seamlessly.

2 Create another keyframe (F6) at frame 8.

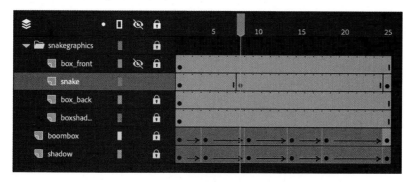

3 With the Asset Warp tool, double-click the first joint from the root joint.

● **Note** Recall that double-clicking a joint allows you to isolate the joint from the rest of the rig to manipulate it.

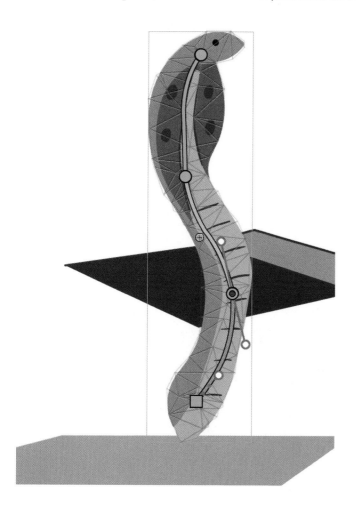

4 Move the joint to the left to shift that portion of the snake's body.

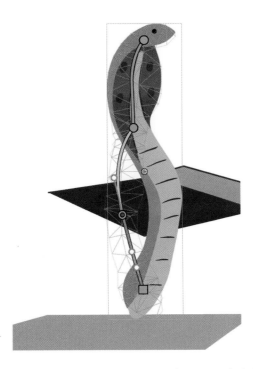

5 Double-click the next joint, and move it slightly to the right to shift that portion of the snake's body.

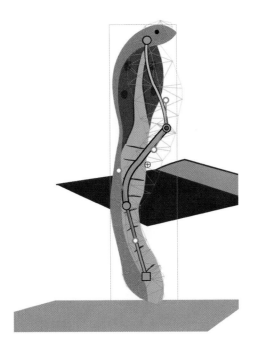

6 Drag the handles of the joint to smooth out the curvature of the snake. Hold the Option+Shift/Alt+Shift keys to move both sides of the handles together.

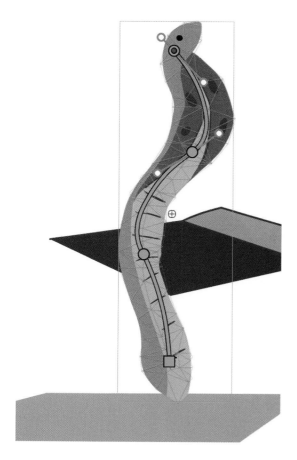

7 Create another keyframe (F6) at frame 15.

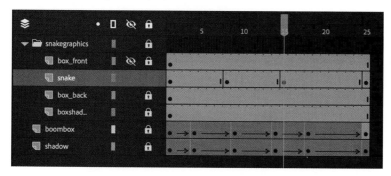

8 As you did in the previous keyframe, use the Asset Warp tool to move the joints of the snake and modify the curvature of the Flexi bones with the joint handles. You can follow the positioning and curves in the following image, or you can try your own snake moves.

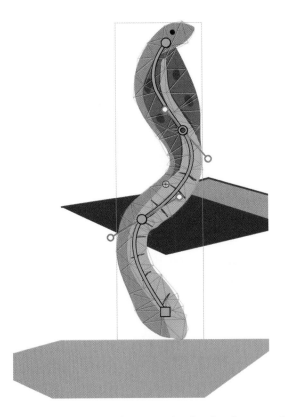

9 Select all the frames between the first keyframe and the last keyframe in the snake layer and choose Create Classic Tween.

Animate applies a tween between your four keyframes in the snake layer and smoothly interpolates the sinewy movements between keyframes.

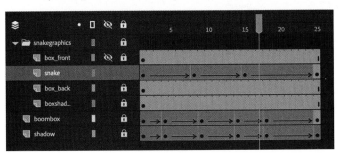

10 Select the Loop option on the timeline, move the brackets to cover all your frames, and press Return/Enter to preview your animation.

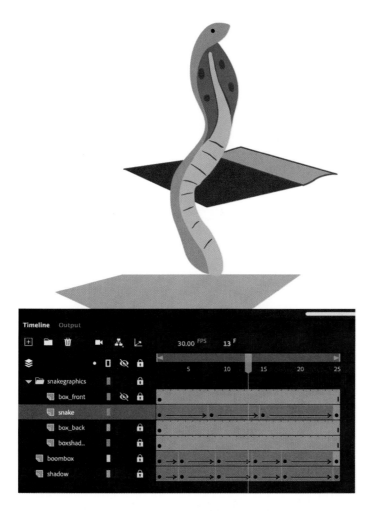

11 Watch your snake do its slinky dance to the music of the boom box! If you're not satisfied with the motion, you can always return to any of the keyframes to modify the positioning of the joints or curvature of the Flexi bones in the rig.

Tip You can hold down the Option/Alt key and drag the Flexi bone itself to change its curvature instead of using the Bezier handles at the joints.

Making envelope deformations

Now you'll add the musical notation pouring from the boom box. The musical notation will ripple to represent the smooth melodies. The Asset Warp tool's envelope deformer option provides controls around the boundaries of your graphic to create those changes.

Adding the musical notation

The musical notation is a bitmap, which you will place in a separate layer.

1   Unhide the box_front layer.

2   Insert a new layer and rename it **music**.

3   Drag the music layer to the bottom of the layer stack.

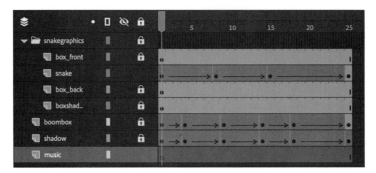

4   In the Library, find the music bitmap and drag it to the Stage in the music layer.

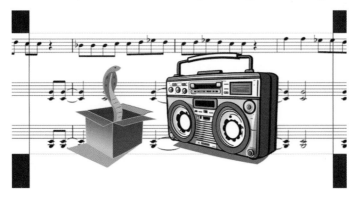

5   Use the Free Transform tool to scale the bitmap smaller (about 80%) and move it so that the right edge of the bitmap is hidden behind the boom box.

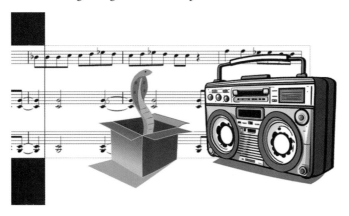

Applying the envelope deformer

The envelope deformer is an option in the Asset Warp tool that adds control points around the boundaries of your warp asset.

1   Select the Asset Warp tool.

2   In the Tool tab of the Properties panel, enable the envelope deformer option. Leave Create Bones off.

3   Click the musical notation bitmap.

The bitmap becomes a warp asset and a mesh is superimposed on it.

Notice that there are additional control points on the four corner points. Because you chose the envelope deformer option, the additional control points allow you to deform the contours of the graphic.

If the graphic were not rectangular, Animate would add enough control points to define the contours of your warped asset.

Note You cannot add additional control points to the envelope deformer.

Animating the music

A warped asset can just have an envelope deformer without a rig inside it, or it can have both an envelope deformer and a rig. In this example, you'll just use the envelope deformer to create a sense of the music ebbing and flowing by making the notes shrink and swell by deforming the contours of the graphic.

1 Select the Asset Warp tool.

2 Click the bottom-right corner control point on the envelope deformer.

3 Pull down on the handle that is connected to the corner control point.

The bottom edge of the warped asset bends and deforms the graphic.

4 Move the corner control point upward.

5 Move your pointer to the edge of the mesh until a curved line appears near your cursor, indicating you can modify a curve. Pull up on the top edge to deform it.

The top edge deforms. You can either use the handles or push and pull directly with the Asset Warp tool.

6 Reposition the deformer handles on the left side of the music to create organic curves.

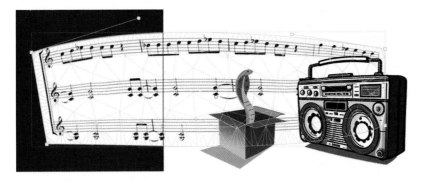

7 Insert a new keyframe (F6) in frame 13 and in the last frame of the music layer.

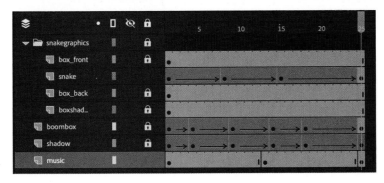

The last keyframe will remain identical to the first to ensure a smooth loop for the animation.

▶ **Tip** If you make a mistake in deforming the envelope of your graphic, you can reset it to its original state. In the Warp Options section of the Property inspector, click the Reset warped asset icon.

8 Deform the contours of the warped asset in the keyframe at frame 13. You don't have to move the control points or handles too far—subtle movements can go a long way, and they will also create fewer issues for Animate to tween.

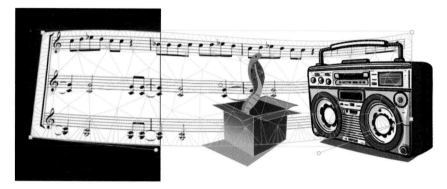

9 Select all the frames between the first keyframe and the last keyframe in the music layer and choose Create Classic Tween.

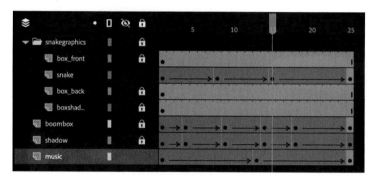

Animate applies a tween between your keyframes in the music layer and creates the undulating musical notation animation.

10 Select the Loop option on the timeline, move the brackets to cover all your frames, and press Return/Enter to preview your animation.

Your animation is complete! The Flexi bones in the snake, combined with the envelope deformations of the music, make possible the fluid, organic motions of this animation.

Think of the countless creative ways you can use modern rigging and envelope deformation in your animations!

Review questions

1 The Asset Warp tool can be used to create a rig on what kinds of graphics?

2 How do you assign a specific numerical value for the rotation of a rig joint?

3 What's the difference between a hard bone and a soft bone?

4 Why would you use a Flexi bone?

5 What animation technique should be applied to animate a rig created by the Asset Warp tool?

6 How do you edit the positions of the joints in a rig?

7 What does the Freeze Joint option do to a rig?

8 What are two ways you can deform the envelope of a warped asset?

Review answers

1 The Asset Warp tool can be used to create a rig on either a vector shape or a bitmap. When the Asset Warp tool is used on a vector shape, the shape is converted to a bitmap unless you change the drawing preferences in Animate > Preferences/Settings.

2 Select the joint, and in the Warp Options section of the Properties panel, enter a value for the angle of rotation.

3 A hard bone is one that allows you to stretch and squash the mesh, which distorts the associated graphic. A soft bone, in contrast, is an option that attempts to preserve the volume or length of the mesh, which simulates a more flexible connection between joints.

4 The Flexi bone option allows you to create a rig with nonlinear bones and distort the warped asset mesh with Bezier curves.

5 A rig created by the Asset Warp tool can be animated only with classic tweening.

6 To edit a rig, right-click the rig or warped asset on the Stage and choose Edit Rig.

7 The Freeze Joint option fixes the joint to the Stage to prevent it from moving.

8 The first way you can deform the envelope of a warped asset is by moving the control points or dragging the handles of the control points that are around the edges of the warped asset's mesh. The second way is by using the Asset Warp tool to intuitively drag on the edges of the mesh to modify their curves.

6 ANIMATING SYMBOLS WITH MOTION TWEENS

Lesson overview

In this lesson, you'll learn how to do the following:

- Create a motion tween.
- Understand the differences between motion tweening and classic tweening.
- Modify the path of motion of a motion tween.
- Use the Motion Editor to refine and create complex motion.
- Edit a property curve.
- Apply eases to create more realistic motion.

 This lesson will take about 1 hour to complete.

To get the lesson files used in this chapter, download them from the web page for this book at peachpit.com/AnimateCIB2024. For more information, see "Accessing the lesson files and Web Edition" in the Getting Started section at the beginning of this book.

Motion tweening offers another approach to animating symbols. Complex movement can benefit from motion tweening's advanced Motion Editor. Use the Motion Editor to view how the properties of your motion tween change over time, and apply and edit eases for sophisticated effects.

Getting started

● **Note** If you have not already downloaded the project files for this lesson to your computer from your Account page, make sure to do so now. See Getting Started at the beginning of the book.

Start by viewing the finished movie file to see the animated infographic that you'll create in this lesson.

1 Double-click the 06End.html file in the 06/06End folder to play the animation in a browser.

The project is a short, animated infographic illustrating the idea of China as an emerging economic threat to the highest-traded currencies in the world. The animation is something you might see accompanying a story in the business and economy section of a news site. In the animation, you see a globe representing Earth, and at the top of it is a stack of blocks, each one emblazoned with a flag: the American flag to represent the US dollar; the European Union flag to represent the euro; and the Japansese flag to represent the yen. Suddenly a large hand with the Chinese flag attached to it bumps the stack, sending the blocks tumbling down. In this lesson, you'll apply motion tweening for the hand and blocks. You'll also use the Motion Editor to make refinements to the action of the blocks, including the bouncing movements as they fall.

2 Close the 06End.html file.

3 Double-click the 06Start.fla file in the 06/06Start folder to open the initial project file in Animate. This file is an HTML5 Canvas document that contains all the graphics you will use in this lesson, with movie clip symbols saved in the library. Each graphic has its own layer, and instances of the symbols have been placed on the Stage in their initial positions.

4   Choose View > Magnification > Clip To Stage to deselect the option (or deselect the Clip Content Outside The Stage button above the Stage) and enable the pasteboard so that you can see all the graphics positioned just off the Stage.

5   Choose File > Save As. Name the file **06_workingcopy.fla**, and save it in the 06Start folder.

Saving a working copy ensures that the original start file will be available if you want to start over.

Understanding the project file

The 06Start.fla file has five layers. The background layer contains background elements that will not be animated. The China layer contains the movie clip instance of the hand and the Chinese flag representing China. Each of the three middle layers (US, Euro, and Yen) contains a corresponding movie clip instance of a block representing those currencies.

The Stage is set at 800 pixels by 600 pixels, and the color of the Stage is gray.

For this lesson, you'll add motion tweens in the top four layers and refine the movements of the blocks with the Motion Editor.

About motion tweens

Motion tweens are another way of creating animation with symbol instances.

Motion tweens, like classic tweens, animate changes in an instance's position, transformation, color effects, or filters. In addition, motion tweens can animate 3D position or translation.

Motion tweens have more options for controlling property changes. However, with more options comes more complexity.

Motion tweens also tend to be less compatible with other Animate techniques. For example, modern rigging relies on classic tweens and not motion tweens.

For these reasons, much of your work should be based on classic tweens, but learning to create animation with both techniques will help you understand the full scope of the animator's toolkit. Understanding both motion and classic tweens will better prepare you to choose the right approach for any project.

Understanding the differences between motion tweens and classic tweens

The key differences between motion and classic tweens are as follows:

- Only motion tweens have access to the Motion Editor, an advanced editor for adjusting properties and eases.

- Motion tweens are separated into their own tween layer. However, classic and motion tweens share the same restriction that no other object can exist in the same layer as the tween.

- Motion tweens support 3D rotations or translations. Classic tweens do not.

- You can edit the path of motion in a motion tween without having to create a separate Motion Guide layer.

- Motion tweens cannot be used to animate modern rigs with the Asset Warp tool.

Animating the hand

You'll start this project by animating the hand moving from off the Stage to shove the three blocks.

1   First you'll add some time on the timeline for the animation to proceed. Select frame 60 in all five layers (Shift+click, or drag through all layers).

2   Choose Insert Frame (F5).

Animate adds frames in all five layers up to frame 60.

3   Deselect the five layers. Select just the graphic of the hand on the Stage, then choose Create Motion Tween at the top of the Timeline panel (or right-click and choose Create Motion Tween).

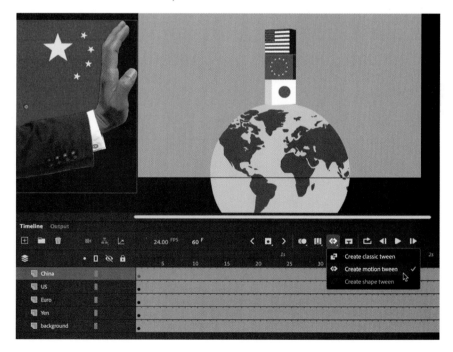

Animate creates a motion tween, indicated by a gold-colored frame span. The China layer becomes a tween layer indicated by a special icon next to the China layer name.

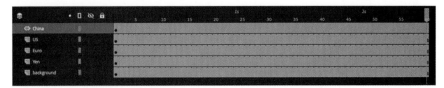

4 Move the playhead to frame 20.

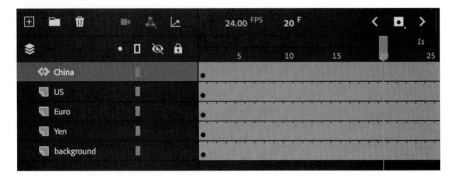

5 Drag the hand graphic so that it just touches the blocks that are balanced on top of the globe. The X-position should be at about 96.

● **Note** Even though the Auto Keyframe option is disabled, Animate inserts new keyframes automatically when you move the instance on the Stage. This is how motion tweening works. If you prefer, you can also manually insert a keyframe (F6) before moving your graphic.

▶ **Tip** Just as you can move the keyframes of a classic tween to adjust the timing of an animation, you can move the keyframes of a motion tween by dragging them within the tween span.

A new keyframe is automatically created at frame 20 to indicate the new position of the graphic. The keyframe appears as a small black diamond.

On the Stage, a series of dots on a line indicates the path of motion for the graphic from its position from the first keyframe to the next keyframe.

6 Preview your animation by pressing Return (macOS) or Enter (Windows).

The hand animates its position from the first keyframe at frame 1 to the next keyframe at frame 20, sliding smoothly across the Stage.

Span-based versus frame-based selection

By default, Animate uses frame-based selection, which means you can select individual frames within a motion tween. However, if you prefer to click a motion tween and have the entire span (the beginning and ending keyframes and all the frames in between) be selected, you can enable Span Based Selection from the Frame View menu in the upper-right corner of the Timeline panel (or you can Shift-click to select the entire span).

Compact
Comfortable

Timeline control - Bottom
Match FPS
Span Based Selection
Customize Timeline Tools

Lock

Help

Close
Close Group

With Span Based Selection enabled, you can click anywhere within the motion tween to select it, and move the entire animation backward or forward along the timeline as a single unit.

If you want to select individual keyframes while Span Based Selection is enabled, hold down the Command/Ctrl key and click a keyframe.

Moving keyframes versus changing time in tween spans

Managing the timing of your animation by moving keyframes and stretching or squashing tween spans can sometimes be frustrating because you will get different outcomes depending on what you've selected on the timeline and how you drag those selections.

If you want to simply move the location of a keyframe within a tween span, make sure that only a single keyframe is selected and that the tiny box appears next to your pointer as you begin dragging the keyframe to a new location.

Consider the following animation, in which a ball moves from the left side of the Stage to the bottom edge and then to the right side, making a letter "V." On the timeline, three keyframes mark the three positions of the ball.

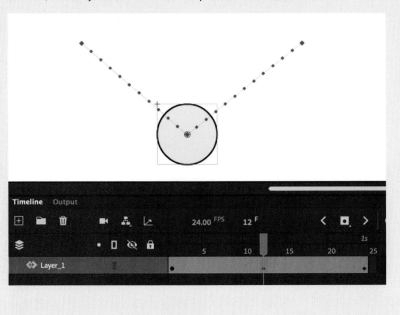

Moving the middle keyframe changes the timing of when the ball hits the bottom of the Stage.

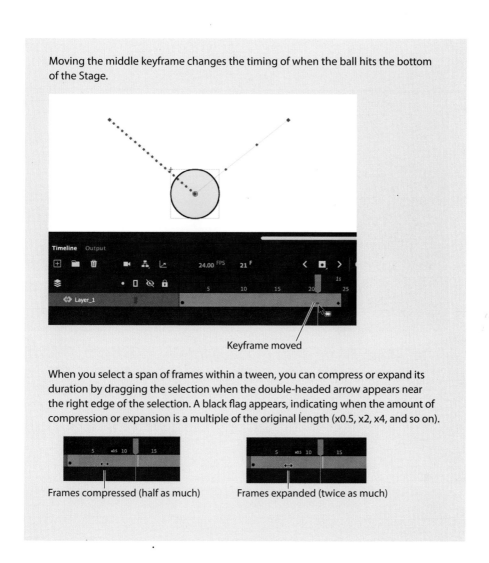

Keyframe moved

When you select a span of frames within a tween, you can compress or expand its duration by dragging the selection when the double-headed arrow appears near the right edge of the selection. A black flag appears, indicating when the amount of compression or expansion is a multiple of the original length (x0.5, x2, x4, and so on).

Frames compressed (half as much)   Frames expanded (twice as much)

Editing the path of motion

The path of motion that is visible on the Stage is fully editable with the Selection, Subselection, or Free Transform tool.

Bending the motion path

You'll use the Selection tool to adjust the motion of the hand so that it moves in a slightly curved path rather than a straight one.

1 With the Selection tool, drag the path of motion down to create a gentle curve.

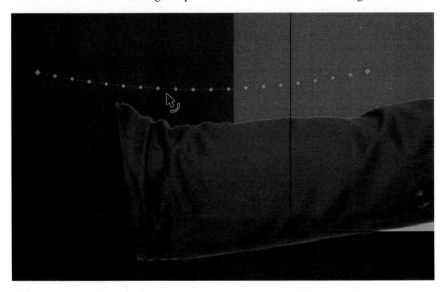

The curve bends slightly.

2 Preview your animation again.

Now the hand follows the curve in a gentle arcing motion.

3 Choose the Subselection tool.

4 Click anchor points on either end of the path and drag the Bezier handles to adjust the curvature.

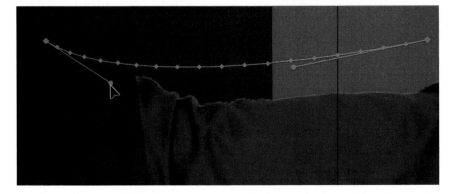

For this task, you won't need to make any precise edits with the Subselection tool, but just understand that the symbol instance follows any adjustments made to the motion path. Unlike classic tweens, with motion tweens you do not have to worry about snapping the registration point of the instance to a path.

About the Motion Editor

The Motion Editor is an advanced panel that is integrated into the Timeline panel and is accessible only when you're editing a motion tween. The panel shows you how the properties of your animation change over the course of the tween as lines on a graph. It takes some time to become familiar with the meaning of the lines and how the curves translate to visual changes on the Stage. But once you recognize how the curves reflect changes in your animation, you have a powerful tool at your disposal.

You can modify the curves on the graph, called *property curves*, by adding or deleting anchor points, and you can change their curvature with Bezier precision.

The Motion Editor also allows you to apply sophisticated eases to your animation similar to the easing options in the Properties panel. However, the Motion Editor visually shows you how your ease affects a property curve. You can even apply different eases to the curves for each property of a tween.

● **Note** The Motion Editor is available only for motion tweens (and not classic tweens, shape tweens, inverse kinematics with the Bone tool, or frame-by-frame animations).

Examining property curves

You edited the animation of the hand by adding a slight dip in its motion. You can apply even more sophisticated movements by editing the X and Y property curves in the Motion Editor.

1 Double-click the motion tween in the China layer on the timeline, or right-click and choose Refine Motion Tween.

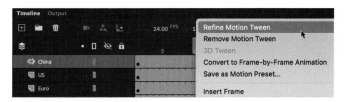

The motion tween expands to reveal the Motion Editor panel. Expand the Location category, if it is not already expanded. The Location category contains two properties: X and Y, each represented by a line on the graph. On the graph, the horizontal axis represents time; the vertical lines correspond to the selected property values (for X and Y, they represent pixel values).

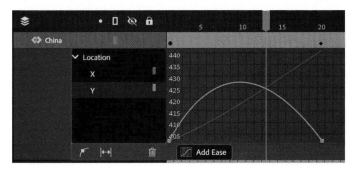

2 Click the X-property to select it.

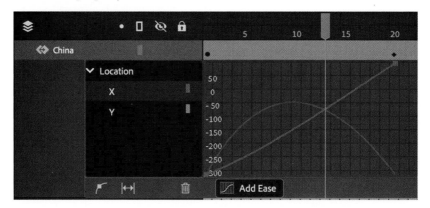

The rising red line becomes bold, and the other line fades. The rising red line represents the changing value of the hand's X-position, which moves from –314 to 96.

3 Now select the Y-property.

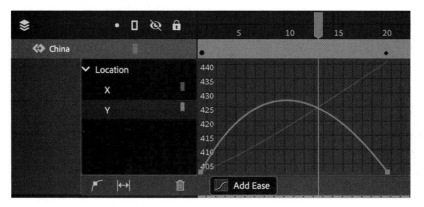

The curved line becomes bold and the other line fades. The curved line represents the changing value of the hand's Y-position, which begins at around 402, then increases to about 430, then decreases back to 402. These changing values describe the hand's gentle downward arcing motion—the arc that you created by adjusting the path of the motion in the previous task.

Editing property curves

To change the shape of the property curve, you add or delete anchor points. At each anchor point you can change the curvature or direction of the curve.

For the next task, you'll edit the X-property so that the hand pauses a bit before reaching the blocks, as if to size them up. Then it backs up and gives the blocks a shove. You'll edit the X-property curve to create this back-and-forth movement.

1 In the Motion Editor, select the X-property under the Location category.

2 Select the Add Anchor Point On Graph option.

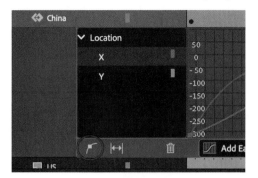

3 Hover your mouse pointer over the property curve.

   Your cursor changes to the Pen tool icon with a plus sign, indicating that you can add an anchor point to the curve.

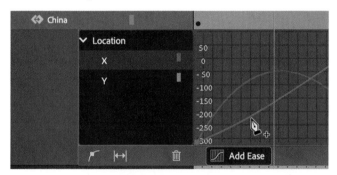

4 Use your mouse to drag the curve upward at frame 11, and release the mouse button when the anchor point is at about the 50-pixel mark.

   This adds a new anchor point to the curve, and a new keyframe is added at frame 11.

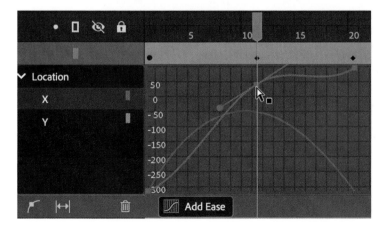

Tip You can also double-click a location on a property curve to add a new anchor point.

Note You can move any of the anchor points, including the ones at the first and last keyframes, to new property values along the vertical axis. You can also move any of the anchor points (except the first one) to new times along the motion tween. In effect, when you move anchor points to new times, you move the keyframes within the tween span.

Tip You can use the arrow keys to nudge a selected anchor point for precise control. Press the Up Arrow key or the Down Arrow key to move the anchor point one property unit up or down, or press Shift-Up or Shift-Down to move the anchor point 10 property units up or down.

5 Select Add Anchor Point On Graph again.

6 Add a new anchor point at frame 17 and drag to about −50.

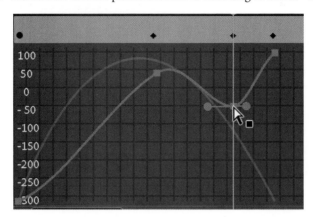

Adding another anchor point to the graph also adds a new keyframe to the motion tween.

7 Each new anchor point comes with direction handles on either side that allow you to change the curvature at that point. Move the handles on each new anchor point so that they are horizontal. This will help create a smooth curve that produces one hill and one dip before reaching its final value.

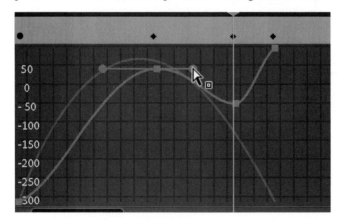

8 Double-click the China motion tween to collapse the Motion Editor. Preview your tween by pressing Return/Enter.

Your newly adjusted X-property curve makes the hand move toward its final keyframe (the first hill), then retreat slightly as it sizes up its target (the dip), and then proceed to its final destination. The path of the motion on the Stage reflects these changes.

▶ **Tip** Hold down the Option/Alt key as you move a direction handle of an anchor point to change the angle of that direction handle independently of the other handle. You can adjust the length of each direction handle without holding down the Option/Alt key. If you adjust the length or angle of one side of a direction handle independently of the other, you can create more dramatic changes to the property curve.

Deleting anchor points

If you've accidentally added too many anchor points, you can always remove them (except for the first and last anchor points). Removing an anchor point has the same effect as removing a keyframe of the motion tween. Hold down the Command/Ctrl key.

Your cursor turns into the Pen icon with a minus sign when you hover over any anchor point. Click any anchor point (except the first or last one).

▶ **Tip** Some anchor points (for example, the first and last anchor points of a property curve) do not have direction handles by default. Select the anchor point you want to add direction handles to, and then hold down the Option/Alt key, pull out a direction handle, and edit the curvature.

Animate removes the anchor point from the property curve. Do not remove any anchor points from your project at this point in the lesson. If you do so inadvertently, press Command+Z/Ctrl+Z to undo the operation.

▶ **Tip** Option/Alt-click an anchor point to remove its direction handles, converting it to a corner point without smooth curves.

Deleting property curves

If you want to delete a curve, click the trash can icon at the bottom of the Motion Editor to delete a tween for a selected property curve.

Viewing options for the Motion Editor

▶ **Tip** You can also hold down the Command/Ctrl key and scroll inside the Motion Editor to change the magnification.

Animate provides different viewing options for the Motion Editor so that you can refine your property curves with greater accuracy.

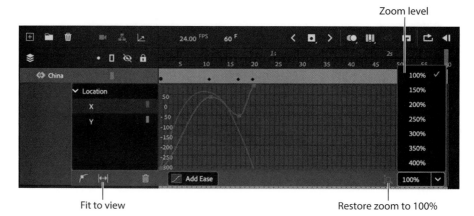

Zoom level

Fit to view   Restore zoom to 100%

● **Note** You can enter a custom magnification level for the Motion Editor, but the minimum value is 100% and the maximum value is 400%.

1   Use the menu at the bottom of the Motion Editor to change the zoom level.

The vertical axis expands to show a more granular level of property values. Scroll up or down to see the top or bottom of the curve.

2   Click Zoom 100% to reset the Motion Editor to its default view.

3   Click Fit To View to expand the Motion Editor to fill the existing space on the timeline. Click the icon again (its name is now Restore View) to return to the default view.

Understanding property keyframes

Changes in properties are independent of one another and do not need to be tied to the same keyframes. That is, you can have one keyframe for the position, a different keyframe for the color effect, and yet another keyframe for a filter. Managing many different kinds of keyframes can become overwhelming, especially if you want different properties to change at different times during the motion tween. Fortunately, Animate provides a few helpful tools for keyframe management.

When viewing the tween span, you can choose to view the keyframes of only certain properties. For example, you can choose to view only the Position keyframes so that you can see when your object moves. Or you can choose to view only the Filter keyframes so that you can see when a filter changes. Right-click a motion tween in the Timeline panel, choose View Keyframes, and then choose the desired property from the list. You can also choose All or None to see all the properties or none of the properties.

You can also insert a keyframe specific to the property you want to change. Right-click a motion tween in the Timeline panel, choose Insert Keyframe, and then select the desired property.

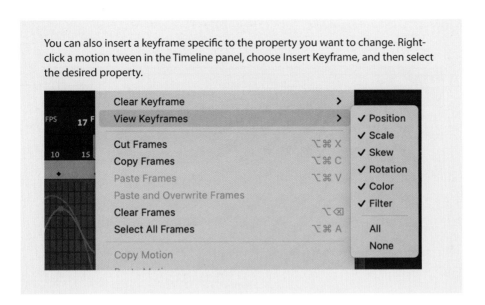

Adding complex eases

Now that the hand gives the blocks a shove, it's time to animate them toppling off the top of the world.

As the blocks fall, they bounce up and down, decreasing in height after each bounce. The Motion Editor provides many different eases that you can apply to create realistic physics-based effects that are quick and easy to edit.

Motion-tweening the blocks

First you'll apply a motion tween for the three blocks to establish their beginning and ending positions.

1 Drag to select frame 21 in the US, Euro, and Yen layers. (If you are using span-based selection, hold down the Command/Ctrl key while you drag.)

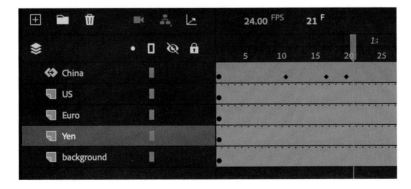

2 Insert a keyframe (F6).

New keyframes are created in the US, Euro, and Yen layers at frame 21.

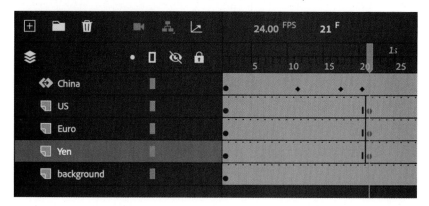

3 While all three keyframes are still selected in the Timeline panel, right-click the blocks on the Stage and choose Create Motion Tween.

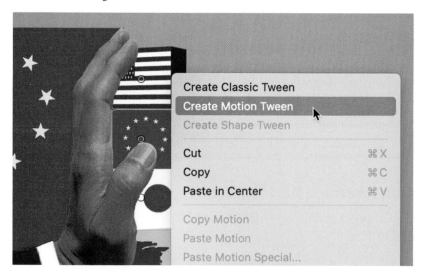

Motion tweens are created for the three blocks, starting at frame 21.

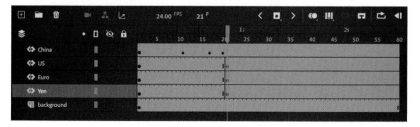

4 Move the playhead to the end of the timeline, at frame 60.

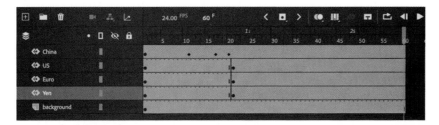

5 With the Selection tool, move the US movie clip instance to the bottom-right of the Stage, at X=700 and Y=531.

6 Using the Free Transform tool, rotate the clip 180 degrees clockwise so that it appears upside down.

7 Move the Euro movie clip instance to the bottom-right of the Stage in the same manner, but just behind the US movie clip, and use the Free Transform tool to rotate it 90 degrees clockwise.

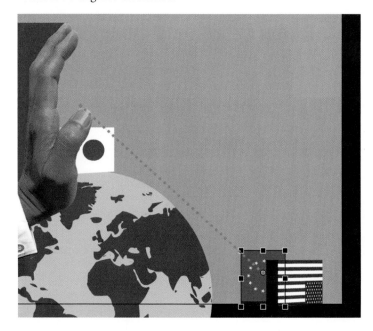

8 Move the Yen movie clip instance to the bottom-right of the Stage, just behind the Euro movie clip, and use the Free Transform tool to rotate it 180 degrees clockwise.

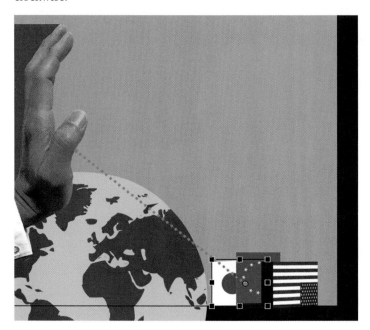

9 Test your new motion by pressing Return/Enter.

The three blocks fall gracefully in a diagonal direction, rotating as they fall. However, you'll want a more violent, realistic tumble, so the next step is to add some eases.

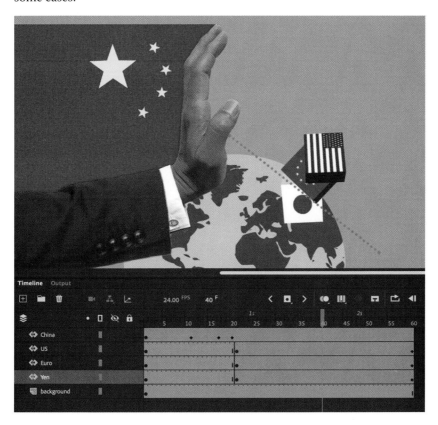

Applying eases from the Motion Editor

One of the preset eases in the Motion Editor is BounceIn, which simulates a bouncing motion. The distance to the final property value gradually decreases as the motion tween approaches its ending keyframe.

1 Double-click the motion tween in the US layer to open the Motion Editor.

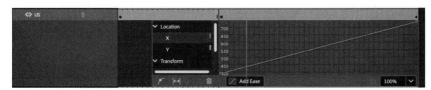

Animate expands the motion tween in the US layer, revealing the Motion Editor panel. The Motion Editor contains property curves for both the X- and Y-properties for Location as well as the Z-property for Transform > Rotation (you may have to scroll down to see the additional properties, or expand the height of your timeline).

2 Select the Y-property under Location.

3 Click Add Ease at the bottom of the Motion Editor to open the Ease panel.

4 Double-click the Bounce And Spring category to reveal the presets within.

5 Select the BounceIn ease preset and enter **5** for the Easing value.

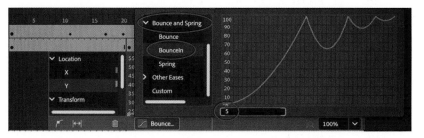

The BounceIn ease simulates a bounce that slowly decays as the motion tween approaches its end. The Easing value for the BounceIn ease determines the number of bounces.

6 Press Tab to confirm the Easing value and press Esc to close the Ease panel.

A dotted line appears in the Motion Editor superimposed on the original property curve. This is the "resulting curve" because it shows the effect of the ease on the tween.

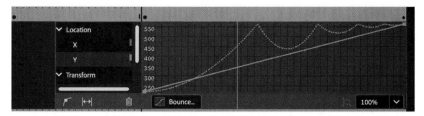

7 Test your new motion by pressing Return/Enter.

The US instance bounces (only in the Y-direction) as it falls to the ground. Note the path of the bounce on the Stage defined by the dots.

8 Collapse the Motion Editor for the US layer, and expand the Motion Editor for the Euro layer.

9 Select the Y-property and apply a BounceIn ease. Change the Easing value to **4** if it's not set to 4 already.

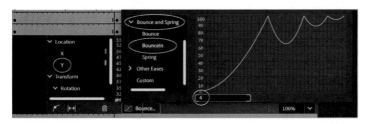

▶ **Tip** To remove an ease, choose No Ease at the top of the ease category list in the Motion Editor.

Note After you've chosen an ease preset, the label on the Add Ease button changes to the name of the preset.

10 Collapse the Motion Editor for the Euro layer, and expand the Motion Editor for the Yen layer.

11 Apply a BounceIn ease to the Y-property of the Yen instance, and change the Easing value to **3**.

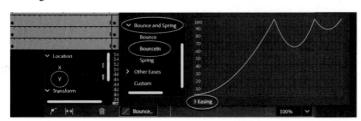

Tip If you're encountering strange, unpredictable behaviors, check to make sure that you've applied the BounceIn ease only to the Y-property curve. You want the bouncing motion to affect only the vertical motion and not the horizontal motion or the rotation. When the three blocks fall, each tumbles with a different number of bounces. The top block bounces the most with five bounces, the middle bounces four times, and the bottom block bounces three times.

12 Test your new motion by pressing Return/Enter.

Applying a second ease to a different property curve

The Motion Editor is powerful because it enables you to treat each property curve of one motion tween independently. For example, you can apply one ease for the Y-property and a different ease for the X-property.

This is exactly what you'll do next. You'll add an ease-out for the horizontal motion of each instance, while maintaining the BounceIn ease for the vertical motion.

Tip You can use the Up, Down, Left, and Right Arrow keys to navigate the ease types in the Ease panel of the Motion Editor.

1 Expand the Motion Editor for the US layer.

2 Select the X-property under Location.

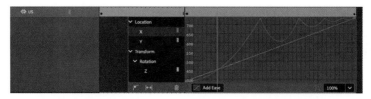

The straight line is highlighted. This represents the linear motion of the object in the horizontal direction.

3 Click Add Ease at the bottom of the Motion Editor to open the Ease panel.

4 Double-click the Simple category.

The category opens, revealing Slow, Medium, Fast, and Fastest presets. The eases in the Simple category affect one side of the motion tween (either the beginning or the end). The eases in the Stop and Start category affect both sides of the motion tween. The eases in the other category are more complex ease types.

5   Select the Fast ease preset, and enter **50** for the Easing value if it's not set to 50 already.

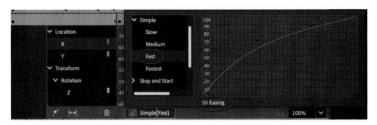

The Fast ease curve is displayed, showing graphically the intensity of the ease. Slower eases are fairly shallow and closer to a straight line; faster eases have progressively greater curvature.

The Easing value determines the strength of the ease for each ease preset and the direction of the ease. A positive number represents an ease-out and a negative number represents an ease-in.

The Easing value of 50 represents a strong ease-out motion.

6   Click outside the Motion Editor or press the Esc key to accept your easing choices.

The dotted line is the resulting ease for the horizontal motion. The block slows down as it reaches its final X-position.

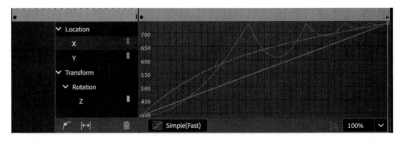

7   Apply Fast eases with an Easing value of 50 for the X-property curves of the other two motion tweens (the Euro and the Yen instances).

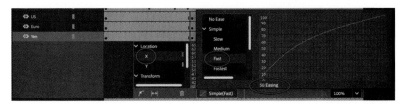

8 Preview your new motion by pressing Return/Enter.

As the three blocks bounce to the ground in the Y-direction, their forward momentum gradually slows down, creating a more realistic animation in the X-direction.

9 Choose Control > Test Movie > In Browser.

Animate publishes all the necessary files to run as an HTML5 Canvas document. Your browser launches and plays the animation.

Property curves versus ease curves

When you apply an ease to a motion tween with the Motion Editor, the original property curve is not altered permanently. In the first section of this lesson, you altered the property curves of a motion tween directly by adding anchor points. Applying eases is akin to applying a filter that influences the outcome of an original property. Like a filter, the ease can be edited or removed altogether.

It is possible to both modify a property curve and add an ease, but the combined result can be unpredictable.

Review questions

1 How is editing the path of motion for a motion tween different from editing a classic tween?

2 How do you access the Motion Editor for a motion tween?

3 What's the difference between a property curve and an ease curve?

4 What does the Easing value do to an ease?

5 How do you change the curvature of a property curve?

Review answers

1 The path of motion for a motion tween is shown on the Stage and can be edited with the Selection, Subselection, or Free Transform tool. The path of motion for a classic tween is a stroke you draw on a separate layer called a Motion Guide layer.

2 To open the Motion Editor panel, double-click a motion tween span on the timeline, or right-click a motion tween span and choose Refine Motion Tween.

3 A property curve is the graphical representation of how a property of a motion tween changes values over time. An ease curve represents a different rate of change that you can apply to an individual property curve. Animate displays the effects of an ease curve on a property curve as a dotted line.

4 The Easing value changes the strength and direction of an ease. Easing values affect eases differently, depending on the type of ease selected. For example, the Easing value for BounceIn eases determines the number of bounces, whereas the Easing value for a Simple Fast ease determines whether the ease is an ease-in or ease-out, and the strength of the ease.

5 To change the curvature of a property curve, select the property in the Motion Editor and select Add Anchor Point On Graph. Click the curve to add a new anchor point, and move the direction handles to change the shape of the curve at that point. You can move the anchor points up or down to change the property value, or you can move the anchor points left or right to change the position of the keyframe within the motion tween.

7 ANIMATING THE CAMERA

Lesson overview

In this lesson, you'll learn how to do the following:

- Understand the kinds of motion that are best animated with the Camera tool.

- Activate the camera.

- Hide and reveal the camera.

- Pan, tilt, roll, and zoom the camera.

- Create depth with the Layer Depth panel.

- Attach layers to the camera to keep them independent of camera motion.

- Apply color effects to the camera.

 This lesson will take about 1 hour to complete.

To get the lesson files used in this chapter, download them from the web page for this book at peachpit.com/AnimateCIB2024. For more information, see "Accessing the lesson files and Web Edition" in the Getting Started section at the beginning of this book.

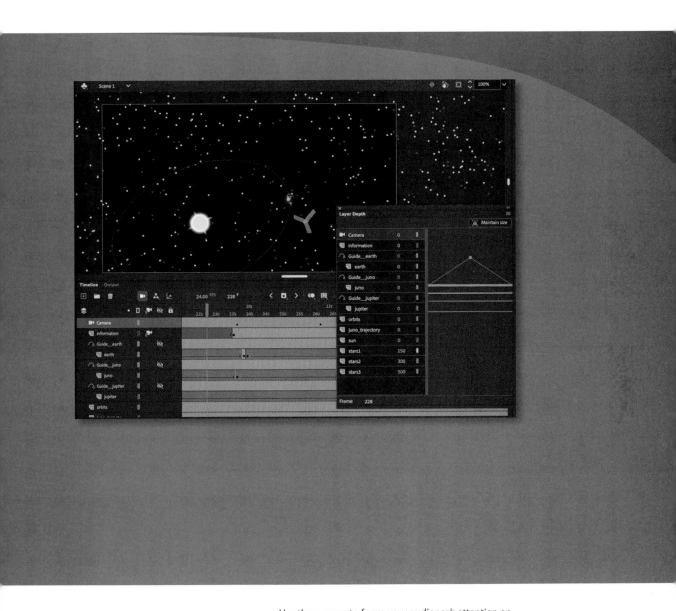

Use the camera to focus your audience's attention on your animation. Use filmmaking techniques such as pan, tilt, roll, and zoom to direct the action for more cinematic approaches. In combination with the Layer Depth panel, achieve a sense of realistic depth.

Animating camera moves

So far, you've learned to animate different properties of symbol instances on the Stage—their position, scale, rotation, transparency, and filters. You've also explored how you can animate complex motion that uses easing, and you've learned how to animate characters with modern rigging or by using layer hierarchies.

However, as an animator you're not just directing the motion of your characters and objects on the Stage, as you would if you were directing a play. You're also in control of the camera, which makes you more like the director of a movie. That means controlling where to point the camera to frame the action, zooming in and out, panning (moving the camera left or right), tilting (moving the camera up or down), and rolling (rotating the camera) for special effects. All of these camera movements are available in Adobe Animate with the Camera tool.

Getting started

● **Note** If you have not already downloaded the project files for this lesson to your computer from your Account page, make sure to do so now. See Getting Started at the beginning of the book.

Start by viewing the finished movie file to see an educational video that you'll create in this lesson.

1 Double-click the 07End.mp4 file in the 07/07End folder to play the video file.

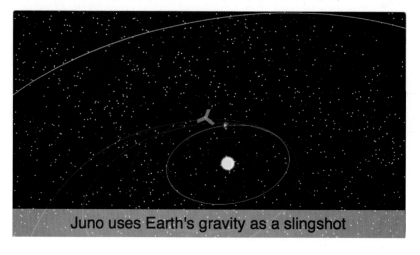

Juno uses Earth's gravity as a slingshot

The project is an animation showing the trajectory of the *Juno* spacecraft, which was launched from Earth in 2011 and reached Jupiter in 2016. The animation is something that you might see on an educational site or at a museum. Notice how the audience's view zooms in and out and how the camera tracks *Juno* as it moves across the solar system. At various points in the animation, captions appear and explain what's happening.

2 Close the 07End.mp4 file.

3 Double-click the 07Start.fla file in the 07/07Start folder to open the initial project file in Animate.

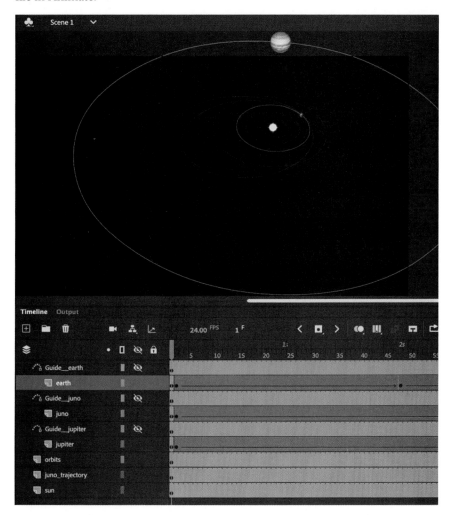

This file is an ActionScript 3.0 document that contains the completed animation of *Juno*'s trajectory and the orbiting Jupiter and Earth. There are no camera moves in this project yet; you'll add those in this lesson. The file also contains graphic elements that have been imported into the library for you to use.

4 Choose File > Save As. Name the file **07_workingcopy.fla**, and save it in the 07Start folder.

Saving a working copy ensures that the original start file will be available if you want to start over.

5 Choose Control > Test.

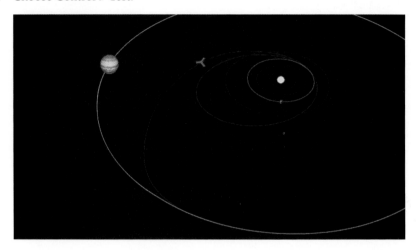

Animate generates a new window for you to preview the animation. You see a partial view of the solar system, with the sun in the middle and Earth and Jupiter orbiting the sun. A spacecraft launches from Earth and follows a gray track. Watch how it circles back toward Earth to be flung away to intercept Jupiter.

The animation is decent, and the Stage shows all the action: the orbiting planets and the movement of the *Juno* spacecraft. However, it lacks drama, and some details get lost because of the different scales we're seeing. When *Juno* circles back toward Earth to use its gravity as a slingshot effect to propel it toward Jupiter, wouldn't it be nice to see it up close as it approaches Earth to get flung back out? That's where the Camera tool can help. You'll animate the camera to direct our attention to the action: get close when you need to, or zoom back out to show the big picture. Use a camera to follow the spacecraft just as you would follow a character across the Stage.

Understanding the project file

Your 07_workingcopy.fla project file includes three animated layers—earth, juno, and jupiter—containing classic tweens with a motion guide layer for each. The motion guides keep the animation on track. Remember that the motion guides for classic tweens are not visible when the animation is published, so to show the orbits of the planets and the trajectory of *Juno*, the guides have been duplicated in the layers called orbits and juno_trajectory. The bottom layer, called sun, contains the sun in the middle of the solar system.

Using the camera

Think of the camera as just another object to which you can apply a motion or classic tween to animate its position, rotation, and scale. If you're already comfortable with managing keyframes and tweens, then the Camera tool should feel familiar.

Enabling the camera

Enable the camera with the Camera tool ![camera icon] in the Tools panel (it may be hidden in the Drag And Drop Tools panel) or by clicking the Add/Remove Camera button at the top of the Timeline panel.

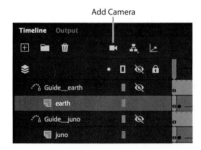

A Camera layer is added to the top of your timeline and becomes active.

On the Stage, the camera controls appear.

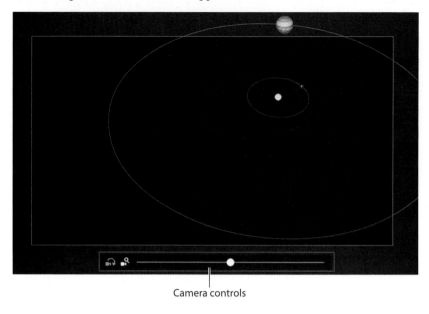

Camera controls

Characteristics of the camera

The Camera layer operates a little differently from a normal layer to which you add graphics.

● Note The Camera tool is not available for all types of Animate documents.

- The size of your Stage becomes the frame of your camera view.

- You can have only one Camera layer, and it is always at the top of all your other layers.

- You cannot rename the Camera layer.

- You cannot add objects or draw in the Camera layer, but you can add classic or motion tweens to the layer, which allows you to animate the camera motion and camera filters.

- When the Camera tool is selected, you cannot move or edit objects in other layers. Disable the camera by selecting the Selection tool or by clicking the Remove Camera button at the top of the Timeline panel.

Setting the camera frame

First you'll use the camera to frame just a small part of the solar system to focus on the beginning of the action: the launch of *Juno* from Earth.

1 Make sure your Camera tool is active and that the on-Stage controls are present. There are buttons for two modes on the controls: one for Rotate and another for Zoom. The Zoom mode should be highlighted.

▶ **Tip** Clicking the Remove Camera button at the top of the Timeline panel doesn't actually delete your Camera layer; it only disables it. You can click the button again to restore the Camera layer. To delete the Camera layer entirely, select it and click the Delete button (trash can icon).

Rotate

Zoom

2 Drag the slider to the right.

The camera view zooms closer into the Stage.

3 When your slider reaches the edge of the camera control, release your mouse button.

The slider snaps back to the center, allowing you to continue dragging to the right to continue zooming.

You can also enter a numerical value for the zoom in the Camera Settings section of the Properties panel.

4 Continue zooming the camera until you've reached about 260%.

Note When using the camera's Zoom mode, be aware of the image resolution. As with any bitmap, zooming in too dramatically will reveal the limitations of the original embedded image.

5 Now drag your camera so that the sun in the middle of the solar system is more or less centered in the Stage, with many of the orbits in view. The Properties panel should display an X value of about −309 and a Y value of about 221.

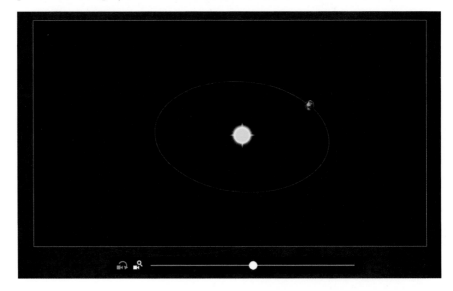

It may seem backward to see the objects on the Stage move in the opposite direction that you drag, but remember that you're moving the camera and not the objects.

As you scrub the timeline to see the animation, notice that your point of view is now closer into the action.

Animating a zoom-out

Since your camera is zoomed in on Earth, you can more easily see the launch of the *Juno* spacecraft. However, at about frame 60, *Juno* leaves the Stage boundaries. You'll want to zoom the camera out to keep the spacecraft in view. For this lesson, disable the Auto Keyframe option on the timeline. You will be inserting all your keyframes manually.

1 Select frame 24 on the Camera layer.

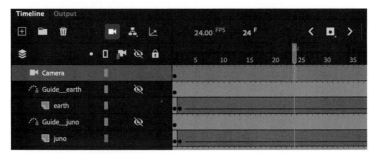

2 Insert a new keyframe (F6) at frame 24.

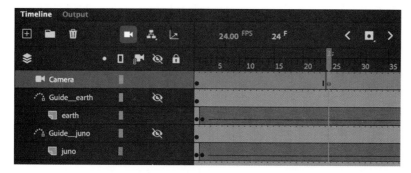

You'll keep the camera in the zoomed-in position from frame 1 to frame 24 and then begin to animate the camera motion from frame 24.

3 Select the keyframe you just created on frame 24 on the Camera layer, and choose Create Motion Tween above the timeline.

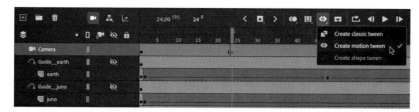

A motion tween is applied starting at frame 24, indicated by the gold tween span on the Camera layer.

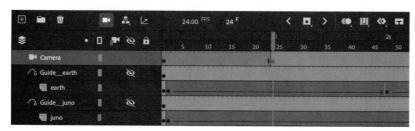

4 Move the playhead to frame 72.

5 Drag the camera zoom slider on the Stage to the left to zoom out and see more of the solar system. The Zoom percentage in the Properties panel should be about 170%.

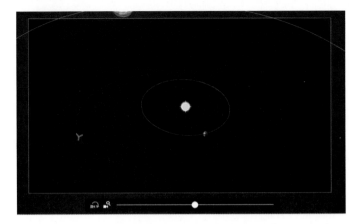

Move the camera so that *Juno* remains roughly in the center of the Stage. The camera position should be close to X=20 and Y=90.

A keyframe is automatically created at frame 72 with the new zoom value and position for the camera.

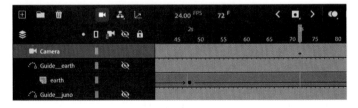

6 Scrub the timeline between frames 24 and 72 to see the animated zoom.

As *Juno* moves farther away from Earth, the camera zooms out to keep it in the frame.

Animating a pan or tilt

A pan is the motion of the camera side to side, and a tilt is motion up or down. You'll pan the camera slowly from left to right to follow the motion of the *Juno* spacecraft.

1 Move the playhead on the timeline to frame 160.

   At this point in time, you'll create another keyframe that establishes a new position for the camera.

2 Move the camera on the Stage to the right. Hold down the Shift key to constrain the movement to the horizontal direction only. You can also just drag the X value in the Properties panel to change the horizontal position to about −250.

The spacecraft should remain roughly at the center of the frame.

3 A new keyframe is automatically created at frame 160.

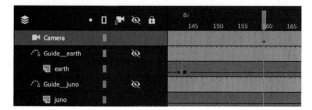

4 Press Return (macOS) or Enter (Windows) to preview the motion tween, which animates your camera zooming out from frames 24 to 72 and then panning from left to right from frames 72 to 160, tracking the spacecraft.

Animating a zoom-in

A crucial part of this animation is when *Juno* does a flyby of Earth, using its gravity as a slingshot to get a boost to Jupiter. You'll zoom in closer to show how the spacecraft approaches Earth.

1 Right-click frame 160 and choose Insert Keyframe > All.

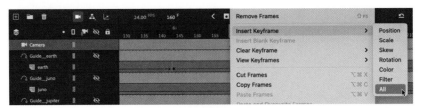

Inserting a keyframe for all the camera properties at frame 160 ensures that any future changes in zoom, position, or rotation occur from frame 160 and not from an earlier point on the timeline.

2 Move the playhead on the timeline to frame 190.

At this point in time, *Juno* is at its closest to Earth.

3 Zoom and move the camera on the Stage so that Earth and *Juno* are close up and nearly centered. The Zoom value should be about 760%, and the Position should be about X=−1309 and Y=767.

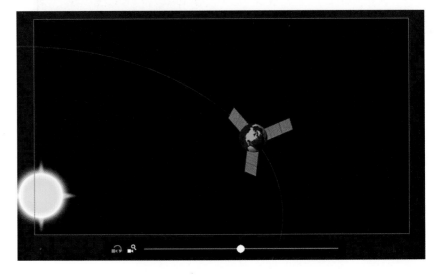

A new keyframe is automatically created at frame 190.

4 Move the playhead to the start of the timeline at frame 1 and press Return/Enter to preview the motion tween.

From frame 160 to frame 190, the camera does a dramatic zoom in as *Juno* flies toward Earth.

Animating a camera roll

A camera roll is when you rotate the camera. The move is unusual, but in some cases, the motion can be quite dramatic and effective. In this project, rotating the camera will intensify the feeling of flying right next to the spacecraft as it approaches Earth.

1 Make sure the playhead on the timeline is still on frame 190.

2 Click the Rotate button on the camera slider.

3 Drag the camera slider to the right so that the camera rotates clockwise (and the objects in view rotate counterclockwise).

The Rotation value should be about −39 degrees.

4 Change the camera option back to the Zoom option and move the camera so that the spacecraft behind Earth is roughly in the center.

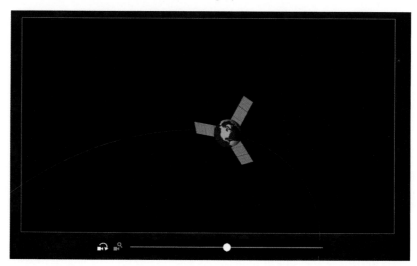

5 Preview the animation by pressing Return/Enter or by scrubbing the timeline.

The dramatic flyby of Earth by *Juno* is captured by the camera zooming in to be close to the action and rolling to intensify the drama.

Finishing the camera moves

After the Earth flyby, *Juno* continues its trajectory toward Jupiter. You'll animate the camera to frame the rest of its journey with additional zooms, rolls, tilts, and pans.

1   Move the playhead to frame 215 and click the Camera frame on the Stage.

2   Reset the rotation value of the camera to **0** degrees by entering **0** for the Rotation value in the Properties panel or by clicking the Reset Camera Rotation button in front of the Rotate label.

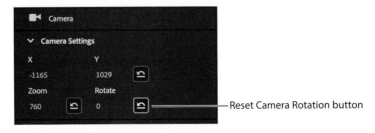

— Reset Camera Rotation button

The camera view rotates back to its default angle.

3   Move the camera so that Earth and *Juno* are at about the center.

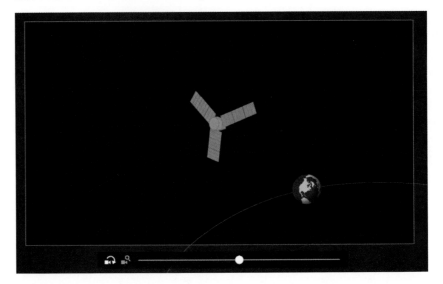

4   Now move the playhead to frame 228.

Juno is moving farther out from the inner solar system, so you'll need to keep backing up the camera.

5   Change the Zoom value to about **90%**. Move the camera so that most of the solar system, including Jupiter's orbit, is in view.

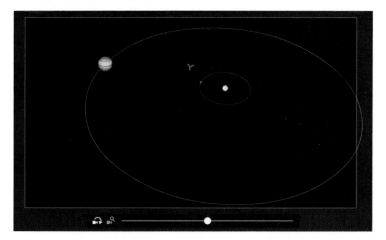

6   Select frame 480. Right-click and choose Insert Keyframe > All to create a new keyframe.

Your final camera move is to zoom in to *Juno*'s approach to Jupiter, so you have to create a beginning keyframe to establish the beginning values for the camera's zoom, position, and rotation.

7   Zoom in for a close-up of Jupiter. The Zoom value of the camera should be about 1400%.

8   Move the camera to keep Jupiter and *Juno* in the frame.

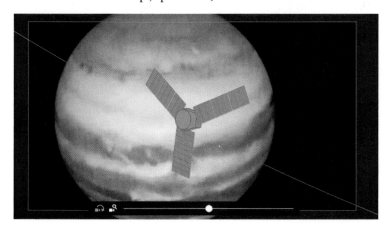

► **Tip** When you zoom in too far all at once, you may lose sight of your graphics and may have trouble putting them back into the camera frame. It's best to zoom a little bit at a time and to move the camera to keep the graphics that you want to zoom in on within the frame.

9 Preview the entire animation by choosing Control > Test.

Animate exports the animation as a SWF in a new window. The animation plays with camera pans, zooms, and rolls that closely follow *Juno*'s journey from Earth to Jupiter.

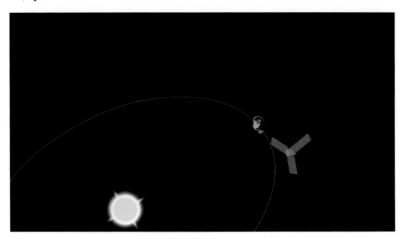

Camera easing, the Motion Editor, and motion paths

Animating the camera is just like animating any other object on the Stage with motion tweening or with classic tweening. As with motion tweening and classic tweening, you can also apply eases to the camera motion to make any of your pans, tilts, zooms, and rolls ease in or ease out for a more natural movement. If you're using motion tweening, you can even access the Motion Editor (see Lesson 6) by double-clicking the tween span (or by right-clicking the span and choosing Refine Motion Tween) in the Camera layer to apply a complex ease or to customize the property curve. The following figure shows the Motion Editor for the camera moves that you just completed.

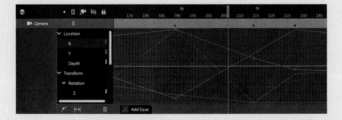

However, not all features of motion tweening or classic tweening are available to the camera. You cannot animate the camera on a path. If you use classic tweens, you can't add a motion guide to the Camera layer for your camera to follow. If you use motion tweens, there is no path on the Stage for you to edit.

Creating depth

When you move a camera to film a scene in real life, you get a sense of depth because foreground elements move across the frame a little quicker than background elements. This is called a *parallax* effect. This is the effect you see when you look out the window of a moving car: closer objects zip past your window, whereas distant objects move very slowly.

Animate offers the ability to create the same sense of depth when you animate camera moves using the Layer Depth panel. The Layer Depth panel allows you to set a layer's *z-depth*, which is its distance from the Camera layer.

By default, all layers have a z-depth value of 0, which means they all are the same distance from the camera. Camera movements do not show a sense of depth, and the overall effect is as if the camera were panning across or zooming into or out of a flat picture. The picture moves or gets bigger or smaller, but there is no differential movement of separate layers.

Adding layers of stars

In the following tasks, you'll enhance the animation of *Juno*'s journey to Jupiter by creating a sense of depth. You'll also add a few layers of stars and position them at different z-depth distances, which will enhance the vastness of space.

1   Add a new layer in your timeline and move it to the bottom of the layer stack.

2   Rename the layer **stars1**.

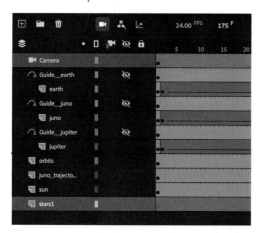

The stars1 layer will contain the first layer of stars.

● **Note** The Layer Depth panel mimics the real-life multiplane camera invented and used by Walt Disney Studios for its traditional animated features, such as *Snow White and the Seven Dwarfs*. The multiplane camera was a gigantic setup that allowed multiple layers of artwork to be filmed for a more realistic sense of depth. However, unlike in Animate, Disney's multiplane camera remained stationary while the individual layers moved at different speeds.

● **Note** The Layer Depth panel can be used independently of the Camera tool. That is, you can place objects in layers with different depth levels and animate them without activating the Camera tool. However, it is the motion of the camera in conjunction with layers at different z-depths that allows viewers to see the three-dimensionality of a scene.

3 In the Library panel, drag the graphic symbol called stars1 from the library onto the Stage.

Instance of stars1 graphic symbol

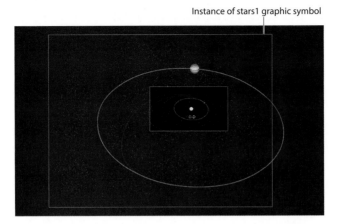

The graphic is simply a collection of gray and white dots randomly scattered over a large area. Don't worry too much about precise placement; using the Selection tool, just position the instance to cover most of the solar system and a little of the space on the left, since that's where the camera moves.

It might be helpful to change the Stage view magnification level so that you can see more of the graphics that may be off the Stage (and out of the camera view).

4 Add a layer called **stars2** below stars1, and add an instance of the stars1 graphic symbol in that layer.

5 Use the Free Transform tool to rotate the instance 180 degrees so that the stars in this layer don't align exactly with the stars in the stars1 layer. Again, make sure the stars cover most of the solar system.

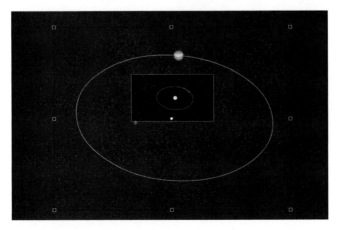

6 Add a third layer of stars, called **stars3**, below all the others, and add an instance of the stars1 graphic symbol in that layer.

7 Use the Free Transform tool to rotate the instance about 55 degrees so that the stars in this bottommost layer don't align exactly with the stars in the layer above it.

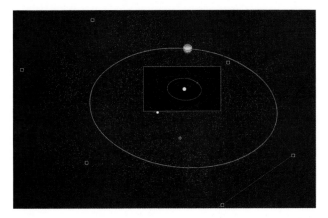

If you select all three instances in the three layers, you can see that they will overlap one another somewhat.

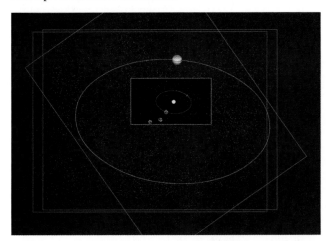

8 Select the first keyframe of the stars3 layer, and in the Properties panel, change the Color Effect so that the Brightness value is at −60%.

The stars in that layer become slightly dimmer, which will reinforce the sense of distance.

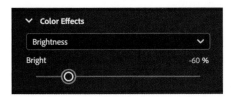

9 Preview your animation by pressing the Return/Enter key.

Although the stars add a nice touch of realism to the highly diagrammatic solar system, the stars are still flat and don't move with any parallax effect. You'll change that next with the Layer Depth panel.

Setting the z-depth in the Layer Depth panel

The Layer Depth panel manages the distances of each layer from the Camera layer.

1 In the Timeline panel, click the Layer Depth button, or choose Window > Layer Depth.

The Layer Depth panel appears, showing all the layers in the order in which they appear in the timeline. Next to each layer is a 0, indicating its current z-depth value. Next to the z-depth value is a color that is coded to the depth diagram on the right of the panel (which is also the color selection in your Layer Properties preferences).

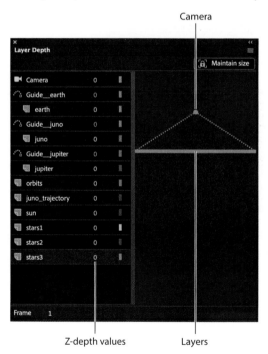

Since all the layers are currently at a z-depth of 0, they are at the same depth level, and they lie at the same plane as the camera frame.

The camera is indicated by the ball with the dotted lines radiating from it. The flat blue line attached to the dotted diagonal lines shows the camera's field of view.

2 Make sure your view of the Stage is at 100% (View > Magnification > 100%). In the Layer Depth panel, drag to the right on the z-depth value for the stars3 layer to increase it to 500. You can also click the value to enter a numeric value, or you can drag the corresponding colored line.

Notice the effect of the stars1 graphic on the Stage as you change the z-depth value. As the z-depth increases, the layer's distance from the camera increases and the stars recede on the Stage. If you drag the opposite way, you can decrease the z-depth into negative values, and you can make the layer appear behind the camera (try it out!).

3 The problem with changing the distance of the stars3 layer is that the graphics in that layer get small—sometimes too small for your animation. You can use the Maintain Size option to prevent your graphics from changing size as you change the layer distance. Move the z-depth value for the stars3 layer back to 0.

4 Now click the Maintain Size option in the Layer Depth panel to select it.

5 Drag the z-depth value for the stars3 layer to increase it to 500.

Notice how the size of the stars remains constant. The Maintain Size option must be clicked before every z-depth change, so if you drag the stars3 layer z-depth value three times to get to 500, make sure you click the Maintain Size option three times.

6 Click the Maintain Size option and set the z-depth value for the stars2 layer to **300** and the z-depth value for the stars1 layer to **150**.

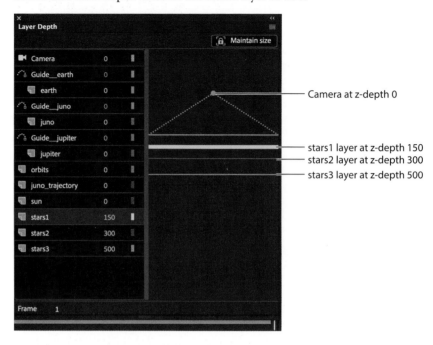

The diagram on the right in the panel indicates the positions of the three layers relative to the camera and the other layers (which remain at a z-depth value of 0). The bold highlighted layer in the diagram is the layer that is currently selected.

7 That's all you have to do! Close the Layer Depth panel. Preview the effects of setting your last three layers farther behind the others.

The parallax effect due to the motion of the camera over layers at varying depth levels is most noticeable if you scrub the timeline between frames 72 and 160. That's when the camera is panning from left to right, tracking *Juno*. You see the orbits sliding by more quickly than some of the stars, which are sliding by more quickly than the more distant stars. The overall effect is a realistic sense of space.

▶ **Tip** To maintain your sanity, it's best to keep your layers' order and their z-depth order the same. As you may have noticed, you could change the z-depth value of a top layer so that it is actually farthest from the camera and, hence, won't overlap graphics in the other layers. This can get very confusing. So you should maintain the same overlapping order of your layers in the Timeline panel as you do in the Layer Depth panel. Change the z-depth values just to change the different spacing between layers.

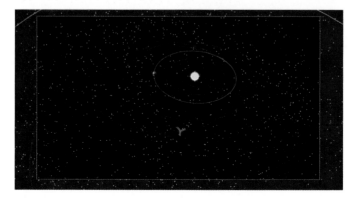

More on the Layer Depth panel: Animating z-depth

Be aware that the z-depth property is tied to an individual keyframe for each layer. That means that the same layer can have a certain z-depth at one keyframe and an entirely different z-depth at another keyframe later in the timeline. Also, objects can jump around, changing distances from the camera. For our project in this lesson, you won't have to worry about different keyframes having different z-depths, since our stars1, stars2, and stars3 layers have only a single keyframe, at frame 1.

However, because the z-depth is tied to individual keyframes, you can apply tweens between the two keyframes to animate motion toward and away from the camera. Animating the z-depth opens up a whole new world of possibilities in three dimensions and is a powerful approach to 3D animation in addition to the 3D Translation and 3D Rotation tools.

Attaching layers to the camera for fixed graphics

There's one last item to add to the animation of the *Juno* spacecraft, and that's the informative captions that pop up to explain the different parts of its trajectory. However, any graphic that we add to the Stage would be subject to all the camera moves—the panning, tilting, rolling, and zooming; that is, unless we fix, or attach, a layer containing the graphic in such a way that it is unaffected by the camera motion.

Animate allows you to do this to one or more layers when you attach them to the Camera layer.

Attaching a layer to the Camera layer

The attached layer is an option in the Layer Properties dialog box. You can also attach a layer by selecting the Attach Layer To Camera option in the timeline.

1 Create a new layer, drag it to the bottom of the layer stack, and rename it **information**.

This new layer will contain the captions that appear at various points along your animation.

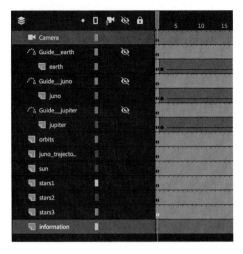

2 Click next to the layer name under the Attach All Layers To Camera icon in the timeline.

A chain-link icon indicates that the layer is currently locked to the Camera layer.

3 Double-click the layer icon in front of its name, or choose Modify > Timeline > Layer Properties.

4 The Layer Properties dialog box appears. Confirm that the Attach To Camera option is selected, and click OK to close the dialog box.

Adding the captions

Now you'll add the information for the animation in keyframes along the timeline.

1   Add about 2 seconds' worth of time (48 frames) at frame 1 before the animation begins (F5). The easiest way to do this is to drag-select frame 1 in all the layers and then press F5 (add frames) 47 times to add 2 seconds of time before the tweens in the earth, juno, and jupiter layers.

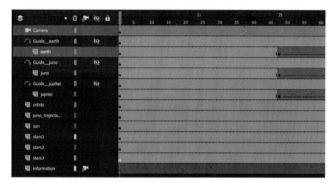

The slight pause before the animation begins will give your audience a chance to read the first caption.

2   Select frame 1 of the information layer.

3   Select the Rectangle tool. Choose None for the Stroke Color and a 50% transparent white for the Fill Color.

4   Create a long rectangle from the upper-left corner about 700 pixels wide and 50 pixels high. The Position for your rectangle should be X=0 and Y=0.

The semitransparent rectangle will be the box for your text.

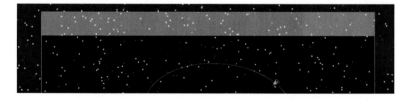

5   Select the Text tool and choose Static Text in the Properties panel.

6   Choose a font that appeals to you by choosing from the Family and Style menus in the Character section of the Properties panel. Make the size 28 points (but note that you may have to increase or decrease the size depending on your font) and the color black. Click the Format: Align Center button in the Paragraph section.

7   Making sure Opacity is set to 100, drag out a text box over the semitransparent white rectangle in your information layer.

8 Type **Juno's journey to Jupiter begins**, and use the Align panel to center the text over the box horizontally and vertically (see Lesson 2 if you don't remember how to use the Align panel).

The first caption is complete.

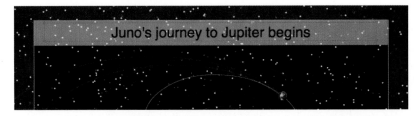

9 You'll make the first caption disappear before the next one appears, so at frame 90 in the information layer, right-click and choose Insert Blank Keyframe (F7).

A blank keyframe appears at frame 90, and the caption disappears from the Stage.

10 The second caption appears as *Juno* doubles back toward Earth, so create another keyframe at frame 118.

11 Copy your text and semitransparent rectangle from frame 1 and paste them into this new keyframe at frame 118.

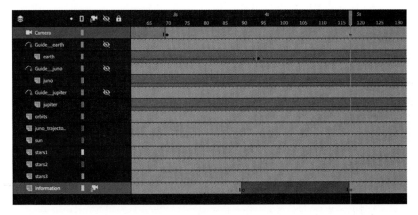

12 Change the contents of the text to read **Juno heads back to Earth**.

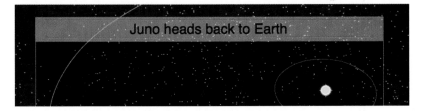

13 Continue in a similar manner to add the third caption. The second caption should disappear at about frame 192, with the third caption appearing at frame 236. The third caption should read **Juno uses Earth's gravity as a slingshot**. The third caption should disappear at frame 336. Feel free to play around with the timing and positioning of the caption!

● **Note** You can still change the z-depth value of a layer that is attached to the Camera layer.

● **Note** You can have more than one layer attached to the Camera layer.

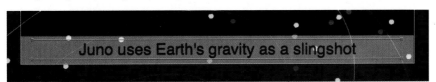

14 The final caption, which should appear at about frame 454 as the camera zooms into Jupiter, should read **Juno arrives at Jupiter 5 years later**.

15 Move the information layer higher in your layer stack just below the Camera layer so that the captions overlap all the other graphics.

16 Test your movie.

As the animation plays, your captions appear one by one. Since the information layer is attached to the Camera layer, the rotations, pans, and zooms do not affect the contents of the layer.

Camera color effects

You can also apply and animate camera color effects to create a color tint and to change the contrast, saturation, brightness, and hue of the entire view on the Stage. The effect simulates a filter that a cameraperson might put on a lens to heighten certain colors for a mood or to create a black-and-white film noir feeling.

To apply a color effect, select a keyframe in your Camera layer and choose the Tool tab in the Properties panel. Expand the Color Effects section and choose Tint. Select the color of the tint or change the Red, Green, and Blue values individually, and then change the value of the Tint to set the amount. A value of 100 is the maximum.

For example, you could apply a sepia tint like this one to your camera to simulate an old-fashioned, aged film reel.

Juno's journey to Jupiter begins

The color effects are applied to each keyframe of the Camera layer. In this project, since you've already animated your camera (and the Camera layer contains multiple keyframes), you would have to apply a color effect to each new keyframe if you want the effect to be consistent throughout the movie.

Exporting your final movie

Create the MP4 movie file by exporting it from Animate and converting it in Adobe Media Encoder, a separate app that is part of Creative Cloud.

1 Choose File > Export > Export Video/Media.

   The Export Media dialog box opens.

2 Keep the Render size at the original 700 pixels by 400 pixels. Select Start Adobe Media Encoder Render Queue Immediately. Click Browse to select the destination filename and location. Click Export.

Animate generates a temporary SWF file and a MOV file from it. Adobe Media Encoder automatically launches.

In Adobe Media Encoder, the exported media file is added to the Render Queue panel.

3 Animate should begin the encoding process automatically. If it doesn't, click the Start Queue button (the green triangle) or press Return/Enter to begin the encoding process.

Adobe Media Encoder converts the MOV file into the default format, shown here as an H.264-formatted video with the standard .mp4 filename extension.

You can upload the final file to Facebook, YouTube, or other video sharing sites, or you can put it on your own website.

Review questions

1 What are the four kinds of camera motion that you can animate with the Camera tool?

2 How do you activate the Camera layer?

3 What are two ways to attach a layer to the Camera layer?

4 What is the z-depth, and how do you change it?

5 What does the Maintain Size option in the Layer Depth panel do?

Review answers

1   You can animate a pan (motion from one side to another), tilt (motion up and down), zoom, and roll (rotation) with the Camera tool.

2   Activate the Camera layer by selecting the Camera tool from the Tools panel or by clicking the Add Camera button at the top of the Timeline panel.

3   Attach a layer to the Camera layer by clicking the empty space in the Attach All Layers To Camera column in the Timeline panel. The layer displays a camera with a chain-link icon, indicating that it is attached to the Camera layer. You can also open the Layer Properties window and select Attach To Camera.

4   Z-depth is a numerical value that indicates a layer's distance from the camera. Open the Layer Depth panel (Window > Layer Depth). You may have to enable Advanced Layers in the Document Settings dialog box (Modify > Document). Change a layer's z-depth by selecting the number to the right of the layer name and typing a new value, or by dragging the colored line that represents a layer relative to the dot that represents the camera.

5   The Maintain Size option in the Layer Depth panel maintains the size of the graphics in a layer when the layer's z-depth value changes. Normally, when a layer's z-depth increases and it moves farther away from the camera, graphics in the layer get smaller since they recede in the distance. The Maintain Size option keeps the size of the graphics constant.

8 ANIMATING SHAPES AND USING MASKS

Lesson overview

In this lesson, you'll learn how to do the following:

- Animate shapes with shape tweens.

- Use shape hints to refine shape tweens.

- Animate gradient fills.

- View onion skin outlines.

- Apply easing to shape tweens.

- Create and use masks.

- Understand mask limitations.

- Animate the masked layers.

 This lesson will take about 90 minutes to complete.

To get the lesson files used in this chapter, download them from the web page for this book at peachpit.com/AnimateCIB2024. For more information, see "Accessing the lesson files and Web Edition" in the Getting Started section at the beginning of this book.

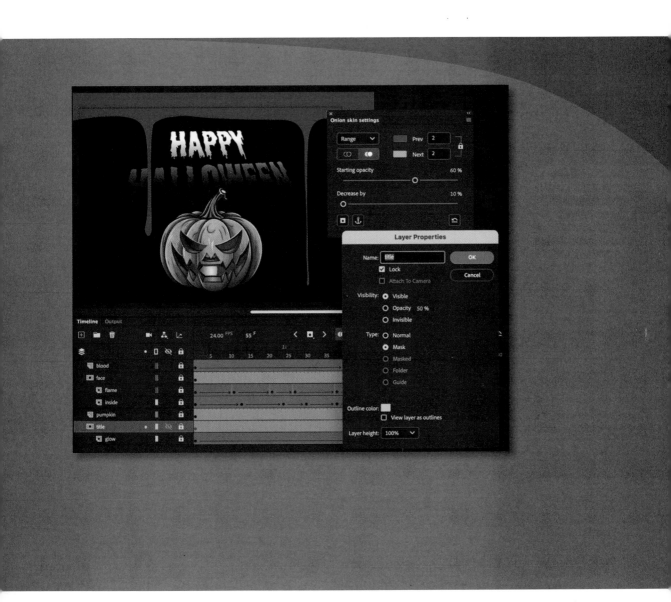

Shape tweening is another technique you can use to deform the contours of a graphic. You can make changes to either the stroke or the fill of any vector shape for organic, fluid animation. Masks provide a way to selectively show only parts of a layer. Together, they can add more sophisticated effects to your animations.

Getting started

● **Note** If you have not already downloaded the project files for this lesson to your computer from your Account page, make sure to do so now. See Getting Started at the beginning of the book.

You'll start the lesson by viewing the animated holiday greeting that you'll create as you learn about shape tweens and masks in Adobe Animate.

1   Switch to a web browser, choose File > Open File, and navigate to 08/08End/08End.gif to play the finished animated GIF. An animated GIF is a single file that often combines multiple images as a looped animation, popular for internet memes.

The project is an animated holiday card for Halloween. The animation shows blood dripping down the card while a flame flickers inside a jack-o'-lantern. The words "Happy Halloween" gradually appear. In this lesson, you'll animate the blood, flame effect, and emerging letters with shape tweens and masking.

2   Close your browser. Double-click the 08Start.fla file in the 08/08Start folder to open the initial project file in Animate.

3   Choose File > Save As. Name the file **08_workingcopy.fla** and save it in the 08Start folder.

Saving a working copy ensures that the original start file will be available if you want to start over.

Animating shapes

In Lesson 5, you learned to deform the envelope of a graphic with the Asset Warp tool for more organic motions, such as the undulations of musical notes.

Another approach to animating the contours of a graphic is to use shape tweening.

Shape tweening is a technique for interpolating the stroke and fill changes of a vector shape between different keyframes. Shape tweens make it possible to smoothly morph one shape into another. Any kind of animation that requires the stroke or fill of a shape to change—for example, animation of smoke, water, or hair—is a potential candidate for shape tweening.

Shape tweens versus the Asset Warp tool's envelope deformer

Both shape tweening and classic tweening with the Asset Warp tool's envelope deformer (see Lesson 5) involve making changes to an object's contours. However, there are key differences between the two techniques.

- Shape tweening can be applied only to vector shapes.

- The envelope deformer can be applied to either vector shapes or bitmap images. However, when the envelope deformer is applied to a vector shape, Animate automatically converts the shape to a bitmap (called a warped bitmap) unless you disable the conversion in Preferences.

- Shape tweening can modify nearly any aspect of a shape's stroke or fill. A gradient fill, the stroke width, and the stroke color can all be tweened.

- In a shape tween, you directly modify the shape's outline with the Selection or Subselection tool; in the envelope deformer, you modify the boundaries of the mesh, which, in turn, distorts the graphic.

- In general, use shape tweening on simple shapes, such as a droplet of water, the curl of a lock of hair, or a puff of smoke. Use the Asset Warp tool's envelope deformer for more complicated illustrations composed of multiple shapes that you want to deform together. For example, you might want to use a shape tween for the changes in just a single eyebrow, but use the envelope deformer for changes to the entire head, which includes the hair and facial features.

Understanding the project file

The 08Start.fla file is an ActionScript 3.0 document that contains most of the graphics in place and organized in different layers. However, the file is static, and you'll be adding the animation.

There are four layers in this animation: a blood layer containing a red shape at the top of the Stage; a face layer containing the shapes of the eyes, nose, and mouth; a pumpkin layer containing a bitmap of the jack-o'-lantern; and a title layer containing the shapes for the Halloween message.

Creating a shape tween

To create the blood dripping effect, you'll animate the changes in the red shape at the top of the Stage. You'll rely on shape tweening to handle the smooth morphing where the curvy edge of the rectangle becomes elongated with vertical drips.

A shape tween requires at least two keyframes on the same layer. The beginning keyframe contains a shape drawn with the drawing tools in Animate or imported from Adobe Illustrator. The ending keyframe also contains a shape. A shape tween interpolates the smooth changes between the beginning keyframe and the ending keyframe.

Establishing keyframes containing different shapes

In the following steps, you'll animate the blood that drips down the Stage.

1   Select frame 72 in all four layers and choose Insert > Timeline > Frame (F5).

    Three seconds' worth of frames are added to all four layers to define the overall length of the animation.

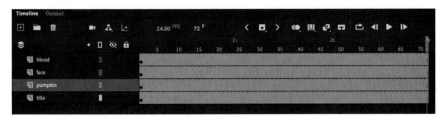

2   Select frame 40 in the blood layer and choose Insert Keyframe above the timeline (or right-click and choose Insert Keyframe, or choose Insert > Timeline > Keyframe [F6]). The contents of the previous keyframe at frame 1 are copied into the new keyframe.

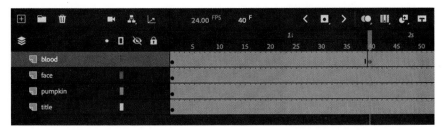

    You now have two keyframes on the timeline in the blood layer, at frame 1 and at frame 40. Next, you'll change the shape of the blood in the ending keyframe.

3   Select the Selection tool.

4   Click away from the shape to deselect it. Move your cursor close to the outlines of the shape, and drag the curve of the bottom edge of the red rectangle down to elongate a drip.

The beginning keyframe and the ending keyframe now contain different shapes—a red rectangle with a mild curve at its bottom edge in the beginning keyframe and one where the curve is elongated in the ending keyframe.

5   The top of the drip will probably look too thick, so use the Selection tool to refine it. Hold down the Option/Alt key, and click the contours of the drip to add anchor points on either side of the bulge where the drip starts. Pull the curves inward to shape the drip. You don't have to copy this screenshot exactly, but do something similar.

Applying the shape tween

Next, you'll apply a shape tween between the keyframes to create the smooth transitions.

1 Click any frame between the beginning keyframe and the ending keyframe in the blood layer.

2 Press and hold the Create Tween button above the timeline and choose Create Shape Tween. Or right-click and then choose Create Shape Tween, or choose Create Shape Tween from the Insert menu.

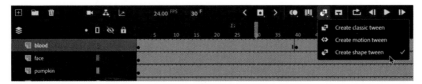

Animate applies a shape tween between the two keyframes, which is indicated by a black forward-pointing arrow and an orange fill in the tween span.

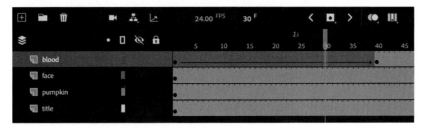

3 Watch your animation by choosing Control > Play (Return [macOS] or Enter [Windows]), or by clicking the Play button at the top of the Timeline panel.

You'll probably be disappointed with the initial results. Don't worry! You'll have a chance to fix it later with shape hints. The red rectangle likely goes through some strange changes in order to get from the first shape to the last, but the important thing is that you have created a smooth animation between the keyframes in the blood layer, morphing between two shapes.

Blend types

In the Properties panel, you can modify your shape tween by choosing either the Distributive or the Angular option for Blend. These two options determine how Animate makes the interpolations to change the shapes from one keyframe to the next.

The Distributive option is the default and works well for most cases. It creates animations in which the intermediate shapes are smoother.

Use the Angular blend if your shapes have many points and straight lines. Animate attempts to preserve apparent corners and lines in the intermediate shapes.

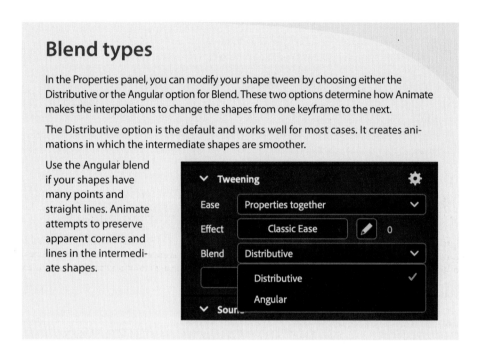

Using shape hints

Animate creates smooth transitions between the keyframes of your shape tween, but sometimes the results are unpredictable. Your shapes may go through strange contortions, flips, and rotations to get from one keyframe to another. You may like the effect, but more often than not you'll want to maintain control of the transformations. Using shape hints can help refine the shape changes.

Shape hints force Animate to map points on the start shape to corresponding points on the end shape. By placing multiple shape hints, you can more precisely control how a shape tween appears.

Adding shape hints

Now you'll add shape hints to the red rectangle to modify the way it morphs from one shape to the next.

1 Select the first keyframe of the blood layer.

The red shape at the top of the Stage is selected.

2 Choose Modify > Shape > Add Shape Hint (Command+Shift+H/Ctrl+Shift+H).

A red-circled letter "a" appears on the Stage. The circled letter represents the first shape hint.

3 Select the Selection tool, and make sure Snap To Objects in the Doc tab of the Properties panel is selected.

Snap To Objects ensures that objects snap to each other when being moved or modified.

4 Drag the circled letter to the top-right corner of the rectangle shape.

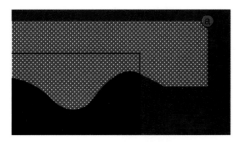

Note Shape hints should be placed on the edges of shapes.

5 Choose Modify > Shape > Add Shape Hint again to create a second shape hint.

A red-circled "b" appears on the Stage.

6 Drag the "b" shape hint to the bottom-right corner of the red rectangle.

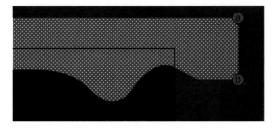

You have two shape hints mapped to different points on the shape in the first keyframe.

7 Select the last keyframe of the shape tween (frame 40).

A corresponding red-circled "b" appears on the Stage, hiding an "a" shape hint that is directly under it.

8 Drag the circled letters to corresponding points on the shape in the second keyframe. The "a" hint goes on the top-right corner, and the "b" hint goes on the bottom-right corner of the rectangle.

The shape hints turn green, indicating that you've correctly placed them so that they correspond to equivalent locations in the first keyframe.

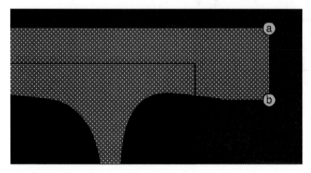

9 Select the first keyframe.

Note that the initial shape hints have turned yellow, indicating that they are correctly placed. When placed properly, the shape hints in the beginning keyframe turn yellow and those in the ending keyframe turn green.

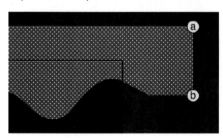

10 Scrub the playhead through the first shape tween on the timeline to see the effect of the shape hints on the shape tween.

The shape hints force the top-right corner of the red shape in the first keyframe to map to the top-right corner of the red shape in the second keyframe and force the bottom-right corners to map to each other. This restricts the transformations and keeps those areas fixed.

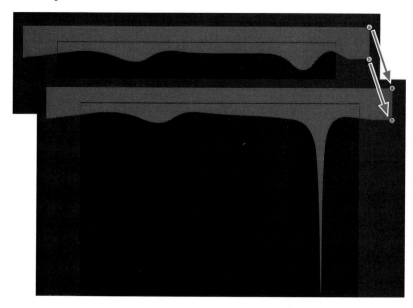

▶ **Tip** You can add a maximum of 26 shape hints to any shape tween. Be sure to add them consistently in a clockwise or counterclockwise direction for best results.

11 Select the first keyframe again and continue adding additional shape hints. Add "c," "d," "e," "f," "g," and "h" shape hints and place them along the contours moving in a clockwise fashion, as in the following screenshot.

12 Select the keyframe in frame 40, and move shape hints "c" through "h" in the corresponding spots on the rectangular shape. Make sure they turn green.

The shape hints keep the areas you want fixed so that the shape tween only morphs the long drip extending from the bottom.

13 As you did with the first drip, use the Selection tool to pull down another drip from the bottom edge of the red rectangle in frame 40. Make sure you are modifying the curve that is between shape hints "e" and "f."

14 If you need more precision, you can use the Subselection tool to be more precise with your curve editing, using the Bezier handles. This will help you make bulges at the bottom of the drips.

Editing shape hints

If you've added too many shape hints, you can easily delete the unnecessary ones. Removing a shape hint in one keyframe will remove its corresponding shape hint in the other keyframe.

- If you want to remove a shape hint, select the first keyframe in which it appears. Right-click (Ctrl+click) and choose Remove Hint from the menu that appears.

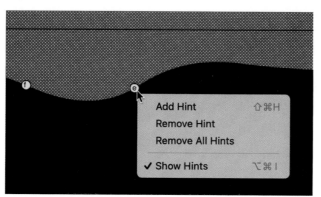

Note If you have several keyframes in a shape tween, and you want to add shape hints for multiple keyframes, you'll have to keep track of which shape hints correspond to the ending keyframe and which ones correspond to the beginning keyframe of each tween.

- If you want to remove all the shape hints, select the first keyframe in which they appear. Right-click (Ctrl+click) and choose Remove All Hints from the menu that appears.

Changing the pace

The keyframes of a shape tween can easily be moved along the timeline to change the timing or pacing of the animation.

Moving a keyframe

The dripping blood slowly animates over a period of 40 frames. If you want the blood to make the shape change more rapidly, you need to move the keyframes closer together.

1 Select the last keyframe of the shape tween in the blood layer.

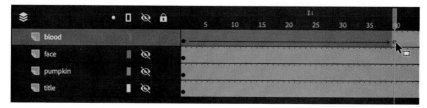

2 Make sure the box icon appears near your cursor as you drag the last keyframe to frame 6.

The shape tween shortens.

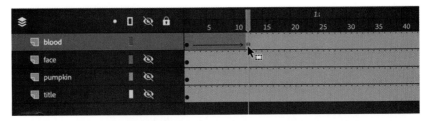

3 Press Return/Enter to play your animation.

The blood drips quickly and then remains static for the rest of the frames on the timeline.

If you want the animation to proceed more slowly, move the keyframes apart. For now, move the last keyframe back to frame 40.

Broken tweens

Every shape tween needs a beginning and an ending keyframe with a shape inside each. If the last keyframe of a shape tween is missing, Animate shows the broken tween as a dotted black line (rather than a solid arrow).

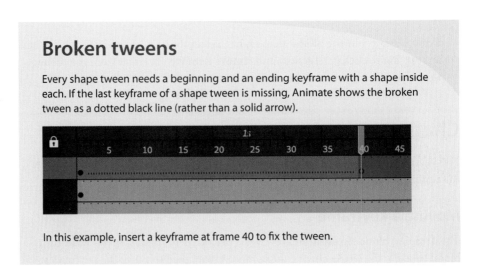

In this example, insert a keyframe at frame 40 to fix the tween.

Easing a shape tween

● **Note** The Motion Editor, which is the advanced panel integrated into the timeline that provides different ease types, is not available for shape tweens.

Eases help your animation give a sense of weight by enabling you to add an acceleration or deceleration component to its motion.

You can use the Properties panel to add an ease to a shape tween. The same eases are available to shape tweens and classic tweens.

Adding an ease-in

You'll make the blood gradually slow down as it drips downward.

1 Click anywhere inside the shape tween in the blood layer.

2 In the Properties panel, click the Effect button and choose Ease Out > Cubic. Double-click to apply the effect.

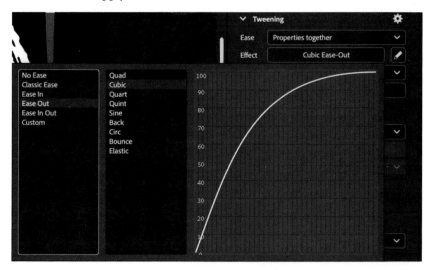

Animate applies an ease-in effect to the shape tween. You can explore the other kinds of ease effects, which vary in kind and intensity.

You'll come back to doing more shape tweens to finish this Halloween greeting card, but for now, it's time to learn how to use mask layers.

▶ **Tip** As with classic tweens, you can apply more advanced eases or even custom eases. Click the Edit Easing button to customize your ease curve.

Creating and using masks

Masking is a way of selectively hiding and displaying content on a layer. It enables you to control the content that your audience sees. For example, you can make a circular mask and allow your audience to see only through the circular area so that you get a keyhole or spotlight effect. In Animate, you put a mask on one layer and the masked content in a layer below it.

For the animated Halloween card you're creating in this lesson, you'll create two mask layers: one for the cutouts in the pumpkin to see the flickering lights inside and another to reveal the title.

Defining the mask layer

You'll convert the face layer to be the mask, which will reveal content in a masked layer below it.

Note Masks do not recognize strokes, so use only fills in the mask layer. Text created with the Text tool also works as a mask.

Tip Animate does not recognize different Alpha levels in a mask created on a timeline, so a semitransparent fill in the mask layer has the same effect as an opaque fill, and edges will always be hard. However, in an ActionScript 3.0 document, you can use ActionScript code to dynamically create masks that will allow transparencies.

1 Double-click the icon in front of the face layer name, or select the face layer and choose Modify > Timeline > Layer Properties.

The Layer Properties dialog box appears.

2 Select Mask and click OK.

The text layer becomes a mask layer, indicated by the mask icon in front of the layer name. Anything in this layer will act as a mask for a masked layer below it. You won't see anything change, however, since you haven't created a masked layer yet.

For this lesson, we're using the white shapes of the eyes, nose, and mouth as the mask, but the mask can be any filled shape. The color of the fill doesn't matter. What's important to Animate are the size, location, and contours of the shape. The shape will be the "peephole" through which you'll see the content on the masked layer below. You can use any of the drawing or text tools to create the fill for your mask.

Creating the masked layer

The masked layer is always indented under the mask layer.

1 Click the New Layer button, or choose Insert > Timeline > Layer.

A new layer appears.

2 Name the layer **inside**.

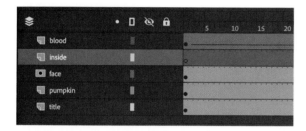

3 Drag the inside layer under the mask layer (named face) and a little to the right so that it becomes indented.

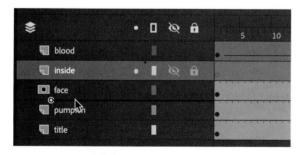

The inside layer becomes a masked layer, paired with the mask layer above it. Any content in the masked layer will be masked by the layer above it.

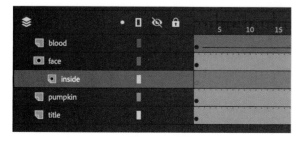

> **Tip** You can also double-click a normal layer under a mask layer, or choose Modify > Timeline > Layer Properties, and select Masked to modify the layer into a masked layer.

4 Choose the Oval tool.

5 For the fill, create a radial gradient that goes from light purple to dark purple. Review Lesson 2 if you're unsure about creating gradients.

6 In the inside layer (the masked layer), draw an oval that covers the shapes in the mask layer.

It may appear strange right now—perhaps like a mistake—but the effects of the mask–masked layer pair aren't visible until the layers are locked.

Seeing the effects of the mask

● **Note** You can have multiple masked layers under a single mask layer.

To see the effects of the mask layer on its masked layer, lock both layers.

1 Click the Lock option for both the face mask layer and the inside masked layer.

Both the mask and masked layers become locked. The shapes in the mask layer reveal parts of the purple radial gradient in the masked layer.

2 Choose Control > Test.

The blood drips down the Stage above a jack-o'-lantern, whose eyes, nose, and mouth are areas through which you see a mysterious purple interior.

Traditional masks

It might seem counterintuitive that the shapes in the mask layer reveal, rather than hide, the content in the masked layer. After all, isn't a mask something that we wear to hide our faces?

That might be true for a face mask, but a traditional mask in photography or painting works differently. When a painter uses a mask, the mask protects the painting from paint splatters so that the underlying painting will be visible. Masking tape protects surfaces so that they aren't affected. When a photographer uses a mask in the darkroom, the mask protects the photosensitive paper from the light, to prevent those areas from getting any darker.

Thinking of a mask as something that protects a lower, masked layer is a good way to remember which areas are hidden and which are revealed.

Animating the mask or masked layers

The jack-o'-lantern is mysterious with a purple interior. However, the client for this fictional project now demands that it have even more drama. Although she likes the look of the purple interior, she wants an animated effect of a candle inside the cavity of the pumpkin.

Fortunately, you can include tweens in either the mask or the masked layer. You can create an animation in the mask layer if you want the mask itself to move or expand to show different parts of the masked layer. Or you can create an animation in the masked layer if you want the content to move under a mask, like scenery whizzing by through a train window.

Adding a warped asset in a masked layer

To make the jack-o'-lantern more compelling for your client, you'll add another masked layer with an animation. The animation will be a flame flickering back and forth.

1   Select the inside (masked) layer and choose the New Layer button to insert a new layer.

    A new layer is added above the inside layer.

2   Rename the new layer **flame**.

Notice that the face (mask) layer now has two masked layers under it. Both layers will be affected by the single mask layer.

3 Hide the layers above your flame layer, which will make it easier to draw.

4 Draw a shape in the form of a flame in the flame layer. For the fill, create a new radial gradient that goes from a bright yellow in the center to red at the edges. (See Lesson 2 if you need a review on how to create gradient fills.)

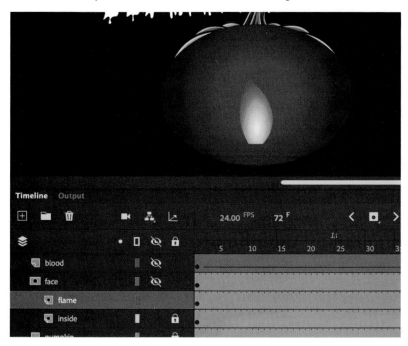

5 Choose the Asset Warp tool.

6 In the Preferences (Animate > Preferences/Settings > Edit Preferences), make sure that in the Drawing section, the Asset Warp tool's Auto Convert Vector To Bitmap For Better Warping And Tweening option is deselected.

For a simple shape like this flame, it's best to keep the vector graphics when using the Asset Warp tool.

7 Click the flame shape to select it, and then click the base inside the flame.

Animate converts the flame shape to a warped asset, which is stored in the Library panel.

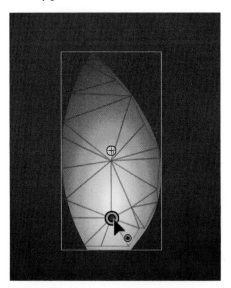

8 In the Properties panel, enable Create bones and select the Flexi option for the Bone type.

The Flexi option allows you to warp the flame with Bezier curves.

9 Drag at the tip of the flame.

Animate creates a bone from the base of the flame to the tip, which you will be able to manipulate to animate the flame.

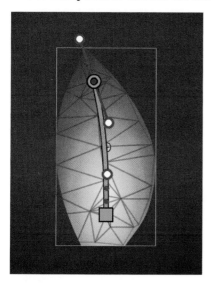

Animating the flame

Your next step is to create variations in the flame and apply classic tweens to animate the warped asset.

1   In the flame layer, insert multiple keyframes (F6) between frames 1 and 72.

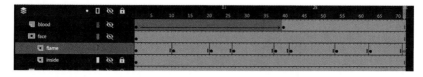

It's not important that you add the same number of keyframes or have them in the same positions as in the figures that accompany this lesson. You will be creating different flame positions in each keyframe.

2 For each keyframe, vary the shape, direction, or curvature of the flame using the bone of the warped asset. Elongate the shape by moving the anchor point at the tip, or move the handles to change the direction of the curve of the bone.

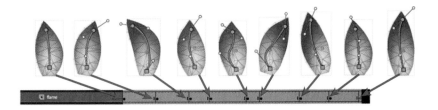

3 Select frames in between each set of keyframes, and apply a classic tween.

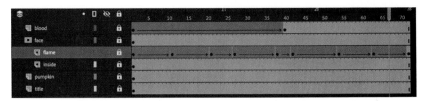

Animate smoothly interpolates the changes in the warped asset flame.

4 Lock the face layer, the flame layer, and the inside layer, and make all your layers visible.

5 Play your animation.

The cutout shapes in the face layer now mask the two layers below it: the flame layer and the inside layer.

Previewing animations with onion skinning

Sometimes it's useful to see how your animation is proceeding from one frame to the next. Seeing how the changes are gradually happening lets you make smarter adjustments to your animation. You can do so using the onion skinning option, available at the top of the Timeline panel.

Onion skinning shows the contents of the frames before and after the currently selected frame.

The term "onion skin" comes from the world of traditional hand-drawn animation, in which animators draw on thin, semitransparent tracing paper known as onionskin. A light box shines a light behind the drawings to allow them to be seen through several sheets. When creating an action sequence, animators quickly flip back and forth between drawings held between their fingers. This allows them to see how the drawings smoothly connect to each other.

Turning on onion skinning

The Onion Skin button is above the timeline, allowing you to toggle it on and off. Pressing and holding the Onion Skin button displays additional options.

1 Unlock the flame layer and hide all the others.

2 Click the Onion Skin button at the top of the Timeline panel.

Animate shows several shapes for the flame, representing the shapes in previous and future frames. Seeing multiple frames on the Stage all at once allows you to compare the changes between frames. The currently selected frame is in red. The previous frames are shown in blue, and the future frames are shown in green. The outlines of the flame fade the farther away they are from the current frame.

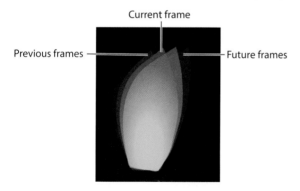

Current frame

Previous frames — — — Future frames

3 On the timeline, Animate displays markers to bracket your currently selected frame. The blue marker (to the left of the playhead) indicates how many previous frames are shown on the Stage, and the green marker (to the right of the playhead) indicates how many future frames are shown.

Note You can even scrub the playhead back and forth along the timeline to see the ghostly images of the onion skins moving along with the animation. You cannot see onion skins during normal playback, however.

4 Move the playhead to a different frame.

Animate keeps the markers around the playhead no matter where you move it, always showing the same number of frames behind and ahead.

Adjusting the markers

You can move either marker to show more or fewer onion skin frames.

- Drag the blue marker to adjust the number of past onion skin frames shown.

- Drag the green marker to adjust the number of future frames displayed.

- Hold down the Command/Ctrl key while dragging either marker to move the past and future markers in equal amounts.

- Hold down the Shift key while dragging either marker to move the onion skin range to a different spot on the timeline (as long as it still encompasses the playhead).

- Press and hold the Onion Skin button at the top of the Timeline panel and choose Anchor Markers. With the Anchor Markers option enabled, you can move your playhead on the timeline and the bracketed onion skinned frames will remain locked in place.

- Press and hold the Onion Skin button at the top of the Timeline panel and choose All Frames. With the All Frames option enabled, the brackets will automatically move to cover the first frame and the last frame on the timeline.

Advanced onion skin options

If you want to change the blue and green color coding of previous and future frames, or if you want to change the opacity of the onion skins, you can do so, and more, in the Advanced Settings.

- Press and hold the Onion Skin button at the top of the Timeline panel and choose Advanced Settings.

  The Onion Skin Settings dialog box appears.

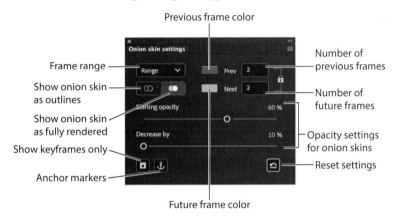

Previous frame color

Frame range

Show onion skin as outlines

Show onion skin as fully rendered

Show keyframes only

Anchor markers

Number of previous frames

Number of future frames

Opacity settings for onion skins

Reset settings

Future frame color

You can fine-tune how the onion skin frames appear by adjusting the following settings:

- Choose the previous and future frame ranges numerically.
- Click the color swatches to change the color of the previous and future frames.
- Choose between seeing the onion skin frames only as outlines, as shown here, or fully rendered.

▶ **Tip** Animate remembers the most recent preferences set in the Onion Skin Settings panel. Clicking the Onion Skin button above the timeline will toggle onion skins with those settings on and off.

- Move the opacity sliders to change the starting opacities and how quickly the onion skin frames fade.
- Choose to see only keyframes.
- Anchor the frame markers.

Shape tweening the fills of shapes

Earlier in this lesson you used shape tweening to change the contours, or stroke, of a shape. That allowed you to create the dripping blood effect. Shape tweening can be used to animate not just the stroke of a shape, but also its fill.

Animating the gradient fill

Next, you will shape-tween the gradient fill of the inside layer to mimic the flickering effect of the flame on the inner wall of the pumpkin.

1 Turn off Onion Skin, unlock the inside layer, and hide the face and flame layers above it.

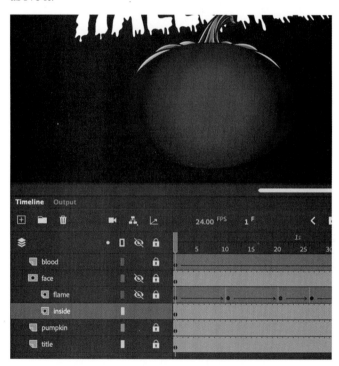

2 Choose the Gradient Transform tool (F), which is hidden under the Free Transform tool.

3 Click on the purple radial gradient on the Stage.

Control points appear over your shape that determine how the radial gradient is applied to the fill.

Focal point ⎯⎯⎯⎯⎯⎯⎯⎯⎯⎯⎯⎯⎯

Width

Center point ⎯⎯⎯⎯⎯⎯⎯⎯⎯⎯⎯⎯

Size

Rotation

4 Adjust any of the controls to vary the way the radial gradient is applied to the fill of the circle.

5 Insert additional keyframes in the inside layer, including a keyframe at frame 72.

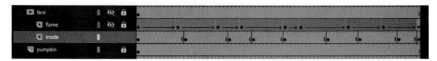

You don't have to have the same number of keyframes as are shown here, or follow where they are exactly.

6   In each additional keyframe in the inside layer, adjust the gradient with the Gradient Transform tool so that each keyframe shows a different gradient fill.

The variations in the purple radial gradient will mimic the animated shadow and light on the inside surface of the pumpkin.

7   Select the span of frames between the first keyframe (frame 1) and the last keyframe (frame 72) and apply a shape tween.

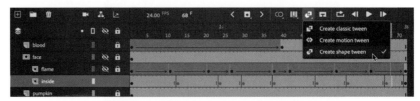

Animate applies a shape tween between all the keyframes of the inside layer, smoothly interpolating all the changes.

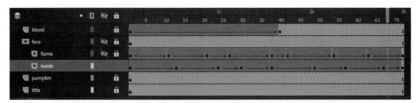

8   Lock the inside layer and unhide the layers above it, then play your animation (Return/Enter).

The flickering flame (using a warped asset animated with classic tweens) and the shifting purple radial gradient (animated with shape tweens) are both masked by the cutout shapes. This demonstrates how combining multiple techniques can help create a more impactful overall effect.

● **Note** Shape tweens can smoothly animate solid colors or color gradients, but they can't animate between different types of gradients. For example, you can't shape-tween a linear gradient into a radial gradient.

Animating the text reveal

Finally, you'll animate a shape tween in a masked layer behind the text to slowly reveal the "Happy Halloween" message.

1 Insert a new layer and rename it **glow**. Move the layer to the bottom of the layer stack.

2 Hide all your layers except for the glow layer and the title layer. Lock all your layers except for the glow layer.

3 In the glow layer, create a large white rectangle just above the letters. Make wavy curves for the bottom edge of the rectangle.

4 In the glow layer, insert a new keyframe at frame 72.

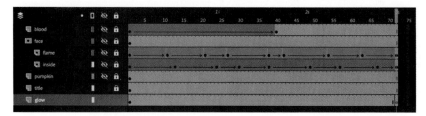

5 In the keyframe at frame 72, pull the corners and the wavy curves of the bottom edge of your rectangle down the Stage, past the letters so that they are covered.

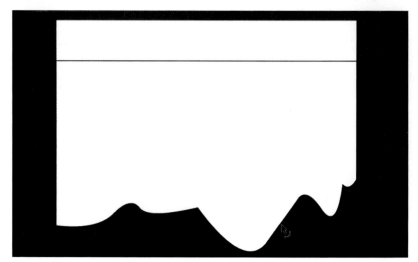

6 Apply a shape tween between the first and last keyframes of the glow layer.

7 Double-click the icon in front of the title layer name, and in the Layer Properties panel, change the Type to a Mask layer.

8 Double-click the icon in front of the glow layer name, and in the Layer Properties panel, change the Type to a Masked layer. (Alternatively, just move the glow layer to the right to indent it under the title layer, and it will automatically change to a Masked layer.)

9 Lock both layers.

10 Play your animation (Enter/Return).

The letters of the Halloween message are in a mask layer, so they reveal the shape tween in the glow layer. As the rectangle tweens downward, the white fill shows through the letters, revealing the full message.

Extra! Final touches

As a finishing touch, you may want to replace the simple white fill in the glow layer with a linear gradient. Applying a linear gradient that moves from an opaque white to a transparent white can soften the advancing hard edge of the shape tween.

1   In the Color panel, create a linear gradient. On one end of the gradient, set the fill color to white at an alpha of 100% (totally opaque). On the other end, set the fill color at an alpha of 0% (totally transparent).

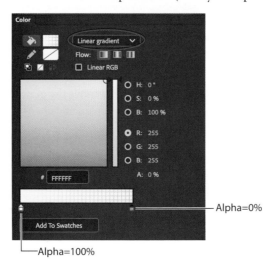

2   With the Paint Bucket tool, apply the linear gradient to your white rectangle in the glow layer.

3   Use the Gradient Transform tool to rotate and narrow the gradient so that the opaque white is at the top and the transparent white is at the bottom.

4   Apply the linear gradient to the shape in the last keyframe of the glow layer, and modify the gradient so that the bottom edge is slightly transparent.

5 Lock all layers and play your animation.

The gradient softens the curved edge of the shape tween to create a spookier, subtler effect to the reveal of the Halloween message.

Shape tweening with variable-width strokes

Any aspect of a shape can be shape-tweened, including variable widths of a shape's stroke. In Lesson 2, you learned to use the Width tool to create lines with thick and thin variations for more expressive graphics. You can change the width of the strokes in different keyframes, and when you apply a shape tween between those keyframes, Animate creates smooth interpolations of those stroke widths.

Considering the ability to animate the thickness of a shape's stroke, the contours of the stroke itself, and the inside fill (with solids, gradients, or transparencies) of a shape, the creative possibilities are nearly limitless.

Exporting the finished animated GIF

Your project is done, and you'll export the animated GIF to be used as a holiday greeting. There is a quick way to create an animated GIF and a more complicated way, depending on whether you want to fine-tune your animated GIF settings.

1 For the quick method, choose Quick Share And Publish > Publish > Animated GIF (.gif).

2   Click Publish.

Animate exports an animated GIF and saves it to the same location as your
Animate file.

3   If you want more control over the export settings, choose File > Export > Export
Animated GIF.

Animate opens the Export Image dialog box. It shows a preview of the image and
various options for optimizations. In the Preset area, make sure the Matte option
is set to Black.

4   In the Preset area, choose GIF from the Optimized File Format menu. Choose
0 from the Lossy menu and 256 from the Colors menu. This will maximize the
quality of your image. You can select Selective and Diffusion for the other two
menus. These options determine how the 256 colors are chosen and mixed to
create the final image.

5   In the Image Size area, keep all the values at their default settings. The Width
and Height should match the original Stage size.

6   In the last area, Animation, you can choose the type of looping behavior for your
animated GIF. Select Forever, which will make your animated GIF loop endlessly.
You can preview the animation by clicking the Play button. You can also examine
each of the 72 frames individually by moving forward or backward one frame at
a time.

7   Click Save, and in the dialog box that appears, provide a filename and navigate to
the 08End folder to save your animated GIF.

Review questions

1 What is a shape tween, and how do you apply it?

2 What are shape hints, and how do you use them?

3 What does the color coding of the onion skin markers indicate?

4 How is shape tweening different from tweening with the Asset Warp tool's envelope deformer?

5 What is a mask, and how do you create one?

6 How do you see the effects of a mask?

Review answers

1 A shape tween creates smooth transitions between keyframes containing different shapes. To apply a shape tween, create different shapes in an initial keyframe and in a final keyframe. Then select any frame between the keyframes in the timeline, and choose Create Shape Tween from the Create Tween button above the timeline.

2 Shape hints are labeled markers that indicate how one point on the initial shape of a shape tween will map to a corresponding point on the final shape. Shape hints help refine the way the shapes will morph. To use shape hints, first select the initial keyframe of a shape tween. Choose Modify > Shape > Add Shape Hint. Move the first shape hint to the edge of the shape. Move the playhead to the final keyframe, and move the corresponding shape hint to a matching edge of the shape.

3 By default, Animate shows the onion skins in previous frames in blue and the onion skins in future frames in green. The onion skin in the currently selected frame is in red. The colors can be customized in the Advanced Settings options in the Onion Skin menu.

4 A shape tween uses shapes, whereas the Asset Warp tool's envelope deformer can be applied to either shapes or bitmaps. A shape tween smoothly interpolates the change of stroke or fill of a shape between two keyframes. The envelope deformer can only deform the mesh around the graphic, and not the stroke or fill.

5 Masking is a way of selectively hiding and displaying content on a layer. In Animate, you put a mask on the top mask layer and the content in the layer below it, which is called the masked layer. Both the mask and masked layers can be animated.

6 To see the effects of the mask layer on the masked layer, you must lock both layers, or test your movie by choosing Control > Test.

9 INVERSE KINEMATICS WITH BONES

Lesson overview

In this lesson, you'll learn how to do the following:

- Use the Bone tool to build armatures with connected movie clips.

- Use the Bone tool to build armatures inside shapes.

- Animate armatures using inverse kinematics.

- Constrain and pin the armature joints.

- Edit the position of armature bones and joints.

- Refine shape deformations with the Bind tool.

- Simulate physics with the Spring feature.

- Use rig mapping to swap armatures with new graphics.

This lesson will take approximately 2 hours to complete.

To get the lesson files used in this chapter, download them from the web page for this book at peachpit.com/AnimateCIB2024. For more information, see "Accessing the lesson files and Web Edition" in the Getting Started section at the beginning of this book.

You can create complex and natural motion with articulations—joints between linked objects and within shapes—using the Bone tool for animation, a process called inverse kinematics.

Getting started

● **Note** If you
have not already
downloaded the project
files for this lesson to
your computer from
your Account page,
make sure to do so now.
See Getting Started at
the beginning of the
book.

In this lesson, you'll create an animation of a character riding a bike using inverse kinematics, and then you'll use rig mapping to apply an animated armature from the Assets panel to a different character.

You'll start the lesson by viewing the bicycle-riding animated character that you'll create as you learn about the Bone tool and armatures.

1 Double-click the 09End.fla file in the 09/09End folder to open it. Choose Control > Test, or click the Test Movie button.

The animation depicts a woman riding a bicycle and waving, her hair blowing in the wind. In this lesson, you'll build an armature (similar to a rig with the Asset Warp tool) and then animate the motion of the character's limbs pedaling the bicycle. You'll also animate the wheels and pedals turning.

2 Double-click the 09Start.fla file in the 09/09Start folder to open the initial project file in Adobe Animate.

3 Choose File > Save As. Name the file **09_workingcopy.fla**, and save it in the 09Start folder.

Saving a working copy ensures that the original start file will be available if you want to start over.

Character animation with inverse kinematics

You learned to animate characters with layer parenting in Lesson 4 and by building rigs with the Asset Warp tool in Lesson 5. In this lesson, you'll learn to use the Bone tool, which gives you another option for character animation.

The Bone tool allows you to build an armature, which is similar to the rig you build with the Asset Warp tool. Both are made up of joints and bones in a hierarchical structure. However, that's where the similarity ends.

The Bone tool uses a method called *inverse kinematics* as a way to move your armature. Inverse kinematics is a mathematical way of calculating the different angles of a jointed object to achieve a certain configuration. In inverse kinematics, you move the child bone, and the parent bone moves along with it. For example, if you drag the hand of a character, the upper arm moves accordingly. The hand is the child and the upper arm is the parent.

By contrast, layer parenting and modern rigging with the Asset Warp tool are based on *forward kinematics*, where moving the parent bone will control its child bones. For example, if you drag the upper arm of a character, the hand moves with it, but the opposite is not true—dragging the hand does not affect the upper arm.

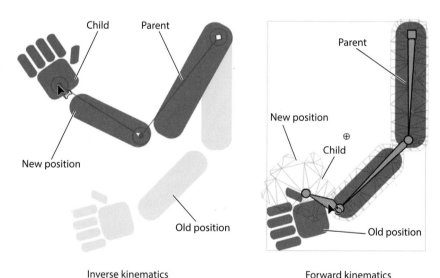

Inverse kinematics   Forward kinematics

In this lesson, you'll animate the pedaling motion of a bicycle rider. By just positioning the character's foot (the child bone), the upper leg and lower leg (the parent bones) are automatically adjusted.

Key differences between the Bone tool and the Asset Warp tool

There are a few basic differences between the Bone tool and the Asset Warp tool in terms of their capabilities, how they work, and how you use them, including the following:

• The Asset Warp tool uses forward kinematics, while the Bone tool uses inverse kinematics.

• You use the Bone tool to connect movie clip symbols or inside vector shapes. You use the Asset Warp tool on vector shapes or bitmaps.

• The Bone tool can create only a single continuous armature in its layer. The Asset Warp tool, on the other hand, can create a rig that contains multiple separate bones or single joints.

• You animate a Bone tool armature in a special armature layer. You animate an Asset Warp tool rig with classic tweens.

Building your armature to animate a character

When animating a character with limbs and joints, first determine which pieces of the character need to move. At the same time, examine how those pieces connect and move. This will almost always be a hierarchical structure, like a tree, starting from a root and branching out in various ways. For the Bone tool, this structure is called the *armature*. Like a real skeleton, each rigid piece that makes up the armature is called a *bone*. The armature defines where your object can bend and how the different bones are connected.

You use the Bone tool to create your armature. The Bone tool tells Animate how a series of movie clip instances is connected, or provides the jointed structure within a shape. A connection between two or more bones is called a *joint*.

1 In your 09working_copy.fla file, view the graphics for the bicycle and Ruby, the rider, which have already been created and placed on the Stage for you.

The pieces of the rider have been positioned so that it is easy to see how they relate to one another. Keeping some space between the pieces will make connecting the bones for your armature easier. Don't worry that Ruby doesn't look exactly right, because you'll move her pieces together in a later step.

2 If necessary, click the Edit Toolbar option to add the Bone tool to the Tools panel, then select the Bone tool.

3 Click the middle of Ruby's chest, and drag with the Bone tool to the top of her right upper arm. Release the mouse button.

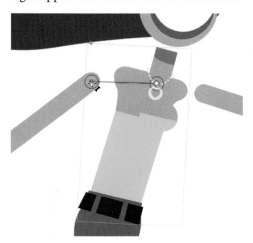

Your first bone is defined in a new armature. Animate shows the bone as a straight line with a square at its base joint and a circle at its tip joint. Each bone is defined from one joint to the next.

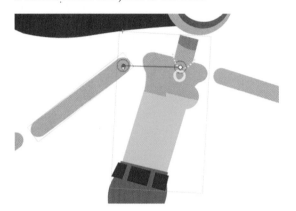

In the timeline, your newly created armature is automatically put in a new layer with a new icon and the default name, Armature_#. This special type of layer keeps your armatures separate from other objects on the timeline, such as graphics and motion tweens.

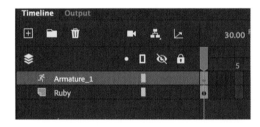

4 Now click the end of your first bone (at Ruby's shoulder) and drag it to the top of Ruby's lower arm (her elbow). Release the mouse button.

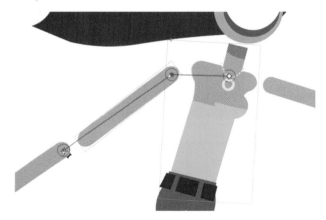

Your second bone is defined.

5 Select the Selection tool, and experiment with grabbing the last bone in the chain (Ruby's right forearm) and moving it up and down the Stage.

Because the bones connect the whole arm to Ruby's torso, moving the lower arm causes the upper arm and torso to move as well, albeit in a somewhat unnatural manner. Don't worry, though; later in this lesson you'll learn how to constrain joints for better control.

Extending your armature

You'll continue to build out the armature by connecting Ruby's other arm, her legs, and the bicycle.

1 With the Bone tool selected, click the base of your very first bone (in Ruby's chest), and drag the Bone tool to the top of Ruby's other upper arm. The first bone is considered your "root bone." Release the mouse button.

2 Continue creating more bones in her lower arm.

Your armature now extends in two directions: one for Ruby's left arm and one for her right arm.

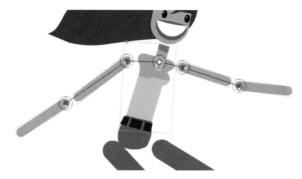

3 Click the base of your very first bone (in Ruby's chest) and drag the Bone tool to the middle of Ruby's pelvis.

4 Extend the armature from the pelvis down to both of Ruby's lower legs. The pelvis will branch off to the right and left thighs, lower legs, and black pedals. You can move objects around to make things easier to connect.

Note You might wonder why we need to include the bicycle as part of Ruby's armature. The bicycle doesn't move, but it needs to appear between her legs so that one leg will be behind the bicycle and the other will be above it. Since all the parts of an armature are on one layer, one solution to managing overlapping objects is to have them in the armature itself.

5 Connect Ruby's torso to her head, and connect her pelvis to the seat of the bicycle.

Your armature now connects all the pieces of Ruby, including her bicycle, and defines how each piece can rotate and move in relation to the other pieces in the armature.

Armature hierarchy

The first bone of an armature is the root bone and the parent of the child bones linked to it. A bone can have more than one child attached to it, as you have for your Ruby armature, making for a very complex relationship. The bone in the chest is the parent, each bone to the upper arm is a child, and the arms are siblings to each other. As your armature becomes more complicated, you can use the Properties panel to navigate up and down the hierarchy using these relationships.

When you select a bone in an armature, the top of the Properties panel displays a series of arrows.

You can click the arrows to move through the hierarchy and quickly select and view the properties of each bone. If the parent bone is selected, you can click the down arrow to select the child. If a child bone is selected, you can click the up arrow to select its parent or click the down arrow to select its own child if it has one. The sideways arrows navigate between sibling bones.

Moving the bones of the armature

Now that you've connected each movie clip with your bones in a complete armature, you can edit each bone's relative position. Initially, there were gaps between the movie clips to make connecting them easier. Holding down the Option/Alt key allows you to move the position of any bone in your armature.

1 Select the Selection tool, and click an empty part of the Stage to deselect the armature.

2 Hold down the Option/Alt key, and move Ruby's right upper arm closer to her body. You can also use the Free Transform tool.

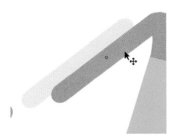

The upper arm is repositioned, but the armature remains intact.

3 Hold down the Option/Alt key, and move all the parts of Ruby's body and the bicycle closer together to eliminate the gaps in her joints.

The character and her armature should look similar to the following figure.

Removing and adding bones and movie clips

To remove a bone, simply select the Selection tool and click the bone to select it; then press Backspace/Delete. The bone and all its child bones will be removed, but the movie clip will remain.

To remove a movie clip, select it on the Stage and press Backspace/Delete. The movie clip and its associated bone will be removed.

If you want to add more movie clips to your armature, drag new movie clip instances onto the Stage in a *different* layer. You cannot add new objects to an armature layer. Once the movie clip instance is on the Stage, you can use the Bone tool to connect it to the bones of your existing armature. The new instance will be moved to the same layer as the armature.

Modifying the position of the joint

If you want to change the point where one bone connects to another—the joint—use the Free Transform tool to move its transformation point. This also moves the rotation point of the bone.

If, for example, you made a mistake and attached the end point of your bone to the middle of the next movie clip rather than to the base, that body part would rotate unnaturally.

1   To modify the position of the joint, select the Free Transform tool and click the movie clip to select it. Move the transformation point to a new position.

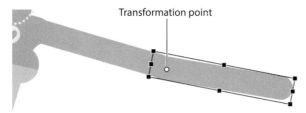

Transformation point

2   The bone now connects to the new transformation point of the movie clip.

Rearranging the stacking order

When you build an armature, the most recent bone will move to the top of the stack in your graphics. Depending on the order in which you connected your bones, the individual movie clips may not overlap correctly. For example, in the previous task, Ruby's legs may not overlap with the bicycle in a way that makes sense. One leg should be behind the bicycle and the other leg should be in front. Use the Modify > Arrange command to change the stacking order of the movie clips in your armature so that they overlap each other correctly.

1   Select the Selection tool, and Shift-select the three movie clips that make up Ruby's back leg, including the pedal.

2   Choose Modify > Arrange > Send To Back, or right-click and select Arrange > Send To Back (Shift+Command+Down/Shift+Ctrl+Down).

▶ **Tip** Use Modify > Arrange > Send To Back to move selected graphics all the way to the bottom of the stacking order, or use Modify > Arrange > Send Backward to move the selected graphics just one level back. Similarly, use Bring To Front to move graphics to the top of the stacking order, or use Bring Forward to move graphics just one level up.

The selected bones of the armature move to the bottom of the stacking order, so Ruby's left leg is now behind the bicycle and the bicycle seat now sticks out from in between her legs.

3   Select the two clips that compose Ruby's left arm, and use the Modify > Arrange command to move the objects to the back.

4   Select Ruby's head and choose Modify > Arrange > Bring To Front, or right-click and choose Arrange > Bring To Front (Shift+Command+Up/Shift+Ctrl+Up).

The head of the armature moves to the top of the stacking order, so Ruby's head is now above her neck.

5   Select the Selection tool, and move the armature around to see how Ruby's right and left arms and legs move behind or in front of her body. Make any corrections, if needed.

Creating the pedaling cycle

Ruby's pedaling is a basic looping animation in which her feet will go around in a circle.

Armatures help make animating the pedaling motion easier because you only have to position her feet on the pedals correctly in keyframes (called poses), and since her feet are connected to the rest of her body, those upper limbs will follow naturally.

Posing your armature

In the first pose, you'll establish Ruby's starting position with her feet and pedals at opposite sides of the rotation motion.

1   Using the Selection tool, drag Ruby's right foot to the top of the pink circle, which represents the path of the pedaling motion. Move the black pedals that are attached to her feet so that they are parallel to the ground.

As you drag her leg and pedal, the bones that are connected to them also move. If you have trouble controlling the armature, don't worry! It takes practice, and in the following sections, you'll learn more tips and tricks to constrain or isolate certain joints for precision positioning.

2   Move Ruby's left foot and pedal to the bottom of the pink circle. Try to keep the black pedal on the curve of the circle.

3   Move Ruby's arms to position them on the handlebars of the bicycle.

Your first pose is completed at frame 1 of your armature layer.

Isolating the rotation of individual bones

As you pull and push on the armature to create your pose, you may find it difficult to control the rotation of individual bones because of their linkages. Holding down the Shift key as you move individual bones will isolate their rotation.

1   Select the back pedal below her left leg.

2   With the Selection tool, drag the pedal.

The leg moves to follow the motion of the pedal.

3   Now, while holding down the Shift key, drag the pedal.

The pedal rotates around the leg, but the rest of the armature doesn't move. The Shift key isolates the rotation of the selected bone.

Holding down the Shift key helps you isolate the rotations of individual bones so that you can position your poses exactly as you want them. Return to Ruby's legs and pedals to make any necessary adjustments using the Shift key.

Pinning individual bones

Another way you can more precisely control the rotation or position of your armature is to fix individual bones in place. For example, currently, the bicycle is free to move and rotate under the rider (as seen in this figure), so pinning it will lock it in place.

1   Select the Selection tool.

2   Select the bone of the bicycle near the bicycle seat.

The bone becomes highlighted, indicating that it is selected.

3   In the Properties panel, select the Pin option.

The bicycle is fixed to the Stage in the current position. A white circle with a black dot appears on the joint to indicate that it is pinned.

4 You can also select a joint and click it when your cursor changes to the icon of a pushpin. That selected bone will be pinned. Click again to unpin the bone.

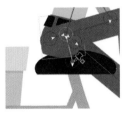

The armature motion is different when using the Pin option versus using the Shift key. The Shift key isolates an individual bone and all the rest of the bones connected to it. When you pin a bone, the pinned bone remains fixed, but you're free to move all the child bones.

Disabling and constraining joints

Before you insert the rest of the poses, you can add refinements to your armature that will make it easier to position Ruby. The various joints of the armature can rotate freely, which isn't particularly realistic. Many armatures in real life are constrained to certain angles of rotation. For example, your forearm can rotate up toward your bicep, but it can't rotate in the other direction beyond your bicep. Your hips can wiggle around your torso but not by very much. These are constraints that you can also impose on your own armature. When working with armatures in Animate, you can choose to constrain the rotation for various joints or even constrain the translation (movement) of the various joints.

Disabling the rotation of joints

If you drag Ruby's head, you'll see that the bone that connects the torso with the pelvis can rotate freely, which allows wildly unrealistic positions.

1 Select the bone that connects Ruby's head with her torso.

The bone is highlighted.

2 In the Properties panel, if necessary, deselect the Enable option in the Joint: Rotation section.

The circle around the joint at the head of the selected bone disappears, which means that the joint is no longer able to rotate.

3 Now drag Ruby's head.

Her head can no longer rotate around the joint in the torso (but it can still rotate around its last joint).

Constraining the range of rotation

There's still some work to do with the armature. You can allow rotation but also constrain that range of rotation for various joints.

1 Select the bone that connects Ruby's chest to her left upper arm.

    The bone becomes highlighted.

2 In the Properties panel, if necessary, deselect the Enable option in the Joint: Rotation section.

    Rotation about the joint in the torso is disabled so that the upper arm cannot move as wildly around the torso.

3 Select the child bone (the bone from the upper arm to the forearm).

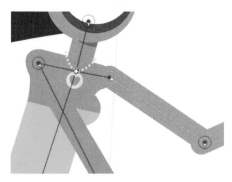

4 In the Properties panel, select the Constrain option in the Joint: Rotation section.

The angle indicator changes from a full circle to a partial circle on the joint, showing the minimum and maximum allowable angles and the current position of the bone.

▶ **Tip** In real life, joints only allow bones to rotate. However, in Animate, you can allow joints to slide in either the *x* (horizontal) or the *y* (vertical) direction, and you can set the limits on how far those joints can travel. Use Joint: X Translation and Joint: Y Translation in the Properties panel to enable and constrain this kind of motion, just like you do with rotation.

5 In the Properties panel, set the Left Offset rotation angle to **−90** degrees and the Right Offset rotation angle to **90** degrees.

6 Drag the upper arm.

You can move the arm, but its rotation is constrained to the extremes of rotating straight up or straight down, preventing your armature from being positioned unrealistically and making it much easier to control and position your poses.

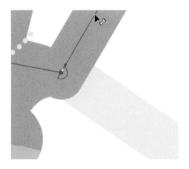

Adding poses

Your armature is now ready. You've connected your bones and applied the appropriate constraints to make the armature easier to pose. In the timeline, you insert poses just as you would insert keyframes for a motion tween.

Inserting poses

● **Note** When dealing with armature layers, "poses" and "keyframes" are essentially the same thing.

Recall that your goal is to define unique poses that will allow a natural pedaling motion. You'll create eight additional poses for Ruby's feet to approximate the circle in which they will travel. The whole cycle will last 48 frames, so each pose will take six frames. For this task, enable the Auto Keyframe option in the controls at the top of your timeline. Recall that the option automatically creates keyframes when you change content on the Stage.

Using on-Stage controls for joint constraints

You can make quick adjustments to any joint rotation or translation constraints by just using the on-Stage controls that appear over joints, rather than making those adjustments in the Properties panel. Using the on-Stage controls lets you see the constraints in context with the other bones and graphics on the Stage.

Simply select a bone, and move your mouse pointer over the joint in the head of the bone. A circle with four arrowheads highlights in blue. Click it to access the on-Stage controls.

To change the constraints for rotation, move your mouse over the outer edge of the circle, which will highlight in red, and click it.

Click inside the circle to define the minimum and maximum angles for the joint rotation. The shaded area is the range of permissible rotation. You can also drag to change the angles within the circle. Click outside the circle to confirm your adjustments.

If you want to disable the rotation at that joint, click the lock icon that appears when you roll over the center of the circle.

To change the constraints for translation (movement up and down or side to side), move your mouse over the arrows inside the circle, which will highlight in red.

Click either the horizontal or the vertical arrow, and then drag the offsets to constrain the translation of the joint in either direction.

1 On the timeline, select frame 6.

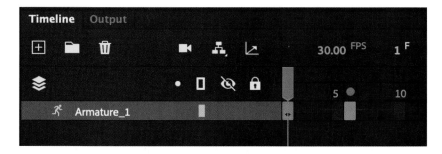

2   Make sure that the Auto Keyframe option in the controls at the top of your timeline is turned on, and move Ruby's feet and pedals so that the front foot/pedal is at the northwest position (about 1 o'clock) and the back foot/pedal is on the opposite side.

A new pose/keyframe is inserted at frame 6.

3   On the timeline, select frame 12.

4   Move Ruby's feet and pedals so that the front foot/pedal is at the northeast position (about 3 o'clock).

5   Continue adding new poses every six frames and positioning Ruby's feet along the pink circle. You'll end up with nine poses, each at roughly every 7 minutes of a clock face, along 48 frames.

The first and last poses will be the same.

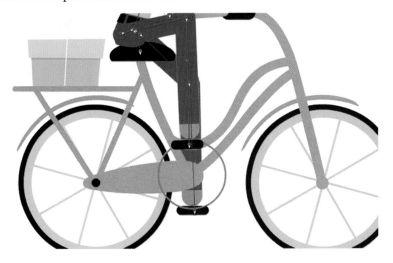

Tip You can edit poses on the timeline just as you can with the keyframes of a motion tween. Right-click along the timeline and choose Insert Pose to insert a new pose. Right-click any pose and select Clear Pose to remove the pose from the layer. Command-click/Ctrl-click a pose to select it. Drag the pose to move it to a different position along the timeline.

6 Select Loop Playback at the bottom of the timeline (Shift+Option+L/Shift+Alt+L), and extend the markers to cover the entire animation span from frame 1 to frame 48.

Tip You can add eases to your inverse kinematics animations by selecting the animation on the timeline and choosing an ease type and strength in the Properties panel. Eases can change the animation by starting slowly (ease-in) and by ending gradually (ease-out). For more about applying eases, see Lesson 3.

7 Click the Play button at the bottom of the timeline (press the Return [macOS] or Enter [Windows] key) to view your animation loop.

Changing joint speed

Joint speed refers to the stickiness, or stiffness, of a joint. A joint with a low joint speed value will be sluggish. A joint with a high joint speed value will be more responsive. You can set the joint speed value for any selected joint in the Properties panel.

The joint speed is apparent when you drag the very end of an armature. If there are slow joints higher up on the armature chain, those particular joints will be less responsive and will rotate to a lesser degree than the others.

To change the joint speed, click a bone to select it. In the Properties panel, set the Joint Speed value from 0% to 100%.

The joint speed doesn't affect the actual animation; it affects only how the armature responds to the way you pose it on the Stage, making it easier to move.

Tip Make sure the first and last poses are identical by copying the first keyframe and pasting it in the last frame. Hold down the Option/Alt key and drag the first keyframe to frame 48.

Adding a wave and head nod

Now that the pedaling motion is complete, you'll add additional movements that give Ruby some personality.

1   Select frame 18, and move Ruby's left arm up in the air to wave.

2   Select frame 24, and move her forearm to a straighter position.

3   Select frame 30, move Ruby's left arm up, and angle her forearm close to her head to complete the wave.

4   In one of the poses (you choose), rotate Ruby's head slightly so that she gives a nod during the wave.

Inverse kinematics with shapes

Ruby and her bicycle are an armature made with various movie clip symbols. You can also create armatures inside shapes, which is useful for animating objects that do not have obvious joints and segments but can still have an articulated motion.

For example, the arms of an octopus have no actual joints, but you can add bones to a smooth tentacle to animate its undulating motion. You can also animate other organic objects, such as a snake, a waving flag, blades of grass bending in the wind, or, as you will do in the next task, Ruby's hair blowing in the wind.

Defining bones inside a shape

Ruby's hair is a shape with a red fill and no stroke. You'll add bones to it in order to animate it.

1   In the library, open the Girl Bicycle__assets__ folder and double-click the Ruby_Head movie clip symbol.

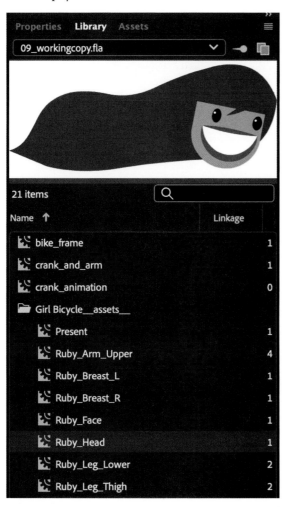

2 In symbol editing mode, note that her hair is in the bottom layer.

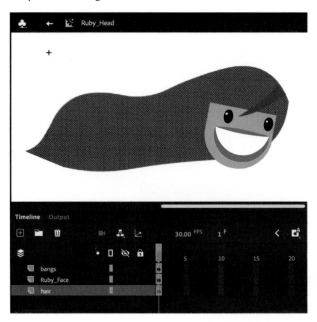

3 Choose the Bone tool.

4 Click inside the shape starting from the right side, and drag a bone part of the way inside the hair.

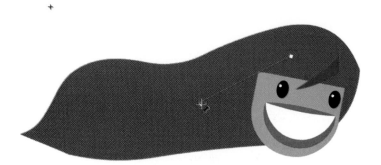

Animate creates an armature inside Ruby's hair and moves it to its own armature layer.

5 Click the end of the first bone, and drag out the next bone a little farther down toward the tip of the hair.

The second bone is defined.

6 Continue building the hair armature with a total of about four bones.

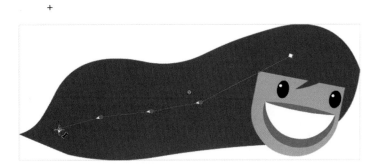

7 When the armature is complete, use the Selection tool to drag the last bone to see how the deformation of the hair follows the bones of the armature.

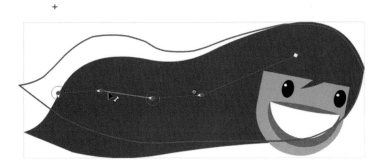

Animating the hair

Animating an armature within a shape follows the same process as animating an armature built with movie clips. You establish different poses for your armature with keyframes along the timeline.

1 Select frame 40 for all three layers, and choose Insert > Timeline > Frame (F5).

Animate adds frames up to frame 40 on the timeline. Making the number of frames in the nested animation of Ruby's hair different from the main timeline of the pedaling will ensure that the animations are not synchronized, resulting in a more natural loop.

2 Move the playhead on the timeline to frame 15.

3 Move the armature in Ruby's hair to deform it. You can also hold down the Shift key as you move a bone to isolate its rotation.

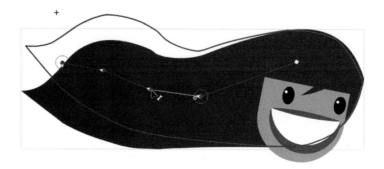

Animate inserts a new pose for Ruby's hair at frame 15.

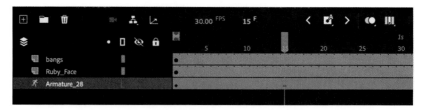

4 Move the playhead to frame 25.

5 Move the armature in Ruby's hair to position it in a different way.

Animate inserts a new pose for Ruby's hair at frame 25.

6 Hold down the Option/Alt key, and drag the first pose to the last frame (40).

Animate duplicates the first pose into frame 40 so that the animation will end at the same place as it begins.

7 Exit symbol editing mode, and test your movie. Because the hair animation is a nested animation in a movie clip symbol, simply pressing Play/Enter on the main timeline won't show her hair moving.

Ruby's hair waves and blows as she pedals her bicycle.

Tip Ruby's flowing hair could also be animated with a shape tween (see Lesson 8) or with classic tweens using the Asset Warp tool (see Lesson 5). All three approaches would work, but each technique has its own advanced options that are beneficial in different situations. For example, only the Bone tool gives you control over springiness (explained in the next section); only shape tweens give you control over the shape with shape hints; and only the Asset Warp tool gives you Bezier curve control with Flexi bones.

8 To complete the animation, add an armature to Ruby's bangs in the bangs layer, and animate the wisp of hair fluttering in her face.

Tip The organic control of a shape by its armature is a result of a mapping between the anchor points along the shape and its bones. You can edit the connections between the bones and their control points and refine the behavior with the Bind tool. The Bind tool must be added to the Tools panel from the Edit Toolbar option. Consult the Animate Help documentation for more information on how to use this advanced tool.

Simulating physics with springiness

So far, you've seen how armatures can help you easily pose your characters and objects in different keyframes to create smooth, natural motion. But you can also add a bit of physics to your armatures so that they react to how they move from pose to pose. The Spring feature helps you do this easily.

Spring simulates physics in any animated armature, whether you're using movie clips or a shape. A flexible object normally would have some "springiness" that would cause it to jiggle on its own as it moved and continue to jiggle even after motion of the entire body stopped. The amount of springiness depends on the object—for example, a dangling rope would have a lot of jiggle, but a diving board would be much stiffer and have less jiggle. You can set the strength of the spring depending on your object, and you can even set different springiness amounts for each bone in an armature to help you get the exact amount of rigidity or flexibility in your animation. In a tree, for example, the larger branches will be less springy than the smaller end branches.

Adding springiness to Ruby's hair

Adding spring to the armature in Ruby's hair allows it to have additional residual motion after a pose in a keyframe. The strength values for spring can range from 0 (no spring) to 100 (maximum spring).

1   In the library, double-click the Ruby_Head movie clip symbol to enter symbol editing mode if you're not there already.

2   In symbol editing mode, select the last child bone in Ruby's hair.

3   In the Properties panel, in the Spring section, set the Strength to 100.

The last bone has the maximum spring strength since the tip is the most flexible part of the whole armature and would have the most independent motion.

4   Select the next bone in the armature. You can simply click it on the Stage, or you can navigate up the armature hierarchy with the arrows in the Properties panel.

5   In the Properties panel, in the Spring section, set the Strength to 70.

The middle of the bone is a little less flexible than the tip, so it has a smaller strength value.

6 Select the next parent bone, and in the Spring section of the Properties panel, set the Strength to 30.

The base of the hair armature is even less flexible than the middle, so it has a smaller strength value.

The effects of the Spring feature are more apparent when there are additional frames on the timeline after the armature's final pose. The additional frames allow you to see the residual bouncing effect after the last pose.

7 Add frames to all the layers until frame 100.

8 Test your movie.

Ruby's hair moves from the first pose to the next, but even past the last pose, the hair continues to sway slightly. The back-and-forth rotation of the hair armature, combined with the addition of springiness to the bones, can simulate the responses to physical forces on an object and makes the animation more realistic.

Go back and experiment with different values for the spring strength, and see what works for your animation.

Adding damping effects

Damping refers to how much the spring effect decreases with time. It wouldn't be realistic if the swaying of the hair continued indefinitely. Over time, the swaying should lessen and eventually stop. You can set a damping value for each bone from 0 (no damping) to 100 (maximum damping) to control how rapidly these effects diminish.

1 Select the last bone of the hair (at the tip), and in the Properties panel, in the Spring section, set the Damping value to 50.

The Damping value will decrease the swaying of the hair over time.

2 Select the next bone (its parent) in the armature, and in the Spring section of the Properties panel, set the Damping to its maximum value (100).

3 Continue selecting bones with Strength values, and add Damping values to slow the springiness.

4 Choose Control > Test to see the effects that the Damping values have on the motion of Ruby's hair.

The hair still sways, but the motion quickly subsides. The Damping values help add a sense of weight to the armature. Experiment with both the Strength and Damping values in the Spring section of your armature to get the most realistic motion.

Tweening automatic rotations

You're almost done! Ruby pedals and waves, and her hair blows in the breeze, but her bicycle's wheels and crank need to turn.

Adding a nested animation of rotating wheels

Now you'll animate rotating wheels inside the movie clip of the bicycle frame.

1 Double-click the bicycle frame on the Stage.

You enter symbol editing mode for the bike_frame movie clip symbol, but you're editing in place to see all the other graphics on the Stage (dimmed).

2 Double-click the back wheel to drill down to the Wheel_Turning movie clip symbol.

3 Select the wheel on the Stage, and click the Create Motion Tween button above the timeline.

Animate creates a tween layer and adds 30 frames.

4 Click inside the tween, and in the Properties panel, select Clockwise for Rotate, and leave Count at 1.

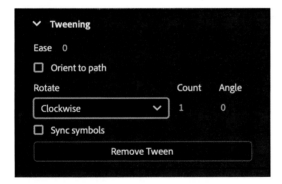

The wheel automatically rotates on its transformation point (which is in the center) for one complete clockwise turn.

Since there is another instance of the Wheel_Turning movie clip for the front wheel of the bicycle, you don't have to create another tween. Your bicycle wheels are complete.

Adding the crank arm

Finally, the bicycle's pedals need to be connected to the bicycle with the crank arm that spins the gears.

1 Double-click the crank_animation movie clip symbol in the library.

You enter symbol editing mode for the movie clip symbol.

2 Select the movie clip instance on the Stage or the first keyframe on the timeline, and click Create Motion Tween above the timeline.

Animate creates 30 frames in a motion tween layer.

3 Add frames so that the tween layer has 48 frames.

The animation of the crank arm rotating must be synchronized to Ruby's pedaling, so the number of frames must match (48 frames).

4 Select the tween. In the Properties panel, select Clockwise for Rotate and 1 for Count.

Animate automatically tweens a clockwise rotation for one turn.

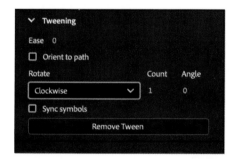

5 Frame 1 and frame 48 are identical, so to make a seamless loop, you'll have to make a slight adjustment. Drag the right edge of the tween to extend the tween to frame 49.

6 Insert a new keyframe at frame 48.

7 Remove frame 49.

You still have a total of 48 frames for the rotation, but the ending keyframe doesn't repeat the beginning keyframe, and the loop will be seamless.

8 Now go to symbol editing mode for the bike_frame movie clip symbol, and add an instance of the crank_animation symbol to the front_pedal layer. The instance should fit right inside the pink circle.

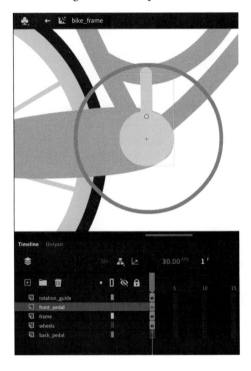

9 Copy the crank_animation instance.

10 Select the back_pedal layer, and choose Edit > Paste In Place (Command+Shift+V/Ctrl+Shift+V).

The Paste In Place command pastes the copied items exactly where you copied them from.

11 Make sure the transformation point is at the center of the crank, and then choose Modify > Transform > Flip Vertical.

The instance flips so that the crank arm now points downward. If the transformation point is not at the center, you can move it with the Free Transform tool.

If you hide the layers above the back_pedal layer, you can see the pedal, its transformation point, and how it flips. However, the crank arm will now rotate counterclockwise.

12 Choose Modify > Transform > Flip Horizontal.

The crank_animation instance flips horizontally so that now the rotation will continue to turn clockwise.

13 Right-click the icon in front of the rotation_guide layer, and choose Properties.

14 In the Layer Properties dialog box that appears, select Guide for the Type. Click OK.

Note A guide layer doesn't show up when you publish the project. It shows up on your timeline as an icon of a T square.

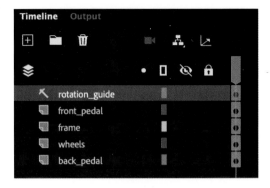

15 Exit symbol editing mode, and test your movie.

Ruby rides her bicycle, and the spinning crank arms synchronize with her pedaling. The pink circle that acted as your guide to position her feet and pedals doesn't appear now that it is in a guide layer.

Rig mapping

Rig mapping is a feature that lets you apply saved armatures to different graphics so that, for instance, a walking animation can be reused with many different characters.

You can save your own armature and armature poses in the Assets panel, or you can use the many assets provided by Adobe.

Saving an animated armature in the Assets panel

To save an armature animation in the Assets panel, you must first save it in your library as a movie clip symbol.

1 Select the armature layer of your Ruby animation. Right-click and choose Convert Layers To Symbol.

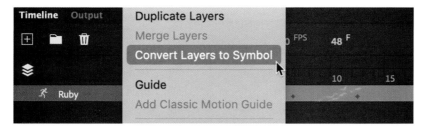

2 In the Convert Layers To Symbol dialog box, enter **Ruby_bike_animation** as the animation's name, select Movie Clip as the type, and click OK.

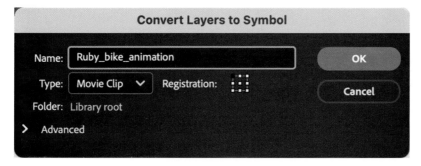

Animate saves the armature layer inside a movie clip symbol, which appears in your library.

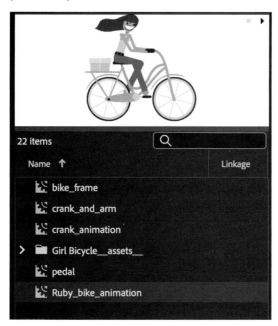

3 Right-click the new movie clip symbol, and choose Save As Asset.

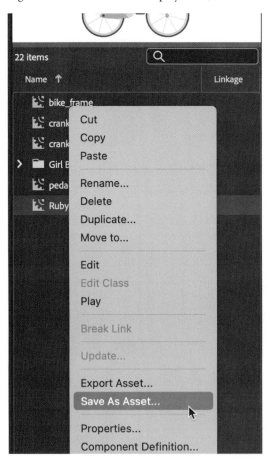

4 In the Save As Asset dialog box, enter a few keywords, separated by commas, that will serve as searchable reminders of the asset. Since you want to save the graphics, the armature, and the animation, keep Objects, Bones, and Motion selected. Click Save.

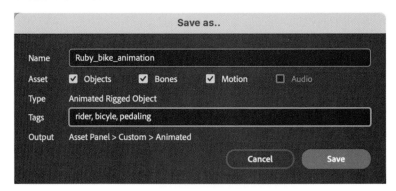

Animate saves the animation in the Custom tab of the Assets panel.

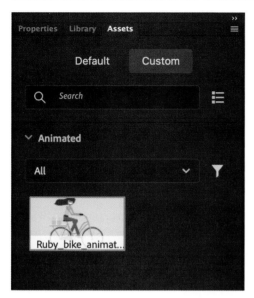

If you choose to save only Bones and Motion (and deselect Objects), your animated armature will be saved to the Assets panel, as the following figure shows.

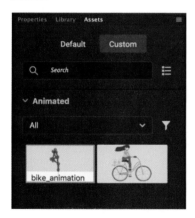

Using rig mapping to apply an armature to new graphics

In this task, you'll see how you can apply a previously saved animated armature to new graphics.

1   Open 09Start_rigmapping.fla in the 09Start folder.

This sample file contains a character on the Stage made up of several movie clips.

2 Select all the instances on the Stage.

3 In the Assets panel, select the Default tab and open the Animated section.

4 In the Filters section, select Characters and Rigs and then choose the Character Walk_Side asset.

5 Drag the Walk Rig asset and drop it on the selected character instances.

The Rig Mapping panel appears.

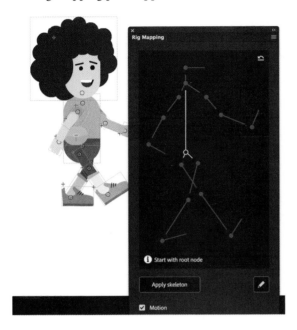

Animate will attempt to map the armature onto the movie clip. If Animate can't map the armature to the graphics automatically, you'll need to manually identify which movie clip instances belong to which bones.

6 Select the root node, which is the hip, highlighted in the Rig Mapping panel.

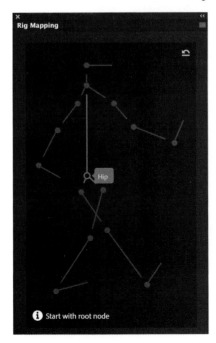

7 On the Stage, click the movie clip corresponding to the character's hip.

When the movie clip instance is matched to its corresponding armature part, both are highlighted in green.

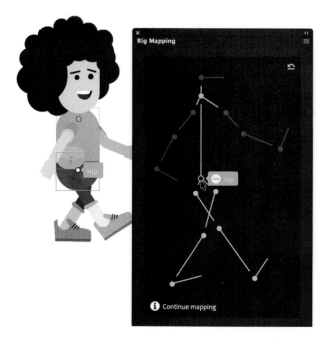

8 Click the next bone in the Rig Mapping panel and the corresponding movie clip instance on the Stage.

If you make a mistake, click the minus sign near each bone to remove that linkage, and choose another bone.

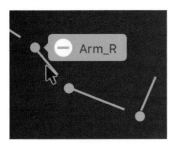

9 Continue manually matching up the armature with the corresponding graphics on the Stage until the entire rig is complete. Click Apply Skeleton.

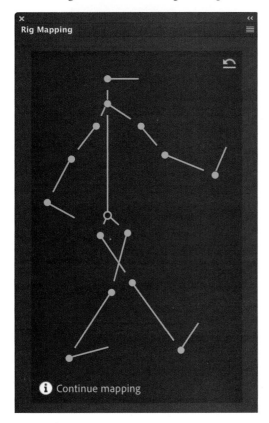

When the rig mapping process is complete, the armature is applied to the movie clips and the rig mapping diagram turns pink.

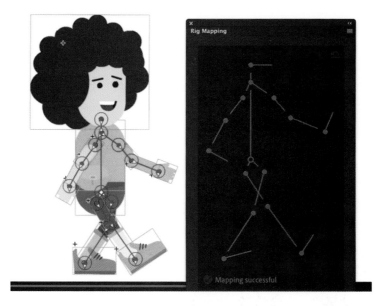

The armature poses appear in the timeline.

10 Test your movie.

The character performs the walk cycle.

Review questions

1   What are the two ways of using the Bone tool?

2   Define and differentiate these terms: bone, joint, and armature.

3   What is the hierarchy of the armature?

4   How do you constrain or disable the rotation of joints?

5   What do strength and damping refer to in the Spring feature?

6   How do you save just an armature to the Assets panel?

Review answers

1   The Bone tool can connect movie clip instances to form an articulated object that can be posed and animated with inverse kinematics. The Bone tool can also create an armature within a shape, which can be posed and animated with inverse kinematics as well.

2   Bones are the objects that connect individual movie clips or that make up the internal structure of a shape for motion with inverse kinematics. Joints are the articulations between bones. Joints can rotate as well as translate (slide in both the x and y directions). Armatures refer to the complete articulated object. Armatures are separated on their own special armature layers on the timeline where poses can be inserted for animation.

3   An armature is made up of bones that are ordered in a hierarchy. When one bone is connected to another bone, one is the parent and the other is the child. When a parent bone has many child bones, each child bone can be described as a sibling of the others.

4   Hold down the Shift key to temporarily disable the motion of the armature and isolate a single bone's rotation. Use the Properties panel to pin a bone to prevent it from rotating, or deselect the Enable option in the Rotation section of the Properties panel to disable a particular joint's rotation.

5   Strength is the amount of springiness of any individual bone in an armature. Add springiness with the Spring feature to simulate the way different parts of a flexible object jiggle when the entire object moves and continue to jiggle when the object stops. Damping refers to how quickly the springiness effect subsides over time.

6   To save an armature to the Assets panel, the armature must be a movie clip symbol. Right-click the movie clip in the library and choose Save As Asset. In the Save As Asset dialog box, select Bones as the option. Animate will save the armature in the Custom tab of the Assets panel.

10 CREATING INTERACTIVE MEDIA

Lesson overview

In this lesson, you'll learn how to do the following:

- Create button symbols.

- Duplicate symbols.

- Swap symbols and bitmaps.

- Name button instances.

- Understand how ActionScript 3.0 and JavaScript create interactive Animate documents.

- Use the wizard in the Actions panel to quickly add JavaScript.

- Create and use frame labels.

- Create animated buttons.

This lesson will take about 2 hours to complete.

To get the lesson files used in this chapter, download them from the web page for this book at peachpit.com/AnimateCIB2024. For more information, see "Accessing the lesson files and Web Edition" in the Getting Started section at the beginning of this book.

Let your viewers explore your project and become active participants. Button symbols and code work together to create engaging, user-driven interactive experiences.

Getting started

Note If you have not already downloaded the project files for this lesson to your computer from your Account page, make sure to do so now. See Getting Started at the beginning of the book.

To begin, view the interactive animated banner ad that you'll create as you learn to make interactive projects in Animate. Banner ads (also called display ads) are common advertisements that generate revenue for websites. They are often animated and eye-catching to attract attention and get users to click through to the advertiser's site for the product. In this lesson, you'll integrate interactivity with animation to create an engaging banner ad.

1   Double-click the 10End.fla file in the 10/10End folder to open the banner ad in Animate. Choose Control > Test to see the final project.

The project opens in your default browser. You can ignore any warnings that appear in the Output panel.

Note This project contains buttons and bitmaps that may generate security errors when you try to play the HTML file locally (from your own computer). Your browser may be blank or simply show a static picture when you double-click the HTML file to open it in a browser. Upload all required files to your server to test the project over the internet, or test the movie within Animate.

The project is a square banner ad for an imaginary store that sells running shoes. Viewers see a quick animated introduction, and then they can click either of the two buttons to see more information about a particular shoe. You can click the "Shop now" button to go directly to the product website, which in this case goes to the Adobe site.

In this lesson, you'll be working in an HTML5 Canvas document to create interactive buttons and structure the timeline properly. You'll learn to add JavaScript code to provide instructions for what each button will do.

2   Close the 10End.fla file.

3   Double-click the 10Start.fla file in the 10/10Start folder to open the initial
    project file in Animate. The file is an HTML5 Canvas document that will play in
    a browser. The document already contains the initial animation on the timeline
    with several assets already in the Library panel.

● **Note** Animate
makes it easy to create
new documents for
banner ads. In the
New Document panel,
the Ads category
contains preset
HTML5 documents
for the standard sizes
of banner ads, such
as leaderboards,
skyscrapers, and mobile
formats.

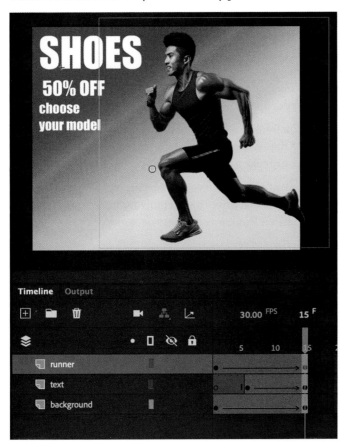

▶ **Tip** Animate
may warn you if your
computer doesn't
have the same fonts
contained in an FLA
file. Choose substitute
fonts, or click Use
Default to have Animate
automatically make the
substitutions.

4   Choose File > Save As. Name the file **10_workingcopy.fla** and save it in the
    10Start folder.

    Saving a working copy ensures that the original start file will be available if you
    want to start over.

About interactive media

Interactive media change based on the viewer's actions. For example, when the
viewer clicks or taps a button, a different graphic with more information is displayed. Interactivity can be simple, such as a button click, or it can be complex,
receiving inputs from a variety of sources, such as the movements of the mouse,
keystrokes from the keyboard, or even the tilting of a mobile device.

ActionScript and JavaScript

In Animate, you add interactivity with either ActionScript 3.0 or JavaScript, depending on the kind of document you're working in.

You use ActionScript to achieve interactivity if you're working in an ActionScript 3.0, AIR for Desktop, or AIR for iOS or Android document. The published file for an ActionScript 3.0 document containing ActionScript interactivity is a projector, which is a self-contained file that plays on a user's computer. An AIR for Desktop document also publishes a file to play on a computer or an AIR-supported platform. An AIR for iOS or Android document publishes a mobile app.

ActionScript provides instructions that enable an animation to respond to the user. Those instructions could be to play a sound, skip to a keyframe on the timeline where new graphics appear, or make a calculation.

In an HTML5 Canvas document like the one you're working on for this banner ad, you use JavaScript, the same code that drives interactivity for web pages in a browser. The WebGL glTF, VR 360, and VR Panorama Animate documents also use JavaScript.

ActionScript 3.0 and JavaScript are very similar (in fact, both are based on an ECMA coding language standard), but there are slight differences in syntax and usage.

In this lesson, you'll use JavaScript in an HTML5 Canvas document to learn to create nonlinear navigation—that is, the movie doesn't have to play straight from the beginning of the timeline to the end. You'll add JavaScript to tell the Animate playhead to jump around and go to different frames of the timeline based on which button the user clicks. Different frames on the timeline contain different content. The user doesn't actually know that the playhead is jumping around the timeline; the user just sees (or hears) different content appear as the buttons are clicked on the Stage.

Don't worry if you don't think you're good at programming! You don't have to be a code ninja, because Animate provides an easy-to-use, menu-driven wizard in the Actions panel that allows you to add JavaScript quickly and simply.

Creating buttons

A button is a basic visual indicator of something users can interact with. Users often click a button with the mouse or tap a button with their finger, but many other types of interactions are possible. For example, something can happen when a user rolls the mouse pointer over a button.

A button is a kind of symbol that has four special states, or keyframes, that determine how the button appears. Buttons can look like virtually anything—an image, a graphic, or a bit of text. They don't have to be those typical pill-shaped gray rectangles that you see on many websites.

Creating a button symbol

In this lesson, you'll create buttons with small thumbnail images. Buttons are a special type of symbol that are stored in the Library panel.

1 Create a new layer above all the existing layers and name it **buttons**.

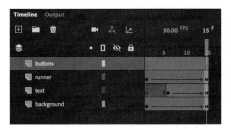

2 Lock the other layers so that you don't accidentally move the other elements on the Stage.

3 Select the Rectangle tool with a white fill and an orange stroke, and create a rectangle on the buttons layer on the Stage about **90** pixels wide and **65** pixels high.

4 In the Library panel, drag the vapormax ultra thumbnail bitmap into the center of the rectangle you just drew.

5 Select both the rectangle and its stroke, and also select the image of the running shoe and choose Modify > Convert To Symbol.

6 In the Convert To Symbol dialog box, choose Button from the Type menu and name the symbol **ultra**. Click OK.

Animate creates a button symbol from the selected graphics, which appears in your library.

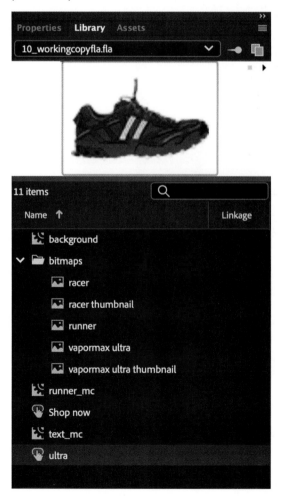

Editing a button symbol

A button symbol contains four special states that are represented on the button's timeline as frames, just like on the main timeline. The four frames include the following:

• The Up state shows the button as it appears when the pointer is not interacting with it.

• The Over state shows the button as it appears when the pointer is hovering over it.

• The Down state shows the button as it appears when the pointer is hovering over it and the user presses the mouse button or trackpad, or taps it.

• The Hit state indicates the clickable area of the button.

You'll understand the relationship between these states and the button's appearance as you work through this exercise.

1 In the Library panel, double-click the **ultra** button symbol.

You enter symbol editing mode for the button symbol where you see a timeline with the Up, Over, Down, and Hit frames. Only the Up frame contains a filled keyframe.

2 Select the Hit frame in the timeline and choose Insert > Timeline > Frame to extend the timeline.

The rectangle and shoe image now extends through the Up, Over, Down, and Hit states.

3 Create a keyframe in the Over frame.

The new keyframe will indicate a change in the graphics when the user's mouse cursor hovers over the button.

4 Double-click the stroke around the rectangle to select it, and then change the color from orange to red.

5 Select the fill of the rectangle and change the color from white to yellow.

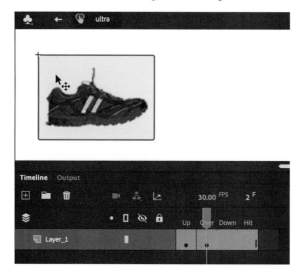

Now the Up keyframe and the Over keyframe are different. The button is normally white with an orange stroke, but whenever the mouse cursor rolls over the button, it will show the Over keyframe that has a yellow fill with a red stroke.

6 Click the left-facing arrow button in the Edit bar above the Stage to exit symbol editing mode and return to the main timeline. Your first button symbol is complete, but your button won't react to your cursor yet. You'll have to test your movie to see how your button changes its appearance depending on its Up, Over, and Down keyframe states.

Invisible buttons and the Hit keyframe

Your button symbol's Hit keyframe indicates the area that is "hot," or clickable by the user. Normally, the Hit keyframe contains a shape that is the same size and location as the shape in your Up keyframe. In most cases, you want the graphics that users see to be in the same area where they click. However, in certain advanced applications, you may want the Hit keyframe and the Up keyframe to be different. If your Up keyframe is empty, the resulting button is known as an invisible button.

Users can't see invisible buttons, but because the Hit keyframe still defines a clickable area, invisible buttons remain active. You can place invisible buttons over any part of the Stage and use code to program them to respond to users.

Invisible buttons are useful for creating generic hotspots. For example, placing them on top of different photos can help you make each photo respond to a click or tap without having to make each photo a different button symbol.

Duplicating buttons

Now that you've created one button, you'll be able to create the second button more easily by duplicating symbols.

1   In the Library panel, right-click the ultra button symbol and choose Duplicate. You can also choose Duplicate from the Library panel menu.

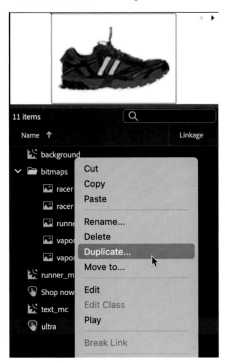

2 In the Duplicate Symbol dialog box, choose Button from the Type menu, and name the symbol **racer**. Click OK.

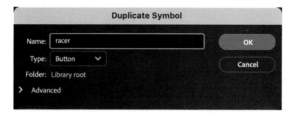

Swapping bitmaps

Bitmaps and symbols are easy to swap on the Stage and can significantly speed up your workflow.

1 In the Library panel, double-click the icon for your newly duplicated symbol (the racer button) to edit it.

2 Select the shoe image on the Stage.

3 In the Properties panel, click the Swap symbol.

4 In the Swap Bitmap dialog box, select the other shoe thumbnail image, called racer thumbnail, and click OK.

The original thumbnail (shown with a dot next to the symbol name) is swapped out for the one you selected. Because they are both the same size, the replacement is seamless. Shift the new bitmap down a bit if you need to center it in the button.

5   Move to the Over keyframe and swap the ultra shoe thumbnail image with the racer shoe.

6   When you're done, take a moment to create a folder in the Library panel, name it **buttons**, and organize your buttons in this folder.

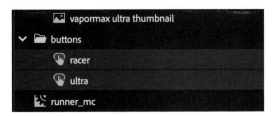

Placing the button instances

Now you'll put the buttons on the Stage and give them names in the Properties panel so that your code can identify them.

1   Drag the racer button from the Library panel to the Stage in the buttons layer, placing it under the ultra button that is already there.

2 Select both buttons and move them under the column of text. The X value should be about **7** and the Y value should be about **140.**

3 Select the keyframe on frame 1 of the buttons layer and move it to the very last frame (frame 15).

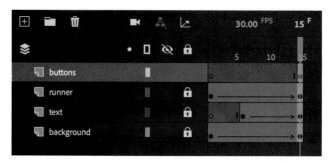

Now the buttons appear only after the animation plays.

4 At this point, you can test your movie to see how the buttons behave. Choose File > Publish Settings.

The Publish Settings panel appears.

5 In the Basic tab for the JavaScript/HTML option selected at the left, deselect the Loop Timeline checkbox and click OK.

● **Note** You can also add JavaScript code to stop the timeline, which you will learn to do later in this lesson.

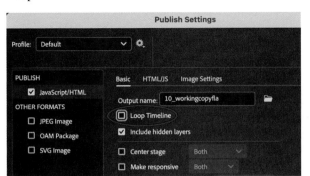

Normally, an Animate project will loop, but for this banner ad, you'll want the animation to play just once and stop.

6 Choose Control > Test.

You can ignore any warnings that show up in the Output panel.

In the browser that opens, the animation plays, and your two buttons appear at the end. Note how the buttons change appearance as your mouse cursor interacts with them.

▶ **Tip** If your browser displays a blank screen when you test your movie (Control > Test), make sure you're connected to the internet. If you're not, open the Publish settings (File > Publish Settings). Select the HTML/JS tab and deselect Hosted Libraries. The Hosted Libraries option links to external JavaScript code, so your published files don't have to include them, but you need to be connected to the internet for your project to work.

At this point, however, you haven't provided any instructions for the buttons to actually do anything. That part comes after you name the button instances and learn a little about coding.

Naming button instances

Next, you'll name each button instance so that your code can reference it. Beginners often forget this crucial step.

1   Click an empty part of the Stage to deselect all the buttons, and then select just the first button.

2   Type **ultra_btn** in the instance name field in the Properties panel.

3   Name the other button **racer_btn**.

Animate is very picky, and one typo will prevent your entire project from working correctly! See the sidebar "Naming rules" for information about instance names.

Naming rules

Naming instances is a critical step in creating interactive projects in Animate. The most common mistake made by novices is not to name, or to incorrectly name, a button instance.

Instance names are important because ActionScript and JavaScript use the names to reference those objects. Instance names are not the same as the symbol names in the Library panel. The names in the Library panel are simply organizational reminders.

Instance naming follows these simple rules and best practices:

- Do not use spaces or special punctuation. Underscores are okay to use.
- Do not begin a name with a number.
- Be aware of uppercase and lowercase letters. ActionScript and JavaScript are case sensitive.
- End your button name with _btn. Although it is not required, it helps identify those objects as buttons.
- Do not use any word that is reserved for an ActionScript or JavaScript command.

Preparing the timeline

To create room on the timeline to add more content, you'll add more frames.

1 Select frame 30 for all your layers.

2 Choose Insert > Timeline > Frame (F5). You can also right-click and choose Insert Frame.

Animate adds frames in all the selected layers up to the selected point, frame 30.

Creating destination keyframes

When the user clicks each button, Animate will move the playhead to a new spot on the timeline according to code that you'll insert. Before adding the code, you'll create all the different options on the timeline that your user might choose.

Inserting keyframes with different content

You will create four keyframes in a new layer and place information about each of the running shoes in the new keyframes.

1 Insert a new layer at the top of the layer stack and name it **content**.

2 Select frame 20 of the content layer.

3 Insert a new keyframe at frame 20 (choose Insert > Timeline > Keyframe, or press F6, or press the Insert Keyframe button above the timeline).

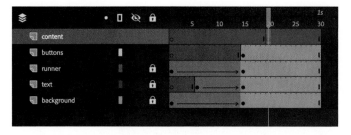

4 Insert a new keyframe at frame 25.

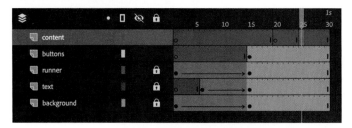

Your timeline has two new empty keyframes in the content layer.

5 Unlock the runner layer and select frame 20.

6 Choose Modify > Timeline > Convert To Blank Keyframes (F7).

An empty keyframe appears at frame 20 of the runner layer. This makes room on the Stage to show more details about the selected running shoe.

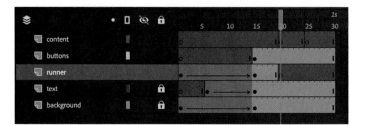

7 Select the empty keyframe at frame 20 of the content layer.

8 In the Library panel, drag the vapormax ultra bitmap to the Stage.

9 Position the bitmap where the runner used to be, and rotate it to give it a little more dynamism. In this example, the Transform panel shows a Rotation of −24 degrees, and the Position And Size section of the Properties panel should show X=65 and Y=−52.

10 With the Text tool, add a description next to the shoe image. Add the text **Vapormax Ultra** in a font and size of your choosing.

11 Select the empty keyframe at frame 25 of the content layer.

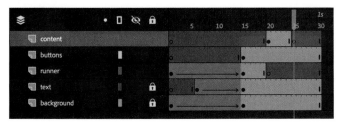

12 Drag the racer bitmap from the Library panel to the Stage.

13 Position the bitmap and rotate it in a similar fashion as the previous shoe.

14 Add the word **Racer** next to this shoe.

The content layer now contains three keyframes: the first keyframe at frame 1 is empty, the second keyframe at frame 20 contains the Vapormax Ultra shoe, and the third keyframe at frame 25 contains the Racer shoe.

Using labels on keyframes

Frame labels are names that you give to keyframes. Instead of referring to keyframes by their frame number, you refer to them by their label, which makes code easier to read, write, and edit.

1   Select frame 20 on the content layer.

2   In the Label section of the Properties panel, enter **ultra** in the Name field.

A tiny flag icon appears on the keyframe.

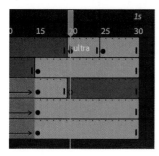

3   Select frame 25 on the content layer.

4   In the Label section of the Properties panel, enter **racer** in the Name field.

A tiny flag icon appears on the keyframe.

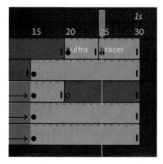

Navigating the Actions panel

The Actions panel is where you enter all your code. If you're using an HTML5 Canvas document, you enter JavaScript. If you're using an ActionScript 3.0 document, you enter ActionScript. Open the Actions panel by choosing Window > Actions, or by selecting a keyframe on the timeline and clicking the ActionScript panel button at the top right of the Properties panel.

You can also right-click any keyframe and choose Actions.

The Actions panel gives you a flexible environment for entering code, as well as different options to help you write, edit, and view your code.

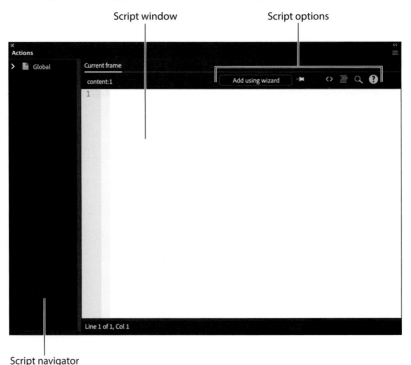

The Actions panel is divided into two parts. On the right of the Actions panel is the Script window—the blank slate where you can write code freely. You enter ActionScript or JavaScript in the Script window just as you would in a text editing application.

On the left is the Script navigator, which shows you where your code is located. Animate places code on keyframes on the timeline, so the Script navigator can be particularly useful if you have lots of code scattered in different keyframes and on different timelines.

At the bottom of the Actions panel, Animate displays the line number and column number (or character in the row) of the current position of the text insertion point.

The upper-right corner of the Actions panel contains options for finding, replacing, and inserting code. The Add Using Wizard button is also located there.

Adding JavaScript interactivity with the Actions panel wizard

Now that you have multiple keyframes on the timeline, your movie will play linearly from frame 1 to frame 30, showing all the shoe choices. However, with this interactive banner ad, you'll want to pause the movie at frame 15 to wait for your viewers to choose a shoe model.

Stopping the timeline

Use a `stop()` action to pause your Animate movie. A `stop()` action simply stops the movie from continuing by halting the playhead.

1   Insert a new layer at the top and name it **actions**.

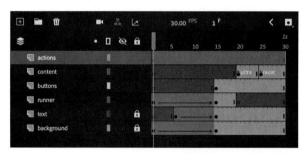

    JavaScript and ActionScript code are generally placed on keyframes on the timeline.

2   Create a keyframe at frame 15 of the actions layer.

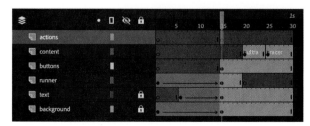

3 Select frame 15 and open the Actions panel (Window > Actions).

4 Click the Add Using Wizard button.

The wizard opens within the Actions panel. The wizard guides you step by step through the code writing process. The code that you generate with the wizard appears in the first field. The wizard is available for inserting JavaScript into HTML5 Canvas, WebGL glTF extended version, VR Panorama, and VR 360 documents. For ActionScript, you can use a different panel called the Code Snippets panel.

5 Step 1 asks you to choose the action, or the behavior that you want Animate to perform, from a list. Scroll down in the list under Select An Action and select Stop (the items are listed alphabetically).

Another menu appears to the right.

6 In the next menu, choose This Timeline.

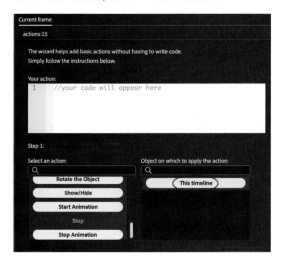

Code appears in the action window. The `stop()` action will apply to the current timeline.

7 Click Next.

Step 2 appears in the wizard.

8 Step 2 asks you to select the trigger that will produce your selected action. Select With This Frame.

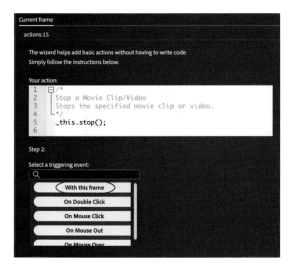

Additional code is added to make reference to the current timeline.

You want the stop() action to be executed as soon as the timeline begins, so the appropriate trigger is when the playhead encounters the current frame.

9 Click Finish And Add.

The finished code is added to the Script window in the Actions panel.

The code is

```
var _this = this;

_this.stop();
```

The first statement creates a variable, or a reference, called _this that refers to the current timeline.

The second statement points to the current timeline and applies the stop() action. The semicolon at the end of each statement acts as a period and indicates the end of a command.

The code in light gray that begins with /* and ends with */ is called a multiline comment, and it is simply a description of what the code does. It acts as a reminder for you and for other developers. Well-commented code is essential. It will save you hours of headaches when you return to a project, and it is considered a best practice for coders.

In the timeline, a tiny lowercase "a" is added to frame 15 in the actions layer to indicate that code has been added there.

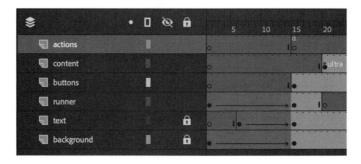

Adding actions for a button click

So far, you have code that stops the timeline at frame 15. Now you'll add an action for a button click. The button click is called a trigger in the wizard, but in JavaScript and ActionScript it is known as an event.

Events are occurrences in your movie that Animate can detect and respond to. For example, a mouse click (or a tap), a mouse movement, and a key press are all events. Pinch and swipe gestures on mobile devices are also events. These events are produced by the user, but some events can happen independently of the user, such as the successful loading of a piece of data or the completion of a sound.

1 Select frame 15 on the actions layer.

2 Open the Actions panel, if it's not already open.

3 Place your text cursor in the last empty line of your Script window. You'll add additional code to the code that's already there.

4 Click the Add Using Wizard button.

The wizard opens within the Actions panel.

5 Step 1 asks for the action. Scroll down and select Go To Frame Label And Stop.

Another menu appears to the right.

6 In the next menu, choose This Timeline.

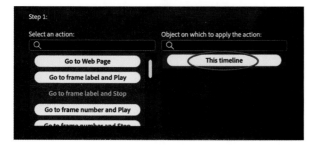

Code appears in the action window. The action will apply to the current timeline.

```
Your action:
1    /*
2      Moves the playhead to the specified frame label in the
3      Can be used on the main timeline or on movie clip timel
4    */
5    _this.gotoAndStop('enterFrameLabel');
6
```

7 Replace the green highlighted letters in the action window with the name of the label you want the playhead to go to. Replace `enterFrameLabel` with **ultra**.

```
Your action:
1    /*
2      Moves the playhead to the specified frame label in the
3      Can be used on the main timeline or on movie clip timel
4    */
5    _this.gotoAndStop('ultra');
6
```

The frame label name appears in green and should be between a set of single quotes.

8 Click Next.

Step 2 appears in the wizard.

9 Step 2 asks for the trigger that will produce your selected action. Select On Mouse Click.

On Mouse Click is an event that happens when the on-screen button is pressed and then released. Another menu appears to the right.

10 The wizard asks for the object for the triggering event. Select ultra_btn, which is the button that corresponds to the first shoe, whose information is displayed in the keyframe labeled ultra.

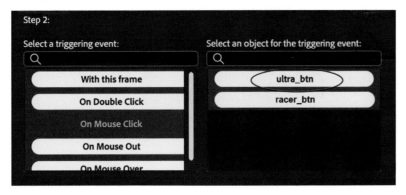

11 Click Finish And Add.

The finished code is added to the Script window in the Actions panel. The code consists of the trigger `'click'` and a function that groups all the code that is executed when the trigger happens. What's important for you to identify are the opening and closing curly brackets of the function. This function has only one statement (a gotoAndStop() action, which moves the playhead), but functions can contain many statements.

```
Current frame

actions:15                          Add using wizard      ◄H ⊕ <> 🖹 Q ?
  1
  2      var _this = this;
  3    ⊟ /*
  4    │ Stop a Movie Clip/Video
  5    │ Stops the specified movie clip or video.
  6    └ */
  7      _this.stop();
  8
  9
 10      var _this = this;
 11    ⊟ /*
 12    │ Clicking on the specified symbol instance executes a function.
 13    └ */
 14    ⊟ _this.ultra_btn.on('click', function(){
 15    ⊟ /*
 16    │ Moves the playhead to the specified frame label in the timeline an
 17    │ Can be used on the main timeline or on movie clip timelines.
 18    └ */
 19    │ _this.gotoAndStop('ultra');
 20    └ });
 21
 22
```

12 Choose Control > Test.

Animate opens your browser to show your project. Click the first button. Animate detects the click trigger on the button and moves the playhead to the ultra keyframe, where the Stage shows information about the Vapormax Ultra shoe.

13 Close your browser and return to Animate.

14 Select frame 15 of the actions layer and open the Actions panel again if it isn't already open.

15 Continue adding actions and triggers to the existing code for the other button. The next button should trigger a `gotoAndStop()` action to the racer keyframe.

Checking for errors

Debugging is a necessary process, for veteran coders as well as novices. Even if you're extra careful, errors will creep into your code. Fortunately, the wizard helps reduce typos and common errors. If you do enter code by hand, a few tips can help prevent, catch, and identify errors.

- If you're working in an ActionScript 3.0 document, Animate automatically displays code errors in the Compiler Errors panel (Window > Compiler Errors) with a description of the error and its location. None of your code will be functional if there is a compiler error in any part of the code.

- Take advantage of color hinting in the code. Animate colors keywords, variables, comments, and other language elements differently. You don't need to know why they are different, but the different colors can give you clues as to where there may be some missing punctuation.

- Click the Format Code button at the upper-right corner of the Actions panel to tidy up your code and make it easier to read. You can change the formatting settings in Animate > Preferences > Edit Preferences > Code Editor (macOS) or Edit > Preferences > Code Editor (Windows).

Creating the "Shop now" button

A crucial component of a banner ad is to direct interested users to the advertiser's site. You'll need to provide another button that will do that.

The "Shop now" button that you'll create next will open a website into a new browser window or tab.

Adding another button instance

The sample lesson file provides a "Shop now" button for you in the Library panel.

1 Select frame 15 in the buttons layer and unlock it if it is locked.

2 Drag the button called "Shop now" from the Library panel to the Stage. Position the button instance under the runner, centered at the bottom edge of the Stage.

3 In the Properties panel, set the X value to **114** and the Y value to **238**.

4 In the Properties panel, name the instance **shopnow_btn**.

Adding code for the "Shop now" button

The action will be Go To Web Page, and the trigger will be a button click/tap.

1　Select frame 15 of the actions layer.

2　Open the Actions panel, if it's not already open.

3　Place your text cursor at a new line after the last line of code in your Script window. You'll add code to the code that's already there.

4　Click the Add Using Wizard button.

　　The wizard opens within the Actions panel.

5　Step 1 asks for the action. Select Go To Web Page.

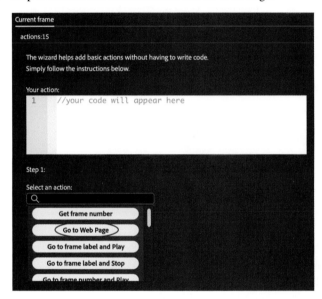

In a real project, you would replace the green highlighted text in the code preview window with the URL of the advertiser's site. For this project, you can leave the default URL, which is Adobe's website.

6　Click Next.

　　Step 2 appears in the wizard.

7   Step 2 asks for the trigger that will produce your selected action. Select On Mouse Click.

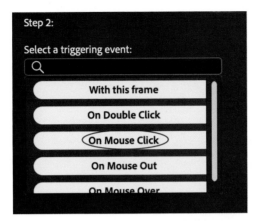

On Mouse Click is an event that happens when the user's mouse is pressed and then released over the button, or if the user taps the button. Another menu appears to the right.

8   The wizard asks for the object for the triggering event. Select shopnow_btn.

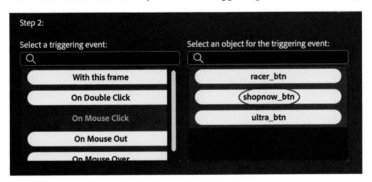

9   Click Finish And Add.

The code to add the "Shop now" button is added to the script. Don't worry if the line numbers for the code in the screenshot here don't match up with your line numbers.

```
28
29
30      var _this = this;
31      /*
32      Clicking on the specified symbol instance executes a function.
33      */
34      _this.shopnow_btn.on('click', function(){
35      /*
36      Loads the URL in a new browser window.
37      */
38      window.open('http://www.adobe.com', '_blank');
39      });
40
```

10 Test your movie.

When you click the "Shop now" button, the Adobe site loads in a browser tab or window.

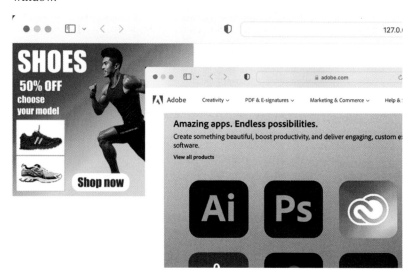

The Code Snippets panel

Animate provides another panel, called the Code Snippets panel (Window > Code Snippets), that offers a way to add ActionScript 3.0 and JavaScript code. The panel is organized into folders for different kinds of interactivity. Simply expand the folder that you want and select the action. Animate guides you for any additional information.

The Code Snippets panel also provides a way for you to save your own code and share it with other developers.

For beginners, it's best to use the Add Using Wizard option in the Actions panel for JavaScript.

Playing animation at the destination

So far, this interactive banner ad works by using the `gotoAndStop()` action to show information in different keyframes along the timeline. But suppose you wanted the running shoe image to animate into the Stage rather than appear suddenly—how would you play an animation after a user clicks a button? One way is to use the action `gotoAndPlay()`, which moves the playhead to the frame number or frame label and plays from that point forward.

Creating transition animations

Next, you'll create a short transition animation for each of the shoes. The transition animation will show the shoe moving onto the Stage from the right edge. Then you'll change your code to direct Animate to go to each of the beginning keyframes and play the animation.

1   Move the playhead to the ultra frame label and select the keyframe in the content layer.

2   Right-click both the selected bitmap and the text on the Stage and choose Create Motion Tween, or choose Create Motion Tween from the Create Tween menu above the timeline.

3   Animate asks whether you want to create a symbol for the selections for the motion tween. Click OK.

Animate creates a separate tween layer for the instance so that it can proceed with the motion tween.

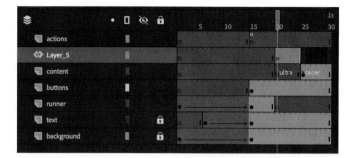

4   Move the instance off the Stage and to the right so that it is no longer visible.

5   Move the playhead to the end of the tween span at frame 24.

6   Move the instance back onto the Stage where it was originally.

The motion tween from frame 20 to frame 24 produces a dramatic entrance.

7 Create a similar motion tween for the second shoe in the keyframe, labeled racer. Don't try to test your movie just yet! You still have to tweak the JavaScript code in the next task to make this work.

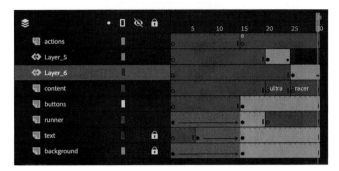

Using the gotoAndPlay() action

The `gotoAndPlay()` action makes the Animate playhead move to a specific frame on the timeline and begin playing from that point.

1 Select frame 15 of the actions layer and open the Actions panel.

2 In your JavaScript code, change the first two `gotoAndStop()` actions to `gotoAndPlay()` actions, but leave the parameter unchanged:

- `gotoAndStop('ultra');` should be changed to `gotoAndPlay('ultra');`.

- `gotoAndStop('racer');` should be changed to `gotoAndPlay('racer');`.

For each of the buttons, the JavaScript code now directs the playhead to a particular frame label and begins playing at that point.

Make sure you keep the function for your "Shop now" button unchanged.

► **Tip** A fast and easy way to do multiple replacements is to use the Find And Replace command in the Actions panel. Click the Find button in the upper-right corner, select Find, and then choose Find And Replace from the menu to the right of the Find Text field.

Stopping the animations

If you test your movie now (Control > Test), you'll see that each button goes to its corresponding frame label and plays from that point, but it keeps playing, showing any remaining animations downstream in the timeline. The next step is to tell Animate when to stop.

1 Select frame 24 of the actions layer, the frame just before the racer labeled keyframe on the content layer.

2 Right-click the frame and choose Insert Keyframe.

A new keyframe is inserted in the actions layer. We'll use the new keyframe to add a stop() action just before the second animation starts to play.

3 Open the Actions panel.

The Script window in the Actions panel is blank. Don't panic! Your code has not disappeared. Your code for the event listeners is on the first keyframe of the actions layer. You have selected a new keyframe in which you will add a stop() action.

Tip If you wish, you can use the Add Using Wizard panel to add the stop() action for each of the keyframes.

4 In the Script window, enter the following: **this.stop();**

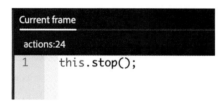

Animate will stop playing when it reaches frame 24.

Tip If you want a quick and easy way to duplicate the keyframe containing the stop() action, hold down the Option/Alt key while you drag it to a new location on the timeline.

5 Insert a keyframe at frame 30.

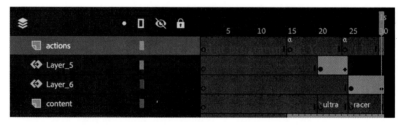

6 In this keyframe, add another stop() action in the Actions panel.

7 Test your movie by choosing Control > Test.

Each button takes you to a different keyframe and plays an animation of a running shoe sliding onto the Stage. At the end of the animation, the movie stops and waits for the viewer to click another button.

Pinning code in the Actions panel

When you have code scattered in multiple keyframes on the timeline, it's sometimes difficult to go back and forth to edit or view your code. The Actions panel provides a way for you to keep the code from particular keyframes "pinned" to the Actions panel. Click the Pin Script button at the top of the Actions panel, and Animate will create a separate tab for the code currently displayed in the Script window.

The tab will be labeled with the frame number where your code resides. You can pin multiple scripts, allowing you to navigate easily between them.

To continue with the rest of this lesson, unpin all the scripts so that you have only the Current frame tab displayed.

Animated buttons

Currently, when you hover your mouse cursor over one of the running shoe buttons, the red stroke and the yellow fill in the box suddenly appear. But imagine if the mouse hover provided an animated effect. It would give more life and sophistication to the interaction between the user and the button.

Animated buttons display an animation in the Up, Over, or Down keyframe. The key to creating an animated button is to nest a movie clip inside a button symbol. Create an animation inside a movie clip symbol and then place that movie clip symbol inside the Up, Over, or Down keyframe of a button symbol. When one of those button keyframes is displayed, the animation in the movie clip plays.

Creating the animation in a movie clip symbol

Your button symbols in this banner ad contain a bitmap of a shoe in their Over states. You will convert that bitmap into a movie clip symbol and then create an animation inside that movie clip.

1   In the Library panel, expand the buttons folder. Double-click the icon for the ultra button.

    You enter symbol editing mode for the button symbol called ultra.

2   Select the shoe bitmap in the Over keyframe.

3   Right-click and choose Convert To Symbol.

    The Convert To Symbol dialog box appears.

4 Choose Movie Clip as the Type and enter **ultra_mc** as the Name. Click OK.

You now have a movie clip instance inside the Over keyframe of your button symbol.

5 Double-click the movie clip instance to edit it in place. Notice how the Edit bar above the Stage shows you the nesting of symbols.

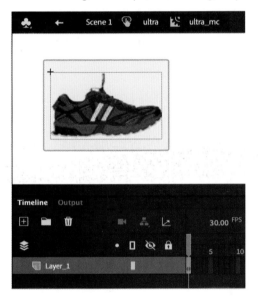

6 Right-click the shoe bitmap and choose Create Motion Tween.

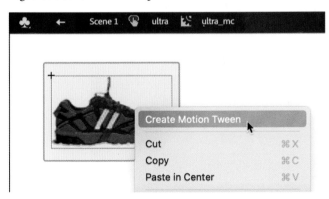

7 In the dialog box that appears asking for confirmation to convert the selection to a symbol, click OK.

The shoe bitmap is converted to a symbol and placed in a motion tween layer. Animate adds 1 second's worth of frames to the timeline.

8 Drag the end of the tween span back so that the timeline has only 10 frames.

9 Move the playhead to frame 10.

10 Choose the Free Transform tool and enlarge the shoe so that it fills, or even breaks, the box into which it is positioned.

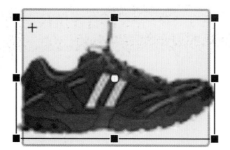

Animate creates a smooth transition between the smaller and larger instances in the 10-frame tween span.

11 Insert a new layer and name it **actions**.

12 Insert a new keyframe in the last frame (frame 10) of the actions layer.

13 Open the Actions panel (Window > Actions) and enter **this.stop();** in the Script window.

Adding the `stop()` action in the last frame ensures that the fade-in effect plays only once. The last keyframe on frame 10 of the actions layer shows a tiny "a," indicating that code is attached there.

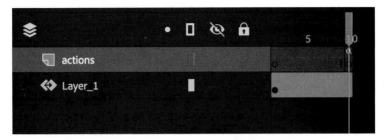

▶ **Tip** If you want an animated button to repeat its animation, leave out the `stop()` action at the end of the movie clip's timeline.

14 Exit symbol editing mode by clicking the Scene 1 button in the Edit bar above the Stage.

15 Choose Control > Test.

When your mouse cursor hovers over the first shoe button, the image of the shoe grows slightly, giving it more emphasis.

● **Note** Notice that you can add JavaScript code to either the main timeline or a movie clip's timeline. Movie clips are the only symbols that support interactivity.

16 Create an identical motion tween for the racer button to animate its Over state, and add a `stop()` action to the end of the tween.

Review questions

1 How and where do you add ActionScript or JavaScript code?

2 How do you name an instance, and why is it necessary?

3 How can you label frames, and when is it useful?

4 What does the stop() action do?

5 What is a trigger in the Actions panel wizard?

6 How do you create an animated button?

Review answers

1 ActionScript or JavaScript code is attached to keyframes on the timeline. Keyframes that contain code are indicated by a small lowercase "a." You add code in the Actions panel. Choose Window > Actions, or select a keyframe and click the Actions panel icon in the Properties panel, or right-click and select Actions. You enter code directly in the Script window in the Actions panel, or you can add code through the Add Using Wizard option. You can also add code with the Code Snippets panel.

2 To name an instance, select it on the Stage and then type a name in the Instance Name field in the Properties panel. You need to name an instance so that ActionScript or JavaScript can identify it with code.

3 To label a frame, select a keyframe on the timeline, and then type a name in the Frame Label box in the Properties panel. You can label frames in Animate to make it easier to reference frames with code and to give you more flexibility.

4 In ActionScript or JavaScript, a stop() action halts the playhead from advancing.

5 A trigger is an event that Animate can respond to with an action. A typical trigger is a button click, or the playhead entering a frame.

6 Animated buttons display an animation in the Up, Over, or Down keyframe. To create an animated button, make an animation inside a movie clip symbol and then place that movie clip symbol inside the Up, Over, or Down keyframe of a button symbol. When one of those button keyframes is displayed, the animation in the movie clip plays.

Next steps

You've made it through the last of 10 lessons. By now you've seen how Adobe Animate, in the right creative hands (yours!), has all the features you need to produce media-rich interactive projects and animations that publish to multiple platforms. You've completed these lessons—many of them from scratch—so you understand how the various tools, panels, and code work together for real-world applications.

But there's always more to learn. Continue practicing your Animate skills by creating your own animation or interactive site. Get inspired by watching animations and seeking out multimedia projects. Expand your Animate knowledge by exploring the Adobe Animate Help resources and other fine Adobe Press publications.

INDEX

NUMBERS

The fastest, easiest, most comprehensive way to learn
Adobe Creative Cloud

Classroom in a Book®, the best-selling series of hands-on software training books, helps you learn the features of Adobe software quickly and easily.

The **Classroom in a Book** series offers what no other book or training program does—an official training series from Adobe Systems, developed with the support of Adobe product experts.

To see a complete list of our Classroom in a Book titles covering the 2024 release of Adobe Creative Cloud go to: peachpit.com/CC2024

Adobe Photoshop Classroom in a Book 2024 Release
ISBN: 9780138262525

Adobe Illustrator Classroom in a Book 2024 Release
ISBN: 9780138263829

Adobe InDesign Classroom in a Book 2024 Release
ISBN: 9780138263911

Adobe After Effects Classroom in a Book 2024 Release
ISBN: 9780138316488

Adobe Animate Classroom in a Book 2024 Release
ISBN: 9780138317713

Adobe Photoshop Lightroom Classic Classroom in a Book 2024 Release
ISBN: 9780138318147

Adobe Premiere Pro Classroom in a Book 2024 Release
ISBN: 9780138318567

Adobe Photoshop, Illustrator, and InDesign Collaboration and Workflow Classroom in a Book
ISBN: 9780137908462

Adobe Creative Cloud Classroom in a Book
ISBN: 9780137914708

Adobe Acrobat Classroom in a Book, 4th edition
ISBN: 9780137983636

 Adobe Press